ESV

SOLO

ESV

ENGLISH STANDARD VERSION: SOLO

AN UNCOMMON DEVOTIONAL

SOLO

NAVPRESS

A NavPress published resource in alliance
with Tyndale House Publishers, Inc.

NAVPRESS®

NavPress is the publishing ministry of The Navigators, an international Christian organization and leader in personal spiritual development. NavPress is committed to helping people grow spiritually and enjoy lives of meaning and hope through personal and group resources that are biblically rooted, culturally relevant, and highly practical.

For more information, go to www.NavPress.com.

© 2007, 2013 by The Navigators

A NavPress published resource in alliance with Tyndale House Publishers, Inc.

ISBN 978-1-61291-491-6

Devotional text by Jan Johnson, J. R. Briggs, and Katie Peckham.

Printed in the United States of America

18	17	16	15	14
6	5	4	3	2

INTRODUCTION TO *SOLO*

The devotional you hold is unique. It isn't designed to teach you to study the Bible but rather to develop a conversation between you and God. The devotions found in *SOLO* are based on the classical method of *lectio divina*: reading, thinking, praying, and living Scripture with the intention of inviting an infinite, omniscient God into your life — as it is, no gloss, no veneer. Lectio divina is more Bible basking than Bible study, as it teaches you to absorb and meditate on Scripture, to converse with God openly, and to live out what has become a part of you — his Word.

But it's not easy. Lectio divina takes practice, and lots of it. You will have to learn to be quiet, to silence the voices of responsibility, self, family, and even religion in order to hear what God has to say to you. Try not to view the elements of lectio divina as steps to be checked off your to-do list. Instead, allow them to meld together in the intentional process of listening to God, of focusing on him and learning what he would have from you and for you, his beloved. Don't worry if no lightning strikes or brilliant revelations come. Sometimes devotion means just sitting in the presence of God.

We know the four elements of lectio divina as Read, Think, Pray, and Live. Each element has a purpose, but don't be surprised if they overlap and weave into each other. Remember as you dive into this devotional that lectio divina is about wholeness: whole practice, whole Bible, whole God.

Read. Thoughtfully, leisurely, faithfully — read the epic love story that is the Bible. Yes, love story. The Bible is the chronicle of God's love for his people from the darkness before Eden to eternity with him in heaven. You are in it; I am in it. But most important, God is in it. Here you will meet him face-to-face.

Eugene Peterson called the Bible "a book that reads us even as we read it." That's an uncommon sort of book, and it requires an uncommon sort of read. Knowing facts about God doesn't change your relationship with him, so take the time to splash around in the Word, to absorb it, to discover what God has to say to you each day.

In each *Solo* devotion, you will find a Scripture passage, but also a reference to an expanded passage. I encourage you to read them both, slowly, attentively, and repeatedly. As Peterson said, "The Bible is given to us in the first place simply to invite us to make ourselves at home in the world of God . . . and become familiar with the way God speaks and the ways in which we answer him with our lives." No Scripture passage exists in a vacuum. Whenever you can, take the time to stretch beyond the passage put before you to understand the larger context in which it is found. The more you read, the more you will understand about yourself and this God who created you.

Think. Each subtle, significant, powerful word of Scripture is meant for you. One word may speak today and another tomorrow, but God sent each of them straight into your life. So listen. Go into your reading with a clean slate. Don't bring what you think you need to hear, what others have said, or what you've been taught about a particular passage. Don't bring fear that you'll misinterpret the text. This is about what God has to say to you.

Our lives are full of static. Whether it's our to-do list, our emotions, or just plain noise, it can be hard to sift God's voice from all the racket. By meditating on each word, by turning it over and over in your mind, you will discover that, as God himself is infinitely complex, so his thoughts have subtle meaning beyond the rote. The more you think about what you read, the more familiar you will become with his voice.

Pray. God yearns to converse with you. And he wants far more than just "thanks for this, can I please have that" prayer. Respond to him in dialogue. That means it's as much about listening as it is about speaking. Open your ears and your heart to hear his voice. Sing praises or laments; write your thoughts in a journal; dance or prostrate yourself before him. Pray.

Maybe God has challenged you. Tell him how you feel, but always remember that what he asks, he asks for your good. He is loving and merciful, not manipulative and harsh. If you come across something in your reading that you don't understand, tell him about it. Ask him about it. Fill your prayers with Scripture. Using the words you have read helps you ensure that your prayers line up with God's Word and intention for your life.

It's easy for us in our culture of doing to want to skim over this part. Don't. Even if you are quiet and he is quiet, you are learning to communicate with God.

Live. You can read, think, and pray all day, but unless you live in God's Word as well, you miss the point. The Bible says, "So also faith by itself, if it does not have works, is dead." (James 2:17). If you have taken God's Word to heart and truly made it part of you, it will by its very nature change you. And when it does, you will find yourself called to act. There will come a time when God takes you to the end of yourself then asks you to go further. He wants you to put yourself at his disposal, to go and do what he asks, even the impossible. When that time comes, you will need the Word he has seared on your heart to give you comfort and strength. This is the abundant life (see John 10:10).

///

SOLO. One-on-one. Just you and God.

The *SOLO* devotions are tailored to help you learn to listen to what God may want to say to you through his Word. You will find that every seventh day is marked as a day of reflection, a time to sit back and let God guide your thoughts and prayers back to themes and Scripture from the previous week. Don't be afraid to reflect, and don't be afraid to go back. Each time you read these devotions, you may find that God has something new to say, for though he is the same always, you change a little each day as he shapes you into the person he designed you to be.

Also, there may be times when you need to hear God's voice on a specific issue. For those times we have provided an index of topics that will guide you to a devotion that may be just what you need.

And so begins the journey.

DESIRE FOR RECONCILIATION

GENESIS 3:1-10

¹Now the serpent was more crafty than any other beast of the field that the Lord God had made.

He said to the woman, "Did God actually say, 'You shall not eat of any tree in the garden'?" ²And the woman said to the serpent, "We may eat of the fruit of the trees in the garden, ³but God said, 'You shall not eat of the fruit of the tree that is in the midst of the garden, neither shall you touch it, lest you die.'" ⁴But the serpent said to the woman, "You will not surely die. ⁵For God knows that when you eat of it your eyes will be opened, and you will be like God, knowing good and evil." ⁶So when the woman saw that the tree was good for food, and that it was a delight to the eyes, and that the tree was to be desired to make one wise, she took of its fruit and ate, and she also gave some to her husband who was with her, and he ate. ⁷Then the eyes of both were opened, and they knew that they were naked. And they sewed fig leaves together and made themselves loincloths.

⁸And they heard the sound of the Lord God walking in the garden in the cool of the day, and the man and his wife hid themselves from the presence of the Lord God among the trees of the garden. ⁹But the Lord God called to the man and said to him, "Where are you?" ¹⁰And he said, "I heard the sound of you in the garden, and I was afraid, because I was naked, and I hid myself."

READ

Read the passage, Genesis 3:1-10, carefully.

THINK

For many of us, these are familiar verses. The first two chapters of Genesis speak of God's amazing Creation. Chapter 3 speaks of the rebellion of humankind. And the remainder of Scripture details God's intricate and loving plan to redeem, restore, and reconcile creation back to himself after what happened in Genesis 3. God's plan hinges on what happened in the garden. How does this passage speak to your situation today?

PRAY

There is no better way to begin to understand God's message than to grasp our separation from him because of sin and our desperate need for him to reconcile our relationship. Take some time to confess those areas where you have deliberately rebelled against God.

LIVE

Knowing that you and everyone else on earth have rebelled against God, what do you feel? In what ways does this knowledge affect the way you live your life?

Reread verse 9. If God knows everything, why did he call out to Adam asking, "Where are you?"

In verse 10, Adam responds to God's question by saying, "I heard the sound of you in the garden, and I was afraid, because I was naked, and I hid myself." When are you most tempted to hide?

WRESTLING IN THE NIGHT

GENESIS 32:22-32

²²The same night he arose and took his two wives, his two female servants, and his eleven children, and crossed the ford of the Jabbok. ²³He took them and sent them across the stream, and everything else that he had. ²⁴And Jacob was left alone. And a man wrestled with him until the breaking of the day. ²⁵When the man saw that he did not prevail against Jacob, he touched his hip socket, and Jacob's hip was put out of joint as he wrestled with him. ²⁶Then he said, "Let me go, for the day has broken." But Jacob said, "I will not let you go unless you bless me." ²⁷And he said to him, "What is your name?" And he said, "Jacob." ²⁸Then he said, "Your name shall no longer be called Jacob, but Israel, for you have striven with God and with men, and have prevailed." ²⁹Then Jacob asked him, "Please tell me your name." But he said, "Why is it that you ask my name?" And there he blessed him. ³⁰So Jacob called the name of the place Peniel, saying, "For I have seen God face to face, and yet my life has been delivered." ³¹The sun rose upon him as he passed Penuel, limping because of his hip. ³²Therefore to this day the people of Israel do not eat the sinew of the thigh that is on the hip socket, because he touched the socket of Jacob's hip on the sinew of the thigh.

READ

Read the passage slowly. (To find out about Jacob's fear of meeting his brother, Esau, whom he had tricked many years before, read the expanded passage.)

THINK

Read the passage aloud this time and pause after each of the three questions in the text (verses 27,29). Jacob, whose name means "manipulator," had made elaborate plans to reconcile with Esau in a generous, peaceful way. Then he stayed behind, which was uncharacteristic of such a quintessential deal maker. There with the night sounds and the smell of the brook, Jacob encountered "a man." Was this man an angel, a God-man, Jesus? (It's okay that we don't know for sure.)

1. Picture yourself in this passage. Are you Jacob? Are you an invisible bystander watching it all?
2. What moment in this passage resonates with you most?

   ☐ wanting desperately to be blessed
   ☐ wanting desperately to know more of God
   ☐ other:

PRAY

Depending on what resonated with you, pray about what you desperately want from God. To avoid letting your mind wander, try writing down your prayer, listening for words from God in response.

LIVE

Sit quietly before God, imagining the night sounds and the smell of running water. Try to be comfortable with God in this wild atmosphere. What does it feel like to trust and to reveal the desires of your heart? Be honest if you feel uncomfortable. What would you like it to feel like? Rest in that.

A PICTURE OF FORGIVENESS

GENESIS 50:15-21

[15]When Joseph's brothers saw that their father was dead, they said, "It may be that Joseph will hate us and pay us back for all the evil that we did to him." [16]So they sent a message to Joseph, saying, "Your father gave this command before he died, [17]'Say to Joseph, "Please forgive the transgression of your brothers and their sin, because they did evil to you."' And now, please forgive the transgression of the servants of the God of your father." Joseph wept when they spoke to him. [18]His brothers also came and fell down before him and said, "Behold, we are your servants." [19]But Joseph said to them, "Do not fear, for am I in the place of God? [20]As for you, you meant evil against me, but God meant it for good, to bring it about that many people should be kept alive, as they are today. [21]So do not fear; I will provide for you and your little ones." Thus he comforted them and spoke kindly to them.

READ

Take some time before you begin to rest in silence. Let your mind settle. Silently read the passage.

THINK

Read the passage again, this time aloud, listening specifically for a word or phrase that touches your heart. When you finish, close your eyes. Recall the word or phrase, taking it in and mulling it over. After a few moments, write it down. Don't write anything else.

PRAY

Read the passage aloud again, searching for how forgiveness is illustrated in the text. Think about what it feels like to be the forgiver, as well as what it feels like to be the forgiven. How is this expression of love meaningful to you? Briefly note your thoughts.

Read the text one last time, then stop and listen for what God is inviting you to do or become this week. Perhaps his invitation will have to do with a new perspective on who you are in his eyes, or maybe you sense an action he is calling you to take. After your prayer, write down what you feel invited to do.

LIVE

Take time to meditate on the following quote from *The Book of Common Prayer*, and let it become your own: "Let not the needy, O Lord, be forgotten; nor the hope of the poor be taken away."[1]

LEARNING TO PAY ATTENTION

EXODUS 3:1-6

[1]Now Moses was keeping the flock of his father-in-law, Jethro, the priest of Midian, and he led his flock to the west side of the wilderness and came to Horeb, the mountain of God. [2]And the angel of the LORD appeared to him in a flame of fire out of the midst of a bush. He looked, and behold, the bush was burning, yet it was not consumed. [3]And Moses said, "I will turn aside to see this great sight, why the bush is not burned." [4]When the LORD saw that he turned aside to see, God called to him out of the bush, "Moses, Moses!" And he said, "Here I am." [5]Then he said, "Do not come near; take your sandals off your feet, for the place on which you are standing is holy ground." [6]And he said, "I am the God of your father, the God of Abraham, the God of Isaac, and the God of Jacob." And Moses hid his face, for he was afraid to look at God.

READ

Read the passage aloud.

THINK

Moses is shepherding his father-in-law's sheep. In the distance he sees a bush in flames, but the bush mysteriously doesn't burn up. He walks closer, perhaps expecting a miracle, only to have a more unique encounter than he ever imagined. He interacts with the living God.

When have you experienced a unique encounter with the living God? What was your burning bush like?

What do you think God meant when he said, "Take your sandals off your feet, for the place on which you are standing is holy ground"?

God is holy. What difference does that make in your life?

PRAY

Ask God to reveal himself to you today in a fresh way, a way that he has never revealed himself before.

LIVE

Moses heard from God when he paid attention. Like Moses, we often encounter God when we pay attention to what's going on around us. Find a quiet place and spend a few moments in utter silence, paying attention to those aspects of your life that you often neglect: people, situations, quiet moments, creation, and so on. As you do this, look for God waiting there to interact with you.

THE BREAD GOD HAS GIVEN

EXODUS 16:9-16

⁹Then Moses said to Aaron, "Say to the whole congregation of the people of Israel, 'Come near before the LORD, for he has heard your grumbling.'" ¹⁰And as soon as Aaron spoke to the whole congregation of the people of Israel, they looked toward the wilderness, and behold, the glory of the LORD appeared in the cloud. ¹¹And the LORD said to Moses, ¹²"I have heard the grumbling of the people of Israel. Say to them, 'At twilight you shall eat meat, and in the morning you shall be filled with bread. Then you shall know that I am the LORD your God.'"

¹³In the evening quail came up and covered the camp, and in the morning dew lay around the camp. ¹⁴And when the dew had gone up, there was on the face of the wilderness a fine, flake-like thing, fine as frost on the ground. ¹⁵When the people of Israel saw it, they said to one another, "What is it?" For they did not know what it was. And Moses said to them, "It is the bread that the LORD has given you to eat. ¹⁶This is what the LORD has commanded: 'Gather of it, each one of you, as much as he can eat. You shall each take an omer, according to the number of the persons that each of you has in his tent.'"

READ

Read the passage aloud. If you'd like, read the expanded passage to get a picture of the complaining that came before this and the obsessive hoarding that came after. Both give us a picture of the neediness of the Israelites at this time.

THINK

Read the passage again slowly, pausing to feel each emotion of the Israelites:

- the deep neediness of complaining
- the excitement of seeing the glory of God visible in the cloud
- the perplexity of seeing this strange bread from heaven
- the satisfaction of having enough

Then consider: If you were to complain to God right now, what would your complaint be? (Don't choose this yourself; wait and let it come to you.) In what ways, if any, have you been perplexed by God's response to your complaining? How might God have truly provided enough but you didn't recognize it as God's bread from heaven — exactly what you needed?

PRAY

If you haven't formally complained to God about this matter, do so. Ask God to show you how he has provided you with enough, even though you still might wonder.

LIVE

Sit in the quiet and feel God's "enoughness" in your body. Where do you feel it? In arms that are full? In a quiet mind? In a stomach that feels full? In muscles that work well? If you can really mean it, try delighting in this enoughness.

GOD REVEALS HIMSELF

EXODUS 33:21–34:7

21And the LORD said, "Behold, there is a place by me where you shall stand on the rock, 22and while my glory passes by I will put you in a cleft of the rock, and I will cover you with my hand until I have passed by. 23Then I will take away my hand, and you shall see my back, but my face shall not be seen."

1The LORD said to Moses, "Cut for yourself two tablets of stone like the first, and I will write on the tablets the words that were on the first tablets, which you broke. 2Be ready by the morning, and come up in the morning to Mount Sinai, and present yourself there to me on the top of the mountain. 3No one shall come up with you, and let no one be seen throughout all the mountain. Let no flocks or herds graze opposite that mountain." 4So Moses cut two tablets of stone like the first. And he rose early in the morning and went up on Mount Sinai, as the LORD had commanded him, and took in his hand two tablets of stone. 5The LORD descended in the cloud and stood with him there, and proclaimed the name of the LORD. 6The LORD passed before him and proclaimed, "The LORD, the LORD, a God merciful and gracious, slow to anger, and abounding in steadfast love and faithfulness, 7keeping steadfast love for thousands, forgiving iniquity and transgression and sin, but who will by no means clear the guilty, visiting the iniquity of the fathers on the children and the children's children, to the third and the fourth generation."

READ

Read the passage slowly. To get a broader feel for what's happening, quickly read the expanded passage.

THINK

During a second read, explore the nooks and crannies of God's communication with Moses, noticing words that embellish your mental picture of who God is or of the situation at hand. The third time, listen for one or two of God's words that especially impress you. Choose one word or phrase, then take time to repeat it to yourself, letting it interact with your thoughts, feelings, and desires.

PRAY

Deeply ponder the quality of God that the word or phrase portrays. Share with him what's striking to you about this aspect of his character. Explore what makes you desirous of someone with this trait. If more thoughts, feelings, or desires come to the surface, open up to them and ask God to clarify how they expand or even alter your understanding of this part of his personality. End your prayer by letting the word or words drift through your mind and heart again.

LIVE

Envision the ways God is present to you right now. What posture does he have (for example, standing tall, sitting near)? What expression is on his face? If he speaks to you, what tones does his voice hold? Ask him to enhance — and correct, if necessary — in the coming months this picture of how you see him, through the Bible passages you read and through your experiences.

DAY 7

GOD ENCOUNTERS

On this seventh day, review and reflect on all you have read this week. Take the time to revel in the ways you've encountered God in the past six days.

THE NECESSITY OF SACRIFICE

LEVITICUS 4:32-35

[32]If he brings a lamb as his offering for a sin offering, he shall bring a female without blemish [33]and lay his hand on the head of the sin offering and kill it for a sin offering in the place where they kill the burnt offering. [34]Then the priest shall take some of the blood of the sin offering with his finger and put it on the horns of the altar of burnt offering and pour out all the rest of its blood at the base of the altar. [35]And all its fat he shall remove as the fat of the lamb is removed from the sacrifice of peace offerings, and the priest shall burn it on the altar, on top of the LORD's food offerings. And the priest shall make atonement for him for the sin which he has committed, and he shall be forgiven.

READ

Read the passage in a very soft voice, maybe even a whisper. Focus on each word as you read, listening intently to each word you are reading.

THINK

We might be tempted to believe that Leviticus is a confusing and irrelevant book, but it has some direct implications for our lives. In Leviticus we find specific rules and regulations from Yahweh, given to distinguish his people, the nation of Israel, from every other culture. God commanded the offering of many different types of sacrifices: burnt, grain, fellowship, sin, and guilt. Each of these served a specific purpose for interaction with God. For example, a sin offering was given for confession, forgiveness, and cleansing.

Why do you think God prescribed offerings to be done in such a unique way? Is he cruel to require that animals be killed to make offerings to him? Why or why not? Why don't we do these types of sacrifices today?

Why does God take sin so seriously? When we sin, what sort of sacrifices are we required to bring to God?

PRAY

Ask God to help you understand the severity of your own sin. Thank God that he sent Jesus, the Lamb of God, to come and be the sacrifice for your sins.

LIVE

Knowing that God has provided the ultimate sacrifice through his Son, Jesus, consider sharing this great truth with someone today. As you drive, walk, work, and relax, whisper under your breath, "Thank you, Jesus," each time you remember the sacrifice he made for your sins.

LETTING GO OF SIN

LEVITICUS 16:20-22

[20]And when he has made an end of atoning for the Holy Place and the tent of meeting and the altar, he shall present the live goat. [21]And Aaron shall lay both his hands on the head of the live goat, and confess over it all the iniquities of the people of Israel, and all their transgressions, all their sins. And he shall put them on the head of the goat and send it away into the wilderness by the hand of a man who is in readiness. [22]The goat shall bear all their iniquities on itself to a remote area, and he shall let the goat go free in the wilderness.

READ

Read the passage slowly. (Read the expanded passage to see how the scapegoat is sent off.)

THINK

The practice in this passage may seem odd today. It was also odd in those days because instead of killing a near-perfect animal, this animal would be allowed to live.

Read the passage again.

1. Picture yourself laying your hands on this precious animal's head. Even better, hold a stuffed animal, figurine, or even your pet, and put your hands on its head.
2. Confess to God your acts of rebellion, your bad attitudes, and your harsh thoughts about others.
3. Experience the feeling of transferring your sin to this animal. (Don't feel sorry for the animal. God didn't give it the capacity to take on hurt or guilt from your sin.)
4. See yourself sending it off as it takes your sin far away from you.

PRAY

What do you wish to say to God about having sent your sins off without you?

LIVE

Quiet your mind and wait on God to show you situations in which you need to remember what you just did. Practice resting assured of God's love in those situations as you are resting assured now.

MY HOLY NAME

LEVITICUS 22:1-8

¹And the LORD spoke to Moses, saying, ²"Speak to Aaron and his sons so that they abstain from the holy things of the people of Israel, which they dedicate to me, so that they do not profane my holy name: I am the LORD. ³Say to them, 'If any one of all your offspring throughout your generations approaches the holy things that the people of Israel dedicate to the LORD, while he has an uncleanness, that person shall be cut off from my presence: I am the LORD. ⁴None of the offspring of Aaron who has a leprous disease or a discharge may eat of the holy things until he is clean. Whoever touches anything that is unclean through contact with the dead or a man who has had an emission of semen, ⁵and whoever touches a swarming thing by which he may be made unclean or a person from whom he may take uncleanness, whatever his uncleanness may be — ⁶the person who touches such a thing shall be unclean until the evening and shall not eat of the holy things unless he has bathed his body in water. ⁷When the sun goes down he shall be clean, and afterward he may eat of the holy things, because they are his food. ⁸He shall not eat what dies of itself or is torn by beasts, and so make himself unclean by it: I am the LORD.'"

READ

Get comfortable. Take time to clear your mind, then focus only on this activity. Read the passage silently. Now read it once more, aloud.

THINK

As you read God's statements about himself and about the priests, what is your reaction? Notice whether you are drawn toward God as you read or repelled from God. Talk to him about this. Explore what might be causing your response. Ask him to show you more of yourself—the memories, opinions, and feelings you bring to him on this day.

PRAY

Silently pray the passage. Praying in your own words by responding to what you're reading is okay at first. But as you continue, use the words of the passage as your prayer. Perhaps you will repeat to your soul, "He is the Lord," or ask him to increase your belief that he is holy. Ask God to show you how this truth interacts with your first reaction.

LIVE

Use this silent time simply to rest in the presence of the holy God who has just made himself known to you. Let go of your own words and let yourself enjoy the experience.

DON'T FORGET

NUMBERS 9:4-5,9-12

⁴So Moses told the people of Israel that they should keep the Passover. ⁵And they kept the Passover in the first month, on the fourteenth day of the month, at twilight, in the wilderness of Sinai; according to all that the LORD commanded Moses, so the people of Israel did. . . .

⁹The LORD spoke to Moses, saying, ¹⁰"Speak to the people of Israel, saying, If any one of you or of your descendants is unclean through touching a dead body, or is on a long journey, he shall still keep the Passover to the LORD. ¹¹In the second month on the fourteenth day at twilight they shall keep it. They shall eat it with unleavened bread and bitter herbs. ¹²They shall leave none of it until the morning, nor break any of its bones; according to all the statute for the Passover they shall keep it."

READ

Read the passage five times, each time focusing on a different aspect of it.

THINK

As humans, we are forgetful people, and as forgetful people we need tangible reminders — symbols — of who God is and what he's done. Therefore, as God commanded, many Jewish homes celebrate Passover around the time of Easter to remember all that God orchestrated to bring them out of bondage in Egypt and into the Promised Land. Under what circumstances are you most prone to forget who God is and what he's done for you?

PRAY

Take a stroll down memory lane. Think about the times when God was evident and at work. Allow your memories to guide your prayers of gratitude for all he has done.

LIVE

Create a symbol that will remind you of God's faithfulness in your life. Maybe it's a photograph of your close friends or a rock you picked up during a hike. Put this symbol in a place where you will see it often. When you look at it, be reminded and thank God for his blessings.

A DIFFERENT STORY

NUMBERS 14:17-24

[17]"And now, please let the power of the Lord be great as you have promised, saying, [18]'The LORD is slow to anger and abounding in steadfast love, forgiving iniquity and transgression, but he will by no means clear the guilty, visiting the iniquity of the fathers on the children, to the third and the fourth generation.' [19]Please pardon the iniquity of this people, according to the greatness of your steadfast love, just as you have forgiven this people, from Egypt until now."

[20]Then the LORD said, "I have pardoned, according to your word. [21]But truly, as I live, and as all the earth shall be filled with the glory of the LORD, [22]none of the men who have seen my glory and my signs that I did in Egypt and in the wilderness, and yet have put me to the test these ten times and have not obeyed my voice, [23]shall see the land that I swore to give to their fathers. And none of those who despised me shall see it. [24]But my servant Caleb, because he has a different spirit and has followed me fully, I will bring into the land into which he went, and his descendants shall possess it."

READ

Read the passage aloud slowly. Keep in mind that this is the prayer of Moses after ten of the twelve members of the Israelite scouting party to the Promised Land expressed doubt that they could make their home in that land, even with God's help. (Read the expanded passage to learn more about the depths of the Israelites' doubt.)

THINK

Read the passage again slowly, noting (a) qualities of God that stand out, (b) qualities of Caleb's response to God, and (c) whatever else comes to you.

What impresses you most about God? Why?

What impresses you most about Caleb? Why?

How do you respond to God's willingness to forgive so many Israelites even though he seems to think they do not have the capacity to be used by him?

PRAY

Ask God to show you where you fit in this passage. How might you be tempted to not obey God? How might God be calling you to live a different story—to be one who has "a different spirit" from others, who follows God passionately even though it might involve risks (for example, loving the unlovely, pursuing a career that makes less money, admitting to others the mistakes you've made)?

LIVE

Imagine what it would feel like to have such trust in God that you would be willing to take whatever next steps God presents to you. Imagine what it would be like to be so different from others that you might be excluded because of it.

GOD OF THE CITY OF REFUGES

NUMBERS 35:9-15

⁹And the LORD spoke to Moses, saying, ¹⁰"Speak to the people of Israel and say to them, When you cross the Jordan into the land of Canaan, ¹¹then you shall select cities to be cities of refuge for you, that the manslayer who kills any person without intent may flee there. ¹²The cities shall be for you a refuge from the avenger, that the manslayer may not die until he stands before the congregation for judgment. ¹³And the cities that you give shall be your six cities of refuge. ¹⁴You shall give three cities beyond the Jordan, and three cities in the land of Canaan, to be cities of refuge. ¹⁵These six cities shall be for refuge for the people of Israel, and for the stranger and for the sojourner among them, that anyone who kills any person without intent may flee there."

READ

Read the passage without worrying about specifics; just try to understand its overall idea.

THINK

God wanted communities to try suspected murderers justly in court, but he also planned "city of refuges" as a refuge from would-be avengers until the trial could be held. Spend time thinking about the God who is making himself known here. Jot down a few words to describe him.

PRAY

For a moment, set aside this passage. Check in with yourself—explore recent thoughts, feelings, and events in your life and how you've responded to them. What's primarily on your heart today? Is anything troubling you?

Bring your thoughts to the God who created cities of refuge. Read the verses again. As you do, picture God entering the room. How do you relate to his presence? Share with him what you've been thinking, if you can. Does doing so make you uncomfortable? Why or why not?

LIVE

Think about what it's been like for you to be with the God who is both a God of justice and a God of refuge. Has it left you with questions or with new thoughts on how you want to deal with your sin in the future? Make note of anything that seems significant.

DAY 14

GOD ENCOUNTERS

On this seventh day, review and reflect on all you have read this week. Take the time to revel in the ways you've encountered God in the past six days.

LISTEN!

DEUTERONOMY 6:1-9

¹Now this is the commandment — the statutes and the rules — that the LORD your God commanded me to teach you, that you may do them in the land to which you are going over, to possess it, ²that you may fear the LORD your God, you and your son and your son's son, by keeping all his statutes and his commandments, which I command you, all the days of your life, and that your days may be long. ³Hear therefore, O Israel, and be careful to do them, that it may go well with you, and that you may multiply greatly, as the LORD, the God of your fathers, has promised you, in a land flowing with milk and honey.

⁴Hear, O Israel: The LORD our God, the LORD is one. ⁵You shall love the LORD your God with all your heart and with all your soul and with all your might. ⁶And these words that I command you today shall be on your heart. ⁷You shall teach them diligently to your children, and shall talk of them when you sit in your house, and when you walk by the way, and when you lie down, and when you rise. ⁸You shall bind them as a sign on your hand, and they shall be as frontlets between your eyes. ⁹You shall write them on the doorposts of your house and on your gates.

READ

Stand in a posture signifying respect for and full attention to God's Word. Read the passage aloud.

THINK

This passage is extremely important among Jewish people. In Jesus' time, every good Jew would recite it as soon as he woke up in the morning and right before he went to bed at night. The passage is referred to as the *Shema,* which comes from the Hebrew "to listen" or "to hear." If you visit the Western Wall in Jerusalem today, you will see Jews fervently praying in front of it. They will have leather straps wrapped around their arms and tiny boxes (called phylacteries) containing Scriptures tied to their arms and foreheads.

How seriously do you take the words of God?

PRAY

Slowly and reverently, pray the words found in verses 4 and 5: "Hear, O Israel: The LORD our God, the LORD is one. You shall love the LORD your God with all your heart and with all your soul and with all your might." Repeat these words over and over again, letting what the words ask of you to sink into your heart.

LIVE

Memorize the words you just prayed, and pray them as often as you remember them.

LIVE IN HIS PRESENCE

DEUTERONOMY 10:12-21

¹²And now, Israel, what does the LORD your God require of you, but to fear the LORD your God, to walk in all his ways, to love him, to serve the LORD your God with all your heart and with all your soul, ¹³and to keep the commandments and statutes of the LORD, which I am commanding you today for your good? ¹⁴Behold, to the LORD your God belong heaven and the heaven of heavens, the earth with all that is in it. ¹⁵Yet the LORD set his heart in love on your fathers and chose their offspring after them, you above all peoples, as you are this day. ¹⁶Circumcise therefore the foreskin of your heart, and be no longer stubborn. ¹⁷For the LORD your God is God of gods and Lord of lords, the great, the mighty, and the awesome God, who is not partial and takes no bribe. ¹⁸He executes justice for the fatherless and the widow, and loves the sojourner, giving him food and clothing. ¹⁹Love the sojourner, therefore, for you were sojourners in the land of Egypt. ²⁰You shall fear the LORD your God. You shall serve him and hold fast to him, and by his name you shall swear. ²¹He is your praise. He is your God, who has done for you these great and terrifying things that your eyes have seen.

READ

Read the passage aloud slowly.

THINK

Read it aloud slowly again.

1. What phrase is most memorable?
2. What quality of God stands out to you? Why?
3. What command stands out to you? Why?

PRAY

Here are some ways to pray back the passage. Use as many of these suggestions as you wish.

- Express to God your thoughts about living in his presence. Has living in his presence been important to you or not?
- Express to God those areas in which you would guess he considers you "stubborn." (Pause and let this come to you. Don't necessarily go with the first thing that comes to mind.)
- Express to God your feelings about the have-nots you know (widows, orphans, foreigners). Talk to God honestly about how willing or unwilling you've been to include such people in your life.

LIVE

Experiment with living in God's presence while caring for the rest of the world. Relax. Quiet yourself. Just be.

YOU WERE ONCE SLAVES

DEUTERONOMY 24:10-15,17-22

[10]When you make your neighbor a loan of any sort, you shall not go into his house to collect his pledge. [11]You shall stand outside, and the man to whom you make the loan shall bring the pledge out to you. [12]And if he is a poor man, you shall not sleep in his pledge. [13]You shall restore to him the pledge as the sun sets, that he may sleep in his cloak and bless you. And it shall be righteousness for you before the LORD your God.

[14]You shall not oppress a hired worker who is poor and needy, whether he is one of your brothers or one of the sojourners who are in your land within your towns. [15]You shall give him his wages on the same day, before the sun sets (for he is poor and counts on it), lest he cry against you to the LORD, and you be guilty of sin. . . .

[17]You shall not pervert the justice due to the sojourner or to the fatherless, or take a widow's garment in pledge, [18]but you shall remember that you were a slave in Egypt and the LORD your God redeemed you from there; therefore I command you to do this.

[19]When you reap your harvest in your field and forget a sheaf in the field, you shall not go back to get it. It shall be for the sojourner, the fatherless, and the widow, that the LORD your God may bless you in all the work of your hands. [20]When you beat your olive trees, you shall not go over them again. It shall be for the sojourner, the fatherless, and the widow. [21]When you gather the grapes of your vineyard, you shall not strip it afterward. It shall be for the sojourner, the fatherless, and the widow. [22]You shall remember that you were a slave in the land of Egypt; therefore I command you to do this.

READ

Read the passage, noting especially the three scenarios and God's instructions for how to respond to them.

THINK

What common theme links the three scenarios? Write it down in one sentence. Get a picture in your mind of what this God is like — One who would give such instructions to his people. What stands out to you about him? Jot that down too.

PRAY

Sit with your eyes closed. Think about a recent encounter with someone who might relate to you like the neighbor, worker, sojourner, or orphan described in the passage. Perhaps you spoke a few words to a homeless beggar, or you listened to someone at school or work who was upset. When faced with the person's need, what did you feel? What thoughts popped into your head? What did you do? Take a few moments to explore with God what was going on in your heart during the encounter.

LIVE

Now look back at the theme you wrote down from the passage and at the traits you noticed about God. How do you picture this God responding to you as you think about the situation you faced? Do you sense him speaking a personal message to you? What is it? (If you have a tendency to assume what God's response would be, say, something similar to what an authority figure in your life might say, resist that.) If you feel clueless about what God might be saying to you, offer this up to him and ask him to show you in the coming weeks.

LEAVING A LEGACY

DEUTERONOMY 34:1-4

[1]Then Moses went up from the plains of Moab to Mount Nebo, to the top of Pisgah, which is opposite Jericho. And the LORD showed him all the land, Gilead as far as Dan, [2]all Naphtali, the land of Ephraim and Manasseh, all the land of Judah as far as the western sea, [3]the Negeb, and the Plain, that is, the Valley of Jericho the city of palm trees, as far as Zoar. [4]And the LORD said to him, "This is the land of which I swore to Abraham, to Isaac, and to Jacob, 'I will give it to your offspring.' I have let you see it with your eyes, but you shall not go over there."

READ

Read the passage the way you might to a room full of children. Articulate your words. Use inflections. Sound excited as you read.

THINK

Moses was the leader of the nation of Israel for the latter part of his life. He was mostly obedient and faithful, but there were times of disobedience. Because of that, God told Moses that the Israelites would enter the Promised Land but that he would not. In chapter 34 Moses dies atop Mount Nebo, located in the modern-day country of Jordan, just to the east of the Dead Sea in Israel.

Why do you think God takes disobedience so seriously? What have been some consequences of your own disobedience?

Are you able to trust the promises of God, even if you never end up seeing them? Why or why not?

PRAY

Ask God to help you live a life of faith and obedience, the kind of life that honors him at all times.

LIVE

Think of Moses-like people you know — older, godly individuals living faithfully for God. Consider connecting with them and getting to know them and their stories.

COURAGEOUS WHEN IT COUNTS

JOSHUA 1:1-9

[1]After the death of Moses the servant of the LORD, the LORD said to Joshua the son of Nun, Moses' assistant, [2]"Moses my servant is dead. Now therefore arise, go over this Jordan, you and all this people, into the land that I am giving to them, to the people of Israel. [3]Every place that the sole of your foot will tread upon I have given to you, just as I promised to Moses. [4]From the wilderness and this Lebanon as far as the great river, the river Euphrates, all the land of the Hittites to the Great Sea toward the going down of the sun shall be your territory. [5]No man shall be able to stand before you all the days of your life. Just as I was with Moses, so I will be with you. I will not leave you or forsake you. [6]Be strong and courageous, for you shall cause this people to inherit the land that I swore to their fathers to give them. [7]Only be strong and very courageous, being careful to do according to all the law that Moses my servant commanded you. Do not turn from it to the right hand or to the left, that you may have good success wherever you go. [8]This Book of the Law shall not depart from your mouth, but you shall meditate on it day and night, so that you may be careful to do according to all that is written in it. For then you will make your way prosperous, and then you will have good success. [9]Have I not commanded you? Be strong and courageous. Do not be frightened, and do not be dismayed, for the LORD your God is with you wherever you go."

READ

As you read the passage, imagine that you wrote these words yourself and are now reflecting on what you wrote.

THINK

Israel is grieving the loss of its trusted leader, Moses. But with every ending comes a new beginning. In the midst of the mourning, God approaches Joshua and assures him that he is the man to lead the people into the Promised Land. God promises Joshua that he will be with him and that the land will be given to the nation of Israel. God commands Joshua to be courageous and tells him to remain committed to the study of his Word.

Read verse 9 again. Is embracing these words in your life hard or easy? At what times are you scared? Why? When you are fearful, what can you do about it?

PRAY

Be blatantly honest with God about your fears, worries, concerns, and anxieties. Tell him exactly why you are scared, and be assured that he hears you. Thank him for listening. Then reread the passage, personalizing the words by making God's words to Joshua your very own.

LIVE

When you find yourself in situations that expose your fears, remember the promises of God—his presence and his guidance for you into the future.

SLOW DOWN AND INQUIRE

JOSHUA 9:3-9,11,14-16

³But when the inhabitants of Gibeon heard what Joshua had done to Jericho and to Ai, ⁴they on their part acted with cunning and went and made ready provisions and took worn-out sacks for their donkeys, and wineskins, worn-out and torn and mended, ⁵with worn-out, patched sandals on their feet, and worn-out clothes. And all their provisions were dry and crumbly. ⁶And they went to Joshua in the camp at Gilgal and said to him and to the men of Israel, "We have come from a distant country, so now make a covenant with us." ⁷But the men of Israel said to the Hivites, "Perhaps you live among us; then how can we make a covenant with you?" ⁸They said to Joshua, "We are your servants." And Joshua said to them, "Who are you? And where do you come from?" ⁹They said to him, "From a very distant country your servants have come, because of the name of the LORD your God. For we have heard a report of him, and all that he did in Egypt. . . . ¹¹So our elders and all the inhabitants of our country said to us, 'Take provisions in your hand for the journey and go to meet them and say to them, "We are your servants. Come now, make a covenant with us." ' . . . ¹⁴So the men took some of their provisions, but did not ask counsel from the LORD. ¹⁵And Joshua made peace with them and made a covenant with them, to let them live, and the leaders of the congregation swore to them.

¹⁶At the end of three days after they had made a covenant with them, they heard that they were their neighbors and that they lived among them.

READ

Read the passage slowly. Keep in mind that the people of Gibeon were afraid because Joshua had conquered Jericho and Ai.

THINK

Read the passage slowly again. The people of Gibeon repeatedly flattered Joshua in order to get their way. He accepted their evidence without inquiring after God. Is there a place in your life where you are susceptible to offers and flattery, so you form attachments without asking God for input? (*Attachments* refers to relationships and commitments to people, tasks, and organizations.)

PRAY

Ask God to help you go over your attachments by moving through the following questions as if God were sitting next to you with his arm around you.

What attachments, if any, have you formed because you think the people involved do something for you?

What attachments, if any, have you rushed into without investigating further, especially by asking God what you need to know about the situation?

Ask God to show you where, if at all, you need to back off from an attachment.

LIVE

Wait with an open heart for anything God might say to you. If nothing comes to you, ask God to make it apparent in the next few weeks if there's anything you need to know about your attachments.

20
21

DAY 21

GOD ENCOUNTERS

On this seventh day, review and reflect on all you have read this week. Take the time to revel in the ways you've encountered God in the past six days.

WE WILL SERVE THE LORD

JOSHUA 24:16-24

¹⁶Then the people answered, "Far be it from us that we should forsake the LORD to serve other gods, ¹⁷for it is the LORD our God who brought us and our fathers up from the land of Egypt, out of the house of slavery, and who did those great signs in our sight and preserved us in all the way that we went, and among all the peoples through whom we passed. ¹⁸And the LORD drove out before us all the peoples, the Amorites who lived in the land. Therefore we also will serve the LORD, for he is our God."

¹⁹But Joshua said to the people, "You are not able to serve the LORD, for he is a holy God. He is a jealous God; he will not forgive your transgressions or your sins. ²⁰If you forsake the LORD and serve foreign gods, then he will turn and do you harm and consume you, after having done you good." ²¹And the people said to Joshua, "No, but we will serve the LORD." ²²Then Joshua said to the people, "You are witnesses against yourselves that you have chosen the LORD, to serve him." And they said, "We are witnesses." ²³He said, "Then put away the foreign gods that are among you, and incline your heart to the LORD, the God of Israel." ²⁴And the people said to Joshua, "The LORD our God we will serve, and his voice we will obey."

READ

Read the passage, paying special attention to what it shows you about the nature of the human heart.

PRAY

As you read of the Israelites' passionate desire to follow God ("Far be it from us that we should forsake the LORD."), what is your reaction to them? When you take a bird's-eye view of the history of Israel, noticing their many rebellions against God and inability to stay committed, what does it make you think and feel? Do you relate to Israel at all — in their desire, in their failure, or both? Talk to God about your thoughts and feelings, eventually sitting quietly to listen for his response.

THINK/LIVE

Write about your prayer experience. What was it like for you? What stood out to you about the Israelites? About yourself? About God? If you contemplated your own fickleness or zeal, do you sense that God is leading or challenging you in some way regarding this? Make a note of anything that seems significant.

WHEN YOU CAN'T TAKE THE CREDIT

JUDGES 7:1-7

¹Then Jerubbaal (that is, Gideon) and all the people who were with him rose early and encamped beside the spring of Harod. And the camp of Midian was north of them, by the hill of Moreh, in the valley. ²The LORD said to Gideon, "The people with you are too many for me to give the Midianites into their hand, lest Israel boast over me, saying, 'My own hand has saved me.' ³Now therefore proclaim in the ears of the people, saying, 'Whoever is fearful and trembling, let him return home and hurry away from Mount Gilead.'" Then 22,000 of the people returned, and 10,000 remained.

⁴And the LORD said to Gideon, "The people are still too many. Take them down to the water, and I will test them for you there, and anyone of whom I say to you, 'This one shall go with you,' shall go with you, and anyone of whom I say to you, 'This one shall not go with you,' shall not go." ⁵So he brought the people down to the water. And the LORD said to Gideon, "Every one who laps the water with his tongue, as a dog laps, you shall set by himself. Likewise, every one who kneels down to drink." ⁶And the number of those who lapped, putting their hands to their mouths, was 300 men, but all the rest of the people knelt down to drink water. ⁷And the LORD said to Gideon, "With the 300 men who lapped I will save you and give the Midianites into your hand, and let all the others go every man to his home."

READ

As you read the passage, underline the words that stick out to you or surprise you.

THINK

The book of Judges is filled with violence. Christians struggle to understand how God's redemptive plan can involve these events. Yet God's power is at work when the Israelites battle foreign, pagan armies. God uses Gideon to lead the nation into battle for his purposes. But as he guides Gideon, he asks much of him. God cuts Gideon's army down from thirty-two thousand men to ten thousand, and eventually to three hundred. God wants to show *his* power through Gideon. He wants Israel to credit him.

When have you accomplished things in your own strength and taken all the credit while forgetting about God? When have you accomplished things that seemed big and impossible, knowing you did so only because God intervened?

PRAY

Write a list of huge requests you have for God—things so large that if they came to fruition, you would know they did so only because God intervened. Spend time praying through this list.

LIVE

Review your list on a regular basis, watching for God's incredible—and at times subtle—intervention. As you see God's faithfulness, thank him often that he is a caring friend.

DAY 24

EXPANDED PASSAGE: JUDGES 13

TALKING WITH GOD

JUDGES 13:2-3,6-9,17-20

²There was a certain man of Zorah, of the tribe of the Danites, whose name was Manoah. And his wife was barren and had no children. ³And the angel of the LORD appeared to the woman and said to her, "Behold, you are barren and have not borne children, but you shall conceive and bear a son." . . .

⁶Then the woman came and told her husband, "A man of God came to me, and his appearance was like the appearance of the angel of God, very awesome. I did not ask him where he was from, and he did not tell me his name, ⁷but he said to me, 'Behold, you shall conceive and bear a son. So then drink no wine or strong drink, and eat nothing unclean, for the child shall be a Nazirite to God from the womb to the day of his death.'"

⁸Then Manoah prayed to the LORD and said, "O Lord, please let the man of God whom you sent come again to us and teach us what we are to do with the child who will be born." ⁹And God listened to the voice of Manoah, and the angel of God came again to the woman as she sat in the field. But Manoah her husband was not with her. . . .

¹⁷And Manoah said to the angel of the LORD, "What is your name, so that, when your words come true, we may honor you?" ¹⁸And the angel of the LORD said to him, "Why do you ask my name, seeing it is wonderful?" ¹⁹So Manoah took the young goat with the grain offering, and offered it on the rock to the LORD, to the one who works wonders, and Manoah and his wife were watching. ²⁰And when the flame went up toward heaven from the altar, the angel of the LORD went up in the flame of the altar. Now Manoah and his wife were watching, and they fell on their faces to the ground.

READ

Read the passage aloud slowly. Manoah and his wife will become Samson's parents, and so God prepares them for this task. (Read the expanded passage to hear even more of the story.)

THINK

Read the passage aloud slowly again, taking note of the back-and-forth conversation between God and this couple. It forms a picture of what an interactive life with God might be like.

Notice the conversational interaction: who listened; who asked questions.

Would you have asked the question Manoah asked ("What is your name?") or a different question?

How would it be to talk to God when lying facedown (see verse 20)?

PRAY

Try this: Lie facedown on the floor or the ground as Manoah and his wife did. Ask God for further instruction about something in your life. Notice what it's like to talk to God in this position. Don't get up too soon.

LIVE

Rest your forehead on the ground with your arms above you. Just "be" before God this way.

LET ME BE AVENGED

JUDGES 16:25-30

²⁵And when their hearts were merry, they said, "Call Samson, that he may entertain us." So they called Samson out of the prison, and he entertained them. They made him stand between the pillars. ²⁶And Samson said to the young man who held him by the hand, "Let me feel the pillars on which the house rests, that I may lean against them." ²⁷Now the house was full of men and women. All the lords of the Philistines were there, and on the roof there were about 3,000 men and women, who looked on while Samson entertained.

²⁸Then Samson called to the LORD and said, "O Lord GOD, please remember me and please strengthen me only this once, O God, that I may be avenged on the Philistines for my two eyes." ²⁹And Samson grasped the two middle pillars on which the house rested, and he leaned his weight against them, his right hand on the one and his left hand on the other. ³⁰And Samson said, "Let me die with the Philistines." Then he bowed with all his strength, and the house fell upon the lords and upon all the people who were in it. So the dead whom he killed at his death were more than those whom he had killed during his life.

READ

Sit quietly and let your thoughts settle. Now read the passage silently. Let the events of the story filter into your heart and interact with your present state of mind.

THINK

What stands out to you about Samson's dramatic action and the ending of his life? Do you resonate with his deep desire for justice to be served? What do you observe about how he acted on that desire for revenge?

PRAY

Read the passage a second time, looking specifically for a word or phrase about Samson's desire for revenge or justice that is meaningful to you. Maybe his act angers you, or you feel a similar desire. When you finish reading, close your eyes. Recall the word or phrase and sit quietly, mulling it over. Let it stimulate you into a dialogue with God.

LIVE

Read the passage a third time, watching how God interacts with Samson and with the Philistines: Although God does not directly act or speak in the passage, he grants Samson's request to avenge himself, and he allows the Philistines to lose their lives. What stands out to you about God's involvement (or lack of involvement)? Talk with him about your perception of him in this passage. Be open to what he may be showing you through what you read.

WELCOMING THE STRANGER

RUTH 3:1-2,4,8-13,16-18

¹Then Naomi her mother-in-law said to her, "My daughter, should I not seek rest for you, that it may be well with you? ²Is not Boaz our relative, with whose young women you were? See, he is winnowing barley tonight at the threshing floor. . . . ⁴But when he lies down, observe the place where he lies. Then go and uncover his feet and lie down, and he will tell you what to do." . . .

⁸At midnight the man was startled and turned over, and behold, a woman lay at his feet! ⁹He said, "Who are you?" And she answered, "I am Ruth, your servant. Spread your wings over your servant, for you are a redeemer." ¹⁰And he said, "May you be blessed by the LORD, my daughter. You have made this last kindness greater than the first in that you have not gone after young men, whether poor or rich. ¹¹And now, my daughter, do not fear. I will do for you all that you ask, for all my fellow townsmen know that you are a worthy woman. ¹²And now it is true that I am a redeemer. Yet there is a redeemer nearer than I. ¹³Remain tonight, and in the morning, if he will redeem you, good; let him do it. But if he is not willing to redeem you, then, as the LORD lives, I will redeem you. Lie down until the morning." . . .

¹⁶And when she came to her mother-in-law, she said, "How did you fare, my daughter?" Then she told her all that the man had done for her, ¹⁷saying, "These six measures of barley he gave to me, for he said to me, 'You must not go back empty-handed to your mother-in-law.'" ¹⁸She replied, "Wait, my daughter, until you learn how the matter turns out, for the man will not rest but will settle the matter today."

READ

Read the passage slowly. Naomi is Ruth's mother-in-law, the mother of Ruth's deceased husband.

THINK

Read the passage again slowly, this time keeping in mind that Ruth is a foreign Moabite woman while Naomi and Boaz are Israelites. Ruth is different from them in nationality, background, and age.

Who do you identify with most: Naomi or Boaz, the older, wiser Israelites, or Ruth, the younger, foreign woman?

Imagining you are the person you identified with, how does it feel to hear or say the term *daughter*? (Again, this was unusual because of their differences in nationality.)

What might God be saying to you about the "strangers" in your life?

What might God be telling you about the places in your life where you feel like a stranger?

PRAY

Thank God for how he provides for those who are strangers and aliens, that he isn't partial to just one group. Ask God how you might partner with him in this.

LIVE

In the quiet, consider God's attentiveness to all people. Is there someone specific he brings to mind? Today and in the next few days, look for opportunities to pay attention to the stranger in the same way God does.

DECIPHERING GOD'S VOICE

1 SAMUEL 3:8-10

[8]And the LORD called Samuel again the third time. And he arose and went to Eli and said, "Here I am, for you called me." Then Eli perceived that the LORD was calling the boy. [9]Therefore Eli said to Samuel, "Go, lie down, and if he calls you, you shall say, 'Speak, LORD, for your servant hears.'" So Samuel went and lay down in his place.

[10]And the LORD came and stood, calling as at other times, "Samuel! Samuel!" And Samuel said, "Speak, for your servant hears."

READ

As you read the passage, imagine yourself in the story, watching the situation from the back of the room.

THINK

At the beginning of 1 Samuel, Hannah wanted to give birth to a son, but she was barren. She prayed earnestly, crying out to the Lord. God heard her prayer, and she gave birth to Samuel. She dedicated him to the temple, where he ministered under Eli the priest. Scholars believe Samuel was a teenager when the events of this passage occurred.

Does hearing God so clearly seem possible? How do you decipher between his voice and the other voices in your life? Samuel needed Eli's guidance for this. What people around you could help you discern when God is trying to communicate with you and what he's saying?

PRAY

Often the most effective way to hear God's voice is to still our minds and quiet our hearts for a considerable amount of time. Set aside twenty minutes in a quiet place and make yourself comfortable. Invite God to communicate with you. Don't read or pray. Just listen and be, bringing your mind back if it wanders.

LIVE

Sometime in the next week, schedule another twenty minutes of silence and once again listen and wait for God to speak to you. Don't give up. Your practice will pay off.

DAY 28

GOD ENCOUNTERS

On this seventh day, review and reflect on all you have read this week. Take the time to revel in the ways you've encountered God in the past six days.

IS GOD ENOUGH?

1 SAMUEL 8:1,3-7,9-10,19-22

¹When Samuel became old, he made his sons judges over Israel. . . . ³Yet his sons did not walk in his ways but turned aside after gain. They took bribes and perverted justice.

⁴Then all the elders of Israel gathered together and came to Samuel at Ramah ⁵and said to him, "Behold, you are old and your sons do not walk in your ways. Now appoint for us a king to judge us like all the nations." ⁶But the thing displeased Samuel when they said, "Give us a king to judge us." And Samuel prayed to the LORD. ⁷And the LORD said to Samuel, "Obey the voice of the people in all that they say to you, for they have not rejected you, but they have rejected me from being king over them. . . . ⁹Now then, obey their voice; only you shall solemnly warn them and show them the ways of the king who shall reign over them."

¹⁰So Samuel told all the words of the LORD to the people who were asking for a king from him. . . .

¹⁹But the people refused to obey the voice of Samuel. And they said, "No! But there shall be a king over us, ²⁰that we also may be like all the nations, and that our king may judge us and go out before us and fight our battles." ²¹And when Samuel had heard all the words of the people, he repeated them in the ears of the LORD. ²²And the LORD said to Samuel, "Obey their voice and make them a king." Samuel then said to the men of Israel, "Go every man to his city."

READ

Read the passage aloud slowly.

THINK

The Israelites wanted God, but they were afraid they'd miss out if they didn't have a king like the other nations. They wanted to fit in with the other nations by having a king lead them and fight their battles for them. Read the passage again, this time deeply feeling the determination of the Israelites and the disappointment of Samuel.

1. Who do you resemble most? (a) Samuel — being confronted by people asking him to make changes he believes are wrong, or (b) the Israelites — wanting to be like others?
2. If you chose *a*, converse with God about this as Samuel did: What would you like to say to God regarding these demands? If *b*, how would you finish this sentence: I want to be like _____. If you continue wanting to be like a certain person, how might it cheat you out of what God wants for *you*?
3. What would your life look like if you trusted God to give you what you need, regardless of how odd that may seem when compared to other people's lives?

PRAY

Be honest with God about any frustration of wanting to be like others or frustration with those who do. Ask God to show you the advantages of trusting him more with these things.

LIVE

While you sit in a quiet place, practice feeling okay being different from other people. If you can, view that difference as special or chosen. Relax with a sense of God's hand on you.

AND THE LORD BE WITH YOU!

1 SAMUEL 17:31-40

³¹When the words that David spoke were heard, they repeated them before Saul, and he sent for him. ³²And David said to Saul, "Let no man's heart fail because of him. Your servant will go and fight with this Philistine." ³³And Saul said to David, "You are not able to go against this Philistine to fight with him, for you are but a youth, and he has been a man of war from his youth." ³⁴But David said to Saul, "Your servant used to keep sheep for his father. And when there came a lion, or a bear, and took a lamb from the flock, ³⁵I went after him and struck him and delivered it out of his mouth. And if he arose against me, I caught him by his beard and struck him and killed him. ³⁶Your servant has struck down both lions and bears, and this uncircumcised Philistine shall be like one of them, for he has defied the armies of the living God." ³⁷And David said, "The LORD who delivered me from the paw of the lion and from the paw of the bear will deliver me from the hand of this Philistine." And Saul said to David, "Go, and the LORD be with you!"

³⁸Then Saul clothed David with his armor. He put a helmet of bronze on his head and clothed him with a coat of mail, ³⁹and David strapped his sword over his armor. And he tried in vain to go, for he had not tested them. Then David said to Saul, "I cannot go with these, for I have not tested them." So David put them off. ⁴⁰Then he took his staff in his hand and chose five smooth stones from the brook and put them in his shepherd's pouch. His sling was in his hand, and he approached the Philistine.

READ

While you read, let the scenario unfold in your mind. When David describes striking a bear, hear the roaring and grunting. Feel the ponderous weight of the bronze helmet, and then the light, smooth weight of the stones in your hand.

THINK

What one particular event, character, or feature of the story stands out to you? Take time to concentrate on that. Are you drawn to David's courage? Maybe you're surprised when David rejects Saul's armor. Consider what your own reaction would be, and then consider how the characters in the story reacted. As you meditate, allow God to show you more about yourself, him, and the way life is.

PRAY/LIVE

Priest and author Henri Nouwen wrote, "Make the conscious choice to move the attention of your anxious heart away from [the] waves and direct it to the One who walks on them and says, 'It's me. Don't be afraid.' . . . Look at him and say, 'Lord, have mercy.' Say it again and again, not anxiously but with confidence that he is very close to you and will put your soul to rest."[2] (To read the rest of the story, see John 6:16-21.)

What do you feel anxious about, if anything? What might happen if you shifted your attention "away from [the] waves" and "to the One who walks on them"? What concrete thing could you do to help redirect your attention?

HONORING AND VALUING OTHERS

1 SAMUEL 26:7-11

⁷So David and Abishai went to the army by night. And there lay Saul sleeping within the encampment, with his spear stuck in the ground at his head, and Abner and the army lay around him. ⁸Then said Abishai to David, "God has given your enemy into your hand this day. Now please let me pin him to the earth with one stroke of the spear, and I will not strike him twice." ⁹But David said to Abishai, "Do not destroy him, for who can put out his hand against the Lord's anointed and be guiltless?" ¹⁰And David said, "As the Lord lives, the Lord will strike him, or his day will come to die, or he will go down into battle and perish. ¹¹The Lord forbid that I should put out my hand against the Lord's anointed. But take now the spear that is at his head and the jar of water, and let us go."

READ

Hold this book in your hands. As you read the passage, pace the room or walk outside. As you do, consider the speed at which you are reading. Take your time and find a rhythm of reading that matches your pace. (For example, if you are reading fast, walk fast.)

THINK

Earlier in 1 Samuel, God anointed David to be the future king of Israel, even though Saul was still on the throne. This man, overcome with cruelty, jealousy, evil, and insecurity, then repeatedly attempted to take David's life. For many years, David hid from Saul's army.

One night, David and Abishai sneak into Saul's camp, and there Abishai notices the perfect opportunity to kill Saul. But David refuses. David is so certain of God's sovereignty that he refuses to kill Saul.

We all have enemies, big or small, and desire for them to come to ruin. Yet ponder the interchange between Saul and David in verses 21-24.

PRAY

Think of the people you consider your enemies. Pray for them and ask God to help you honor them, even though doing so may seem impossible.

LIVE

Seek out intentional opportunities to honor those who dishonor you and to value the lives of those who do not value you.

PAIN, DISAPPOINTMENT, AND HEARTBREAK

2 SAMUEL 1:24-27

24 You daughters of Israel, weep over Saul,
    who clothed you luxuriously in scarlet,
    who put ornaments of gold on your apparel.

25 How the mighty have fallen
    in the midst of the battle!

Jonathan lies slain on your high places.
    26I am distressed for you, my brother Jonathan;
very pleasant have you been to me;
    your love to me was extraordinary,
    surpassing the love of women.

27 How the mighty have fallen,
    and the weapons of war perished!

READ

King Saul (who tried to kill David many times) and his son, Jonathan (David's best friend), are dead. If possible, read the expanded passage, the song of lament David wrote in response to the news of their death.

THINK

Sometimes pain and suffering are the central emotions of our hearts. We cannot avoid pain and suffering, but we can control how we respond to them. David's reaction is to be honest and open about the pain rather than avoid it or pretend it isn't there.

What is your response to heartbreak? Do you think David's response is healthy? Why or why not? What thoughts and feelings go through you as David honors the evil king in death?

PRAY

Think of the pain and heartbreak you have experienced in your lifetime. Maybe that pain is a current reality. Though doing so may be difficult, spend time expressing your pain in a lament to God. See him attentively listening to you and reaching out to comfort you. What does it feel like to be comforted?

LIVE

Live knowing that God is loving enough to listen to you and big enough to care for you in your pain.

GOD'S TRACK RECORD WITH ME

2 SAMUEL 7:18,20-23,28-29

[18]Then King David went in and sat before the LORD and said, "Who am I, O Lord GOD, and what is my house, that you have brought me thus far? . . . [20]And what more can David say to you? For you know your servant, O Lord GOD! [21]Because of your promise, and according to your own heart, you have brought about all this greatness, to make your servant know it. [22]Therefore you are great, O LORD God. For there is none like you, and there is no God besides you, according to all that we have heard with our ears. [23]And who is like your people Israel, the one nation on earth whom God went to redeem to be his people, making himself a name and doing for them great and awesome things by driving out before your people, whom you redeemed for yourself from Egypt, a nation and its gods? . . . [28]And now, O Lord GOD, you are God, and your words are true, and you have promised this good thing to your servant. [29]Now therefore may it please you to bless the house of your servant, so that it may continue forever before you. For you, O Lord GOD, have spoken, and with your blessing shall the house of your servant be blessed forever."

READ
Read the passage aloud slowly.

THINK
Read the passage even more slowly and deliberately, considering every word. Listen for the line that resonates with you and read it again after you finish the passage. Pause. Consider any of the following issues, letting God nudge you.

- In what ways has God changed you that you can be grateful for?
- What has God brought you out of?
- How has God been heroic regarding you ("doing . . . great and awesome things by driving out before your people, whom you redeemed for yourself from Egypt, a nation and its gods")?
- What would you like to ask God for regarding the future?

PRAY
Pray through the above passage, innovating and personalizing your prayer according to the questions in the Think section.

LIVE
Give this a try: Consider the line from the passage that caught your attention and put it to a tune from a song you already know (or make a tune up, if you wish). Sing that line and then sit in the quiet. Sing it again and sit in the quiet. Sing it one more time and sit in the quiet.

DAY 34

EXPANDED PASSAGE: 2 SAMUEL 9

HONORING OTHERS

2 SAMUEL 9:8-13

[8]And he paid homage and said, "What is your servant, that you should show regard for a dead dog such as I?"

[9]Then the king called Ziba, Saul's servant, and said to him, "All that belonged to Saul and to all his house I have given to your master's grandson. [10]And you and your sons and your servants shall till the land for him and shall bring in the produce, that your master's grandson may have bread to eat. But Mephibosheth your master's grandson shall always eat at my table." Now Ziba had fifteen sons and twenty servants. [11]Then Ziba said to the king, "According to all that my lord the king commands his servant, so will your servant do." So Mephibosheth ate at David's table, like one of the king's sons. [12]And Mephibosheth had a young son, whose name was Mica. And all who lived in Ziba's house became Mephibosheth's servants. [13]So Mephibosheth lived in Jerusalem, for he ate always at the king's table. Now he was lame in both his feet.

READ

Read the passage slowly, setting yourself inside the throne room. Look at David up close — the imposing crown, the rugged face that's seen countless wars, the lavish surroundings. Now see Mephibosheth, hunched in fear, embarrassed and uncomfortable. How might he have come into the room, being "lame in both his feet"? What feelings rise up in you as you see the story play out? What questions come to mind?

THINK

Pause to become aware of how you relate to what is unfolding here. Which character do you identify with, if any? Why?

PRAY

Read the story a second time, being aware of memories, thoughts, or ideas it triggers. Read it one last time, listening for how the story's message about honoring others relates to what is in you today. Spend time meditating on what you discover.

LIVE

Ask God if there is something he is specifically inviting you to do based on your reading today. Is there anything standing in your way of responding? Explore it with God. Talk to him about what holds you back from following him completely.

DAY 35

GOD ENCOUNTERS

On this seventh day, review and reflect on all you have read this week. Take the time to revel in the ways you've encountered God in the past six days.

AN ABSALOM MOMENT

2 SAMUEL 15:3-6

[3]Absalom would say to him, "See, your claims are good and right, but there is no man designated by the king to hear you." [4]Then Absalom would say, "Oh that I were judge in the land! Then every man with a dispute or cause might come to me, and I would give him justice." [5]And whenever a man came near to pay homage to him, he would put out his hand and take hold of him and kiss him. [6]Thus Absalom did to all of Israel who came to the king for judgment. So Absalom stole the hearts of the men of Israel.

READ

Read the passage five times.

THINK

There are points in our lives (more often than we would like to admit) when we attempt consciously and subconsciously to promote ourselves in unhealthy and selfish ways. We puff ourselves up, brag about our accomplishments, and embellish the truth.

Absalom, the son of King David, promotes himself for selfish gain in front of those who came to the city gate. The text says he "stole the hearts of the men of Israel."

When are you most tempted to steal the hearts of everyone in _____? Think about your most recent Absalom moment. Consider the roots of your temptation and how you might avoid it in the future.

PRAY

Spend time inviting God to remind you that he loves you just the way you are, that you cannot earn his approval. Welcome God to show you your true identity as his child, an identity that is defined not by what you do, but by who you are and to whom you belong.

LIVE

Ask a good friend to gently keep you accountable when you begin to promote yourself in front of others. Be ready to accept your friend's input.

LOVING THOSE IN THE HERE AND NOW

2 SAMUEL 19:1-8

¹It was told Joab, "Behold, the king is weeping and mourning for Absalom." ²So the victory that day was turned into mourning for all the people, for the people heard that day, "The king is grieving for his son." ³And the people stole into the city that day as people steal in who are ashamed when they flee in battle. ⁴The king covered his face, and the king cried with a loud voice, "O my son Absalom, O Absalom, my son, my son!" ⁵Then Joab came into the house to the king and said, "You have today covered with shame the faces of all your servants, who have this day saved your life and the lives of your sons and your daughters and the lives of your wives and your concubines, ⁶because you love those who hate you and hate those who love you. For you have made it clear today that commanders and servants are nothing to you, for today I know that if Absalom were alive and all of us were dead today, then you would be pleased. ⁷Now therefore arise, go out and speak kindly to your servants, for I swear by the LORD, if you do not go, not a man will stay with you this night, and this will be worse for you than all the evil that has come upon you from your youth until now." ⁸Then the king arose and took his seat in the gate. And the people were all told, "Behold, the king is sitting in the gate." And all the people came before the king.

READ

Read the passage aloud slowly. Absalom had rebelled against his father, David, and took over Israel. As David mourns Absalom, the people who defended him and brought him back with honor are listening.

THINK

Read the passage aloud slowly again. David did what we often do. He lived in regret. He wanted what he used to have and what he couldn't now have. As a result, he undervalued and discouraged the people who had stood by him and helped him.

1. Who do you identify with more: David or the army?
2. Consider their feelings: David living in regret; the army feeling ignored and discarded.
3. Consider their next steps: David turning his heart to the people around him who loved him; the army speaking up and stating their needs to a hurting person.

PRAY

Pray for yourself and others, especially that they'll see and implement any possible next steps (for example, moving out of regret and valuing the people in front of them, or speaking up to someone who is devaluing others).

LIVE

Let your mind rest in glad appreciation for those who stand by you. Ask God for opportunities to bless them. Then in the dailiness of life, look for those opportunities.

GOD FEELS THE PAIN

2 SAMUEL 24:13-17,25

¹³So Gad came to David and told him, and said to him, "Shall three years of famine come to you in your land? Or will you flee three months before your foes while they pursue you? Or shall there be three days' pestilence in your land? Now consider, and decide what answer I shall return to him who sent me." ¹⁴Then David said to Gad, "I am in great distress. Let us fall into the hand of the LORD, for his mercy is great; but let me not fall into the hand of man."

¹⁵So the LORD sent a pestilence on Israel from the morning until the appointed time. And there died of the people from Dan to Beersheba 70,000 men. ¹⁶And when the angel stretched out his hand toward Jerusalem to destroy it, the LORD relented from the calamity and said to the angel who was working destruction among the people, "It is enough; now stay your hand." And the angel of the LORD was by the threshing floor of Araunah the Jebusite. ¹⁷Then David spoke to the LORD when he saw the angel who was striking the people, and said, "Behold, I have sinned, and I have done wickedly. But these sheep, what have they done? Please let your hand be against me and against my father's house." . . .

²⁵And David built there an altar to the LORD and offered burnt offerings and peace offerings. So the LORD responded to the plea for the land, and the plague was averted from Israel.

READ

Skim the expanded passage. Now read the excerpt three times carefully.

THINK/PRAY

Set the text aside and imaginatively replay the story, inserting yourself as a character in it. Perhaps you will be one of David's elders, or David himself.

What do you think and feel as you hear God's words of discipline? What do you experience as you walk through this tension-filled and tragic day? What do you see? Hear? Smell? What questions do you have for God? Are you angry? Afraid? Talk to him.

As the end of the day approaches and you see God's interaction with the angel, what is that like for you? When God's heart is changed by David's prayers, what thoughts and feelings bubble up in you? Express them to God.

LIVE

C. S. Lewis wrote, "[Each sinful act leaves a mark] on that tiny central self which no one sees in this life but which each of us will have to endure — or enjoy — for ever. One man may be so placed that his anger sheds the blood of thousands, and another so placed that, however angry he gets, he will only be laughed at. But the little mark on the soul may be much the same in both."[3] Are there any "little marks" on your soul that you haven't talked about with God? Explore recent experiences, reactions, thoughts, and feelings you've had. What do they tell you about what's inside your heart? Talk to God about this, and make note of any action you feel he is leading you to.

A DREAM FULFILLED

1 KINGS 5:1-5

¹Now Hiram king of Tyre sent his servants to Solomon when he heard that they had anointed him king in place of his father, for Hiram always loved David. ²And Solomon sent word to Hiram, ³"You know that David my father could not build a house for the name of the Lord his God because of the warfare with which his enemies surrounded him, until the Lord put them under the soles of his feet. ⁴But now the Lord my God has given me rest on every side. There is neither adversary nor misfortune. ⁵And so I intend to build a house for the name of the Lord my God, as the Lord said to David my father, 'Your son, whom I will set on your throne in your place, shall build the house for my name.'"

READ

Read the passage aloud slowly.

THINK

Read the passage aloud slowly again, especially verses 3-5.

1. Listen for the words or phrases that stand out to you — perhaps one of these:

   - "build a house for the name of the LORD his God"
   - "warfare with which his enemies surrounded him, until the LORD put them under the soles of his feet"
   - "LORD my God has given me rest on every side. There is neither adversary nor misfortune."
   - "so I intend to build a house for the name of the LORD my God"

   These phrases indicate that David lived an interactive life with God and that Solomon is attempting to do the same. They also refer to David and Solomon's dream coming true. David had wisely let go of his dream of building the temple, while Solomon was now taking the next step by implementing the dream.

2. What dreams have you had?
3. What dreams have you let go of or picked up?

PRAY

Talk to God about the phrases in the passage that hint at dreams you have. Ask God to give you wisdom about whether you need to let go of these dreams or pick them up. Ask God for vision and power to take your next step.

LIVE

Relish the peace that God gives, knowing that dreams don't have to be realized today. Maybe ponder and pursue your next step. Put on the idea of readiness and see if it fits.

LISTEN TO MY PRAYERS

1 KINGS 8:22-30

²²Then Solomon stood before the altar of the LORD in the presence of all the assembly of Israel and spread out his hands toward heaven, ²³and said, "O LORD, God of Israel, there is no God like you, in heaven above or on earth beneath, keeping covenant and showing steadfast love to your servants who walk before you with all their heart; ²⁴you have kept with your servant David my father what you declared to him. You spoke with your mouth, and with your hand have fulfilled it this day. ²⁵Now therefore, O LORD, God of Israel, keep for your servant David my father what you have promised him, saying, 'You shall not lack a man to sit before me on the throne of Israel, if only your sons pay close attention to their way, to walk before me as you have walked before me.' ²⁶Now therefore, O God of Israel, let your word be confirmed, which you have spoken to your servant David my father.

²⁷"But will God indeed dwell on the earth? Behold, heaven and the highest heaven cannot contain you; how much less this house that I have built! ²⁸Yet have regard to the prayer of your servant and to his plea, O LORD my God, listening to the cry and to the prayer that your servant prays before you this day, ²⁹that your eyes may be open night and day toward this house, the place of which you have said, 'My name shall be there,' that you may listen to the prayer that your servant offers toward this place. ³⁰And listen to the plea of your servant and of your people Israel, when they pray toward this place. And listen in heaven your dwelling place, and when you hear, forgive."

READ

Read the passage.

THINK

What's your immediate reaction to Solomon's candid prayer to God? Think about the statements Solomon makes and the things he asks God to do. Are they things you could let yourself ask of God? Or do they indicate a belief in qualities of God that you have not encountered or experienced? Which qualities?

PRAY

Read Solomon's prayer again, this time listening for what stands out to you as representing the lack of belief you noticed in yourself when you read the passage the first time. Explore your reaction more deeply, paying attention to what it tells you about yourself. Maybe you feel that you can bring to God only desires that are completely selfless, or perhaps you don't trust that he shows "steadfast love" to you. Share with God what you uncover.

LIVE

Ignatius of Loyola once said, "Everything that one turns in the direction of God is prayer." No matter what has arisen in you during this time — irritation, fear, desire, disinterest, lack of trust in God — it can all be prayer when shared with him; it's all part of your conversation with God. Notice how Solomon lets his anxiety and insecurity spill into his prayer to God, and allow yourself to do the same.

IDOL FACTORIES

1 KINGS 12:27-33

[27]"If this people go up to offer sacrifices in the temple of the LORD at Jerusalem, then the heart of this people will turn again to their lord, to Rehoboam king of Judah, and they will kill me and return to Rehoboam king of Judah." [28]So the king took counsel and made two calves of gold. And he said to the people, "You have gone up to Jerusalem long enough. Behold your gods, O Israel, who brought you up out of the land of Egypt." [29]And he set one in Bethel, and the other he put in Dan. [30]Then this thing became a sin, for the people went as far as Dan to be before one. [31]He also made temples on high places and appointed priests from among all the people, who were not of the Levites. [32]And Jeroboam appointed a feast on the fifteenth day of the eighth month like the feast that was in Judah, and he offered sacrifices on the altar. So he did in Bethel, sacrificing to the calves that he made. And he placed in Bethel the priests of the high places that he had made. [33]He went up to the altar that he had made in Bethel on the fifteenth day in the eighth month, in the month that he had devised from his own heart. And he instituted a feast for the people of Israel and went up to the altar to make offerings.

READ

Each time you read this passage, focus on the sentence: "Then this thing becomes a sin."

THINK

Israel at this time was split into two sections: the northern and the southern kingdoms. Jeroboam was ruling in the northern kingdom. He erected two golden calves (as Aaron had at Sinai in Exodus). In addition to calves, he erected forbidden shrines and created a sacred holiday.

Instead of placing his entire trust in Yahweh, Jeroboam chose to erect idols to be the center of worship for the people in his kingdom. Under his leadership, the significance of worshipping the Lord God was lessened and eventually lost.

Sneering at such blatant disrespect of the living God is easy for us. But even though we don't erect golden calves, our focus on certain things eclipses our worship of God. John Calvin said that our hearts are idol factories.

Meditate on some of the golden calves in your life that eclipse your worship of God. These could be reputation, power, wealth, identity, fame, church, relationships — anything that takes your eyes off God.

PRAY

Spend time confessing your golden calves. Ask the Holy Spirit to pinch you each time you turn to them.

LIVE

Be aware that your heart is an idol factory. Recognize that idols come in all shapes and sizes. When you find yourself bowing a knee to them, return to the Lord in humility.

41
42

DAY 42

GOD ENCOUNTERS

On this seventh day, review and reflect on all you have read this week. Take the time to revel in the ways you've encountered God in the past six days.

WHEN TRUSTING GOD IS A HANDFUL

1 KINGS 17:7-16

⁷And after a while the brook dried up, because there was no rain in the land.

⁸Then the word of the LORD came to him, ⁹"Arise, go to Zarephath, which belongs to Sidon, and dwell there. Behold, I have commanded a widow there to feed you." ¹⁰So he arose and went to Zarephath. And when he came to the gate of the city, behold, a widow was there gathering sticks. And he called to her and said, "Bring me a little water in a vessel, that I may drink." ¹¹And as she was going to bring it, he called to her and said, "Bring me a morsel of bread in your hand." ¹²And she said, "As the LORD your God lives, I have nothing baked, only a handful of flour in a jar and a little oil in a jug. And now I am gathering a couple of sticks that I may go in and prepare it for myself and my son, that we may eat it and die." ¹³And Elijah said to her, "Do not fear; go and do as you have said. But first make me a little cake of it and bring it to me, and afterward make something for yourself and your son. ¹⁴For thus says the LORD, the God of Israel, 'The jar of flour shall not be spent, and the jug of oil shall not be empty, until the day that the LORD sends rain upon the earth.'" ¹⁵And she went and did as Elijah said. And she and he and her household ate for many days. ¹⁶The jar of flour was not spent, neither did the jug of oil become empty, according to the word of the LORD that he spoke by Elijah.

READ

Read the passage aloud slowly.

THINK

Read the passage slowly again. This time notice the repetitive phrases and words that seem to shimmer. Are there any in this passage that you sense God saying directly to you?

1. How do you resemble Elijah, the loner who was perhaps content by the solitary brook but now has to venture into Palestinian territory and ask a widow for her last dime?
2. How do you identify with the widow and feel that Elijah is asking too much? How difficult is it for you to give up the last handful of flour? Hold out your hand in front of you. Open and close it. Imagine that the amount of flour your hand could hold is all that stands between you and death.
3. How do you think the widow felt every time she put her hand in the jar and there was another handful of flour?

PRAY

Ask God what might be your jar of flour today—something that needs filling up. It's okay to tell God he's asking too much. At first, the widow did just that. Trusting God is a process.

LIVE

Consider how it would feel to trust God this much. How would your life be different if you trusted God with just a little more every single morning, as the widow did?

BECAUSE HE HUMBLED HIMSELF

1 KINGS 21:20-29

²⁰Ahab said to Elijah, "Have you found me, O my enemy?" He answered, "I have found you, because you have sold yourself to do what is evil in the sight of the LORD. ²¹Behold, I will bring disaster upon you. I will utterly burn you up, and will cut off from Ahab every male, bond or free, in Israel. ²²And I will make your house like the house of Jeroboam the son of Nebat, and like the house of Baasha the son of Ahijah, for the anger to which you have provoked me, and because you have made Israel to sin. ²³And of Jezebel the LORD also said, 'The dogs shall eat Jezebel within the walls of Jezreel.' ²⁴Anyone belonging to Ahab who dies in the city the dogs shall eat, and anyone of his who dies in the open country the birds of the heavens shall eat."

²⁵(There was none who sold himself to do what was evil in the sight of the LORD like Ahab, whom Jezebel his wife incited. ²⁶He acted very abominably in going after idols, as the Amorites had done, whom the LORD cast out before the people of Israel.)

²⁷And when Ahab heard those words, he tore his clothes and put sackcloth on his flesh and fasted and lay in sackcloth and went about dejectedly. ²⁸And the word of the LORD came to Elijah the Tishbite, saying, ²⁹"Have you seen how Ahab has humbled himself before me? Because he has humbled himself before me, I will not bring the disaster in his days; but in his son's days I will bring the disaster upon his house."

READ

Read the passage, putting yourself into the scene as much as you can.

THINK

Imagine yourself as Elijah, noticing what you think and feel throughout this tale. (See the expanded passage for more details.) Read the passage again until you reach God's words to Ahab and Jezebel, and the description of what they have done to defy him. Pause there.

PRAY

As you picture yourself speaking God's words of judgment to Ahab, listen to what you are saying. What does God's anger toward this enemy make you feel? Do you feel the same anger God does over the injustice? If not, what does Ahab's sin make you feel? When you picture the three of you there—Ahab, God, you—what position is your body inclined to take toward each of them? Talk to God about your response.

Now return to the passage, and continue reading where you left off. When you reach the part about Ahab's repentance, hear God tell you about his change of mind. What does this make you feel? Where do your thoughts go? Talk to God about your response.

LIVE

Meditate on the following prayer from *The Book of Common Prayer*: "The Lord is full of compassion and mercy: O come, let us adore him."[4] Notice what your response is. If there is something you need to repent of today, go to God and receive his mercy. If you want to adore him for his compassion, spend time doing so. If you don't want to adore God, take time to open yourself to the reality that he is praiseworthy. Don't force yourself to feel things you don't feel or to say things you don't mean, but do consider the reality acknowledged in the prayer.

44

FALSE HOPES?

2 KINGS 4:20,24-29

²⁰And when he had lifted him and brought him to his mother, the child sat on her lap till noon, and then he died. . . .

²⁴Then she saddled the donkey, and she said to her servant, "Urge the animal on; do not slacken the pace for me unless I tell you." ²⁵So she set out and came to the man of God at Mount Carmel.

When the man of God saw her coming, he said to Gehazi his servant, "Look, there is the Shunammite. ²⁶Run at once to meet her and say to her, 'Is all well with you? Is all well with your husband? Is all well with the child?'" And she answered, "All is well." ²⁷And when she came to the mountain to the man of God, she caught hold of his feet. And Gehazi came to push her away. But the man of God said, "Leave her alone, for she is in bitter distress, and the LORD has hidden it from me and has not told me." ²⁸Then she said, "Did I ask my lord for a son? Did I not say, 'Do not deceive me?'" ²⁹He said to Gehazi, "Tie up your garment and take my staff in your hand and go. If you meet anyone, do not greet him, and if anyone greets you, do not reply. And lay my staff on the face of the child."

READ
Read the passage, preferably including the expanded passage.

THINK
Have you ever felt the bitter sting of shattered hopes and desires? The barren woman from Shunem knows the sting intimately — her grief here seems to confirm the doubt she experienced earlier when the holy man, Elisha, prophesied that she would have a son. At the time of the prophecy, not wanting to get her hopes up, she wouldn't even let on that she desired a son. Now she seems to wish she'd never hoped at all.

Notice Elisha's response to the woman in her fear, grief, and regret. Take several minutes to think about this. How might Elisha's response reflect God's response to her? What might God have been feeling as he watched her struggle with her son's death?

PRAY
Explore your own heart to see if there are any deep desires there that you are afraid to trust God with. Can you tell him why you hold back? Ask him to show you his response to your desires and to help you trust him more, just as the Shunammite woman trusted Elisha enough to expose her anguish to him.

LIVE
Henri Nouwen wrote, "At every moment you have to decide to trust the voice that says, 'I love you. I knit you together in your mother's womb' (Ps. 139:13)."[5] Ponder this quote. What might your life look like if you were to take God at his word, believing that he knows all about you and cares for you as tenderly as Elisha cared for the Shunammite? How might you pray differently? Live differently?

INVESTING IN PEOPLE

2 KINGS 11:17–12:2

[17]And Jehoiada made a covenant between the LORD and the king and people, that they should be the LORD's people, and also between the king and the people. [18]Then all the people of the land went to the house of Baal and tore it down; his altars and his images they broke in pieces, and they killed Mattan the priest of Baal before the altars. And the priest posted watchmen over the house of the LORD. [19]And he took the captains, the Carites, the guards, and all the people of the land, and they brought the king down from the house of the LORD, marching through the gate of the guards to the king's house. And he took his seat on the throne of the kings. [20]So all the people of the land rejoiced, and the city was quiet after Athaliah had been put to death with the sword at the king's house.

[21]Jehoash was seven years old when he began to reign.

[1]In the seventh year of Jehu, Jehoash began to reign, and he reigned forty years in Jerusalem. His mother's name was Zibiah of Beersheba. [2]And Jehoash did what was right in the eyes of the LORD all his days, because Jehoiada the priest instructed him.

READ

Read the passage aloud slowly, keeping in mind that Jehoiada is a priest of Judah at a time when Judah has been worshipping Baal instead of God.

THINK

Read the passage again slowly, trying to picture the priest Jehoiada and his young pupil, Joash, who becomes one of the few good kings of Judah.

1. What about Jehoiada do you most admire or dislike?
2. How would you like, or not like, to resemble Jehoiada as a teacher and leader? (Think of a teacher as anyone from whom others learn, and think of a leader as anyone who finds others following him or her. Even in friendships, sometimes one friend is the teacher and the other is the student, although they may not realize it.)

PRAY

Pray for people who look up to you — either for good or bad. In that case, you are their teacher and leader. Ask God who he is asking you to reach out to as an informal teacher or leader. Or you may want to simply pray about what you pass on to others.

LIVE

Sit in the quiet with God, holding before him those who follow you or look up to you. You might wish to ask God, "What do I need to know about myself as a teacher or leader?" Ideas might not come to you right away. Note those that do, and keep watch for them in the coming days and weeks.

GOD'S KINDLED WRATH

2 KINGS 22:11-17

¹¹When the king heard the words of the Book of the Law, he tore his clothes. ¹²And the king commanded Hilkiah the priest, and Ahikam the son of Shaphan, and Achbor the son of Micaiah, and Shaphan the secretary, and Asaiah the king's servant, saying, ¹³"Go, inquire of the LORD for me, and for the people, and for all Judah, concerning the words of this book that has been found. For great is the wrath of the LORD that is kindled against us, because our fathers have not obeyed the words of this book, to do according to all that is written concerning us."

¹⁴So Hilkiah the priest, and Ahikam, and Achbor, and Shaphan, and Asaiah went to Huldah the prophetess, the wife of Shallum the son of Tikvah, son of Harhas, keeper of the wardrobe (now she lived in Jerusalem in the Second Quarter), and they talked with her. ¹⁵And she said to them, "Thus says the LORD, the God of Israel: 'Tell the man who sent you to me, ¹⁶Thus says the LORD, Behold, I will bring disaster upon this place and upon its inhabitants, all the words of the book that the king of Judah has read. ¹⁷Because they have forsaken me and have made offerings to other gods, that they might provoke me to anger with all the work of their hands, therefore my wrath will be kindled against this place, and it will not be quenched.'"

READ

Read the passage once aloud to get a feel for what's happening.

THINK

Read the passage again. As you do, listen for words or images that especially impact you, such as raging anger and "it will not be quenched," or the king tearing his clothes.

PRAY

Take time to silently repeat this word or phrase from the passage or to let the image play itself out in your mind. See how it meshes with your thoughts, feelings, and memories. Eventually let your contemplation lead you to consider whether there are any questionable or sinful areas of your life that you have been ignoring lately. Can you tell why you've been ignoring them? Bring them before God. What is your posture?

LIVE

Picture this God who is provoked to anger. What's it like to be before him? Now see Jesus, the mediator between the holy God pictured in this passage and the sinful people God loves. Turn to Jesus and together examine your heart. Watch his response to the sinful areas you noticed. What is he inviting you to do in response to what you see? Respond to his invitation. Watch God the Father accept Jesus' redemption of your sin — see God's wrath cool — and experience being welcomed back into full fellowship with him once more.

GIVING STRONG SUPPORT

1 CHRONICLES 11:10-11

[10]Now these are the chiefs of David's mighty men, who gave him strong support in his kingdom, together with all Israel, to make him king, according to the word of the LORD concerning Israel. [11]This is an account of David's mighty men: Jashobeam, a Hachmonite, was chief of the three. He wielded his spear against 300 whom he killed at one time.

READ
Read the passage and underline every verb or action word.

THINK
David's Mighty Men were willing to risk their lives by crossing the Philistine military camp in order to bring David water from the Bethlehem well. What incredible friendships!

Discuss this passage with a friend or spiritual mentor. What do you think about the idea of offering strong support to others? Is it awkward? Is it worth the effort?

PRAY
Tell God about any worries or insecurities you have about supporting others. Pray for the discernment to choose a few mature, like-minded people to join in support with you and the boldness to ask them for help.

LIVE
Approach these individuals and ask them to join with you.

DAY 49
GOD ENCOUNTERS
On this seventh day, review and reflect on all you have read this week. Take the time to revel in the ways you've encountered God in the past six days.

SHOUT FROM THE MOUNTAINTOPS

1 CHRONICLES 16:23-29

²³ Sing to the L ORD, all the earth!
   Tell of his salvation from day to day.
²⁴ Declare his glory among the nations,
   his marvelous works among all the peoples!
²⁵ For great is the L ORD, and greatly to be praised,
   and he is to be feared above all gods.
²⁶ For all the gods of the peoples are worthless idols,
   but the L ORD made the heavens.
²⁷ Splendor and majesty are before him;
   strength and joy are in his place.
²⁸ Ascribe to the L ORD, O families of the peoples,
   ascribe to the L ORD glory and strength!
²⁹ Ascribe to the L ORD the glory due his name;
   bring an offering and come before him!
Worship the L ORD in the splendor of holiness.

READ

Read the passage aloud slowly, keeping in mind that "Ascribe to the LORD" here means something like "give credit to."

Read the passage aloud again, but do it this time as if you are speaking convincingly, first to all the earth (verse 23 addresses the entire planet, including the vegetation and animals of the earth), then to all the "families of the peoples" (verse 28, all nations, all tribes, all classes of people).

THINK

Read the passage again silently and ponder the following:

1. Consider the words you most relish. What phrase did you particularly enjoy saying as you read the passage dramatically?
2. What would you most want the earth to know or understand about God?
3. What would you most want the families of the earth to know or understand about God?

PRAY

Begin by asking God to lead you in your prayer. Wait for him. Once you get started, you may wish to say something like, "O God, I'm so glad you are . . ." and finish with ideas from this psalm.

LIVE

If you could shout this psalm from anywhere in the world, where would that be? (It might be on a specific mountaintop or by a certain waterfall or even before an international group, such as the United Nations.) Picture yourself saying these verses from your heart in that setting, without embarrassment or any other reservation. Rest in your boldness.

OUR DAYS ARE LIKE A SHADOW

1 CHRONICLES 29:12-19

[12]Both riches and honor come from you, and you rule over all. In your hand are power and might, and in your hand it is to make great and to give strength to all. [13]And now we thank you, our God, and praise your glorious name.

[14]But who am I, and what is my people, that we should be able thus to offer willingly? For all things come from you, and of your own have we given you. [15]For we are strangers before you and sojourners, as all our fathers were. Our days on the earth are like a shadow, and there is no abiding. [16]O LORD our God, all this abundance that we have provided for building you a house for your holy name comes from your hand and is all your own. [17]I know, my God, that you test the heart and have pleasure in uprightness. In the uprightness of my heart I have freely offered all these things, and now I have seen your people, who are present here, offering freely and joyously to you. [18]O LORD, the God of Abraham, Isaac, and Israel, our fathers, keep forever such purposes and thoughts in the hearts of your people, and direct their hearts toward you. [19]Grant to Solomon my son a whole heart that he may keep your commandments, your testimonies, and your statutes, performing all, and that he may build the palace for which I have made provision.

READ

David is blessing God in this passage. To see his entire prayer, read the expanded passage, seeing how he dedicates to God the money and materials generously given by him and all the Israelites for building the temple.

THINK

When David talks about "our days on earth are like a shadow" — that everything we have is actually only being borrowed from God — how does that strike you? What item do you own, or what relationship do you have, that you hold more tightly than you would a shadow? Be honest.

PRAY

As you approach God in prayer, picture yourself bringing with you the item that is hard to hold loosely. Talk to God about what keeps you attached to it. Don't try to navigate the prayer so that by the end you are letting go of your treasured thing. Don't try to force yourself to be less attached to it than you actually are. Simply talk to God while you imaginatively hold it tightly in your hands, and tell him about why it's so important to you. Keep in mind that if you are still in the same position internally at the end of your prayer time, that's okay.

LIVE

Take a few more minutes to reflect on what talking to God was like as you held on to the item you're unwilling to give up — at least not easily. Did you feel guilty or uncomfortable, or do you have trouble being honest with him? Why might that be?

DEDICATION CEREMONIES

2 CHRONICLES 6:12-18

¹²Then Solomon stood before the altar of the LORD in the presence of all the assembly of Israel and spread out his hands. ¹³Solomon had made a bronze platform five cubits long, five cubits wide, and three cubits high, and had set it in the court, and he stood on it. Then he knelt on his knees in the presence of all the assembly of Israel, and spread out his hands toward heaven, ¹⁴and said, "O LORD, God of Israel, there is no God like you, in heaven or on earth, keeping covenant and showing steadfast love to your servants who walk before you with all their heart, ¹⁵who have kept with your servant David my father what you declared to him. You spoke with your mouth, and with your hand have fulfilled it this day. ¹⁶Now therefore, O LORD, God of Israel, keep for your servant David my father what you have promised him, saying, 'You shall not lack a man to sit before me on the throne of Israel, if only your sons pay close attention to their way, to walk in my law as you have walked before me.' ¹⁷Now therefore, O LORD, God of Israel, let your word be confirmed, which you have spoken to your servant David.

¹⁸"But will God indeed dwell with man on the earth? Behold, heaven and the highest heaven cannot contain you, how much less this house that I have built!"

READ

Read the passage, underlining words that stand out to you.

THINK

King Solomon, son of King David, built the famous temple to the Lord on Mount Zion in Jerusalem as a gathering place for the Jews to worship Yahweh. It took him years to build this temple, and at its completion he assembled all the people for a public dedication. To dedicate something is to set it aside for a special purpose. As you read the dedication prayer of Solomon, notice the gratitude and the humility of the king as he prays.

What precious aspects of your life (for example, people, positions, locations, important events, yourself) do you need to set solely aside for the Lord as a public reminder that all you have belongs to God? What would it take for you to do that . . . and with the attitude of Solomon?

PRAY

Write out a prayer of dedication to God for an individual, situation, event, or position.

LIVE

Keep your dedication prayer so you can occasionally refer to it. In fact, if you wish, make a note on your calendar a few weeks from today to reread your prayer. At that time, think about what's different in your life due to your dedication.

DAY 53
EXPANDED PASSAGE: 2 CHRONICLES 15:1–16:10

FROG:
FULLY RELY ON GOD

2 CHRONICLES 16:7-9

[7]At that time Hanani the seer came to Asa king of Judah and said to him, "Because you relied on the king of Syria, and did not rely on the LORD your God, the army of the king of Syria has escaped you. [8]Were not the Ethiopians and the Libyans a huge army with very many chariots and horsemen? Yet because you relied on the LORD, he gave them into your hand. [9]For the eyes of the LORD run to and fro throughout the whole earth, to give strong support to those whose heart is blameless toward him. You have done foolishly in this, for from now on you will have wars."

READ

Read the passage aloud slowly.

THINK

Read the passage again slowly. Previously Asa had been a good king. After hearing convicting prophecy, he "took courage and put away the detestable idols from all the land." (15:8).

1. Which phrase or idea sticks with you?

   ☐ that Asa "relied on the king of Syria, and did not rely on the LORD."
   ☐ that "the eyes of the LORD run to and fro throughout the whole earth, to give strong support to those whose heart is blameless toward him."
   ☐ that not relying on God results in "from now on you will have wars."
   ☐ other:

2. Why does that idea stick with you?
3. The theme of this passage could be summed up in the acronym FROG, standing for Fully Rely On God. Consider your life — for what large or small issues might you FROG that you have not thought of before? (Don't use this passage to beat yourself up; that's not profitable. Use it instead as a springboard to ask God for guidance.)

PRAY

Thank God that you can fully rely on him. Admire God for his divine alertness and for how relying on him keeps you out of trouble. Take your time so that you fully explore your gratitude and admiration.

LIVE

Take some deep breaths and ponder what it would feel like in your gut to rely on God all the time, every day. Taste the sweetness of reliance so it's not a chore but the absolute best way to live.

OPEN ARMS

2 CHRONICLES 30:1,5-9

¹Hezekiah sent to all Israel and Judah, and wrote letters also to Ephraim and Manasseh, that they should come to the house of the LORD at Jerusalem to keep the Passover to the LORD, the God of Israel. . . . ⁵So they decreed to make a proclamation throughout all Israel, from Beersheba to Dan, that the people should come and keep the Passover to the LORD, the God of Israel, at Jerusalem, for they had not kept it as often as prescribed. ⁶So couriers went throughout all Israel and Judah with letters from the king and his princes, as the king had commanded, saying, "O people of Israel, return to the LORD, the God of Abraham, Isaac, and Israel, that he may turn again to the remnant of you who have escaped from the hand of the kings of Assyria. ⁷Do not be like your fathers and your brothers, who were faithless to the LORD God of their fathers, so that he made them a desolation, as you see. ⁸Do not now be stiff-necked as your fathers were, but yield yourselves to the LORD and come to his sanctuary, which he has consecrated forever, and serve the LORD your God, that his fierce anger may turn away from you. ⁹For if you return to the LORD, your brothers and your children will find compassion with their captors and return to this land. For the LORD your God is gracious and merciful and will not turn away his face from you, if you return to him."

READ

Read the passage several times.

THINK

As you read, listen for a new perspective on the way life is, or the way God is, that stands out to you today. Perhaps you will notice that God can have dangerously "fierce anger," yet under other circumstances he is tender and open to a people who have walked far from intimacy with him. Maybe you'll be struck by the pigheadedness that kept some Israelites from yielding themselves to the Lord.

PRAY

Study the perspective you've absorbed, looking at it from different angles and holding it up against different experiences you've had. Do you ever fear approaching God because you worry he might snub you? Have you ever refused grace? Consider a specific situation. Then become aware of God's presence with you. Tell him what was going on during that time. How does the God of this passage (offering his grace and mercy to the Israelites) compare to your image of God in that situation?

LIVE

Close your time today by saying the Lord's Prayer. Speak the words aloud very slowly. Picture the righteous but compassionate God described in this passage, the One who is hearing your prayer now: "Our Father in heaven, hallowed be your name. Your kingdom come, your will be done, on earth as it is in heaven. Give us this day our daily bread, and forgive us our debts, as we also have forgiven our debtors. And lead us not into temptation, but deliver us from evil" (Matthew 6:9-13).

WHAT SHALL WE SAY AFTER THIS?

EZRA 9:10-15

[10]And now, O our God, what shall we say after this? For we have forsaken your commandments, [11]which you commanded by your servants the prophets, saying, 'The land that you are entering, to take possession of it, is a land impure with the impurity of the peoples of the lands, with their abominations that have filled it from end to end with their uncleanness. [12]Therefore do not give your daughters to their sons, neither take their daughters for your sons, and never seek their peace or prosperity, that you may be strong and eat the good of the land and leave it for an inheritance to your children forever.' [13]And after all that has come upon us for our evil deeds and for our great guilt, seeing that you, our God, have punished us less than our iniquities deserved and have given us such a remnant as this, [14]shall we break your commandments again and intermarry with the peoples who practice these abominations? Would you not be angry with us until you consumed us, so that there should be no remnant, nor any to escape? [15]O LORD, the God of Israel, you are just, for we are left a remnant that has escaped, as it is today. Behold, we are before you in our guilt, for none can stand before you because of this.

READ

Read this prayer, spoken by Ezra on behalf of all the exiled Israelites.

THINK

Think about how you relate to this prayer. Have you ever felt similar remorse to what Ezra expresses here? Maybe you feel frustration with the injustices of your community or nation, or maybe you experience guilt on a deep level — not for anything in particular, but just a general sense of not getting it right, ever. What have you done with that feeling? Stuffed it? Allowed it to constantly criticize what you do and say? Have you ever thought of sharing it with God?

PRAY

Ezra's raw confession of messing up before God indicates that he feels very secure in God's merciful love; otherwise, being this defenseless before anyone is hard.

Read Ezra's prayer again, looking for a word, a phrase, or even something about his tone that resonates with you. Take several minutes to mull this over, and listen for what it gives voice to in your heart. Allow yourself to make Ezra's prayer your own, repeating it and following him in prayer to God. Or perhaps you don't identify with what he says, yet beyond your words is a pain you want to share with God. Sit with him in this.

LIVE

When you mess up today, remember Ezra, and remember God's merciful love.

DAY 56

GOD ENCOUNTERS

On this seventh day, review and reflect on all you have read this week. Take the time to revel in the ways you've encountered God in the past six days.

BURDEN FOR THE POOR

NEHEMIAH 5:6-11

[6]I was very angry when I heard their outcry and these words. [7]I took counsel with myself, and I brought charges against the nobles and the officials. I said to them, "You are exacting interest, each from his brother." And I held a great assembly against them [8]and said to them, "We, as far as we are able, have bought back our Jewish brothers who have been sold to the nations, but you even sell your brothers that they may be sold to us!" They were silent and could not find a word to say. [9]So I said, "The thing that you are doing is not good. Ought you not to walk in the fear of our God to prevent the taunts of the nations our enemies? [10]Moreover, I and my brothers and my servants are lending them money and grain. Let us abandon this exacting of interest. [11]Return to them this very day their fields, their vineyards, their olive orchards, and their houses, and the percentage of money, grain, wine, and oil that you have been exacting from them."

LIVE

In preparation for this lesson, fast from one meal. (Use discernment regarding fasting; check with your doctor before doing it. If you can't do it for whatever reason, that's okay.) When you feel the pangs of hunger, use that discomfort as a catalyst for this devotion.

READ

Read the passage slowly.

THINK

While in Babylonian exile as a cupbearer to a foreign king, Nehemiah has a God-given burden: to rebuild the ransacked walls of the forgotten city of Jerusalem and, in the process, to restore the hope of his people. But in the midst of this massive architectural restoration project, the people are being abused by their own countrymen.

Nehemiah's burden grows larger. His burden now includes poverty and injustice. Imagine yourself in Nehemiah's shoes today. What does this burden feel like? Consider your empty stomach and write down how you feel.

PRAY

Begin praying by listening for God's heart regarding justice. Ask him to show you people who need your prayers. Then ask him to point out when you need to speak up on their behalf, and ask for the courage to actually follow through with it.

ZEAL FOR RIGHTEOUSNESS

NEHEMIAH 13:7-13

⁷I then discovered the evil that Eliashib had done for Tobiah, preparing for him a chamber in the courts of the house of God. ⁸And I was very angry, and I threw all the household furniture of Tobiah out of the chamber. ⁹Then I gave orders, and they cleansed the chambers, and I brought back there the vessels of the house of God, with the grain offering and the frankincense.

¹⁰I also found out that the portions of the Levites had not been given to them, so that the Levites and the singers, who did the work, had fled each to his field. ¹¹So I confronted the officials and said, "Why is the house of God forsaken?" And I gathered them together and set them in their stations. ¹²Then all Judah brought the tithe of the grain, wine, and oil into the storehouses. ¹³And I appointed as treasurers over the storehouses Shelemiah the priest, Zadok the scribe, and Pedaiah of the Levites, and as their assistant Hanan the son of Zaccur, son of Mattaniah, for they were considered reliable, and their duty was to distribute to their brothers.

READ

Read the passage, including the expanded portion for background, if you can.

THINK

In these earlier days, what do you notice about the way of life God required his people to abide by? Why do you think this was important to him? What do you think their relationship with God was like? How might it be different from your relationship with him?

PRAY

Become aware of God's presence with you now. Share your thoughts with him, including what you noticed about your own relationship with him. Let this lead you into silent prayer, pondering what's happened in your life since you last talked with him and whether there is anything you need to clear up. Listen for what he might be saying in response to you. If you don't sense him saying anything directly, be open to other ways he might try to communicate with you (such as through other people or recent experiences).

LIVE

Think about the passion Nehemiah demonstrates for honoring God. What would your life look like with more passion? How might you honor God with your lifestyle the way Nehemiah desires to honor God? Jesus said, "Love the Lord your God with all your heart and with all your soul and with all your mind. . . . Love your neighbor as yourself" (Matthew 22:37,39). With this command in mind, think of one small new habit you could cultivate that would honor God in a particular area of your life.

SUCH A TIME AS THIS

ESTHER 4:7-14

[7]And Mordecai told him all that had happened to him, and the exact sum of money that Haman had promised to pay into the king's treasuries for the destruction of the Jews. [8]Mordecai also gave him a copy of the written decree issued in Susa for their destruction, that he might show it to Esther and explain it to her and command her to go to the king to beg his favor and plead with him on behalf of her people. [9]And Hathach went and told Esther what Mordecai had said. [10]Then Esther spoke to Hathach and commanded him to go to Mordecai and say, [11]"All the king's servants and the people of the king's provinces know that if any man or woman goes to the king inside the inner court without being called, there is but one law — to be put to death, except the one to whom the king holds out the golden scepter so that he may live. But as for me, I have not been called to come in to the king these thirty days."

[12]And they told Mordecai what Esther had said. [13]Then Mordecai told them to reply to Esther, "Do not think to yourself that in the king's palace you will escape any more than all the other Jews. [14]For if you keep silent at this time, relief and deliverance will rise for the Jews from another place, but you and your father's house will perish. And who knows whether you have not come to the kingdom for such a time as this?"

READ

As you read this story, imagine how you might feel if you were Esther: You were chosen to be queen by a king who doesn't know of your ethnicity, and now you're hearing word of a political plot that will wipe out your people and your family.

THINK

Focus your attention on either Esther's fear of putting her life on the line for her people or Mordecai's challenge to her in the face of her fear. Meditatively read that part of the passage again. Picture the speaker, including the situation from which the words are spoken. Select one word or phrase to contemplate during your prayer time.

PRAY

Prayerfully ponder a word or phrase from Mordecai or Esther and identify a memory that relates. Maybe at one time you were called on to do something courageous — big or small — but couldn't bring yourself to do it. Or maybe you wonder why God would allow Esther to bear such a heavy responsibility. Perhaps you were recently helped because someone took a stand for you.

Invite God the Father into your meditation. Try not to analyze or push toward solutions. Just notice what comes up and show it to him, as a child might show Daddy a favorite toy that's broken or tell him about a fascinating discovery.

LIVE

Take some time now to rest with the Father. If you have more to say in your conversation with him about Esther's dilemma, continue it. If you have other subjects you'd like to talk to him about, do so. But if you want to just sit in the presence of your loving Father, go ahead.

PREOCCUPATIONS

ESTHER 5:9-13

[9]And Haman went out that day joyful and glad of heart. But when Haman saw Mordecai in the king's gate, that he neither rose nor trembled before him, he was filled with wrath against Mordecai. [10]Nevertheless, Haman restrained himself and went home, and he sent and brought his friends and his wife Zeresh. [11]And Haman recounted to them the splendor of his riches, the number of his sons, all the promotions with which the king had honored him, and how he had advanced him above the officials and the servants of the king. [12]Then Haman said, "Even Queen Esther let no one but me come with the king to the feast she prepared. And tomorrow also I am invited by her together with the king. [13]Yet all this is worth nothing to me, so long as I see Mordecai the Jew sitting at the king's gate."

READ

Read the passage aloud slowly. Haman is upset because the king ordered all those at the king's gate to bow to him, and Mordecai the Jew does not (see Esther 3:3-6).

THINK

Read the passage again slowly.

1. How did Haman's preoccupations affect him? What did those preoccupations reveal about the kind of person he was inside?
2. What preoccupations have filled your mind for the past twenty-four hours? What do these preoccupations reveal about who you are inside?
3. What things would you like to be preoccupied with?

PRAY

Pray this verse in your own words: "Set your minds on things that are above" (Colossians 3:2). Ask God for guidance in what kind of person you want to be and what to focus on.

LIVE

Dream about becoming the kind of person whose mind is preoccupied with God. Contemplation is a time for receiving from God. Receive an image of yourself from him. Embrace the future you.

JUSTICE SERVED

ESTHER 7:3-10

³Then Queen Esther answered, "If I have found favor in your sight, O king, and if it please the king, let my life be granted me for my wish, and my people for my request. ⁴For we have been sold, I and my people, to be destroyed, to be killed, and to be annihilated. If we had been sold merely as slaves, men and women, I would have been silent, for our affliction is not to be compared with the loss to the king." ⁵Then King Ahasuerus said to Queen Esther, "Who is he, and where is he, who has dared to do this?" ⁶And Esther said, "A foe and enemy! This wicked Haman!" Then Haman was terrified before the king and the queen.

 ⁷And the king arose in his wrath from the wine-drinking and went into the palace garden, but Haman stayed to beg for his life from Queen Esther, for he saw that harm was determined against him by the king. ⁸And the king returned from the palace garden to the place where they were drinking wine, as Haman was falling on the couch where Esther was. And the king said, "Will he even assault the queen in my presence, in my own house?" As the word left the mouth of the king, they covered Haman's face. ⁹Then Harbona, one of the eunuchs in attendance on the king, said, "Moreover, the gallows that Haman has prepared for Mordecai, whose word saved the king, is standing at Haman's house, fifty cubits high." ¹⁰And the king said, "Hang him on that." So they hanged Haman on the gallows that he had prepared for Mordecai. Then the wrath of the king abated.

READ

Take some time before you begin to sit in silence. Let your thoughts settle. Now read the passage once silently.

THINK

Read this story of justice being served again, this time aloud. Listen specifically for a word or a phrase that touches your heart in some way. When you finish reading, close your eyes. Recall the word and sit quietly, mulling it over. After a few moments, write the word down. Don't explain it or say more about it; just note it.

PRAY

Read the passage aloud again, this time looking for a person or an action that accentuates your internal picture of God's justice or heightens your understanding of how he governs the world. Perhaps it will be Haman's response to his fate or King Ahasuerus's authoritative command. How is this depiction of God's justice meaningful to you today? Again sit in silence. Briefly note what comes to you.

LIVE

Read the text one final time. This time, listen for what God, through the text, is inviting you to do or become. Perhaps he is offering a new perspective on how he cares when unjust things happen to you, just as King Ahasuerus was outraged to discover the threat to Esther's people. Or maybe you sense that God is calling you to take a stand for justice in a particular situation, like Esther did. Write down what you are being invited to do.

GOD GIVES, GOD TAKES

JOB 1:1,8-11,20-21

[1]There was a man in the land of Uz whose name was Job, and that man was blameless and upright, one who feared God and turned away from evil. . . .

[8]And the LORD said to Satan, "Have you considered my servant Job, that there is none like him on the earth, a blameless and upright man, who fears God and turns away from evil?" [9]Then Satan answered the LORD and said, "Does Job fear God for no reason? [10]Have you not put a hedge around him and his house and all that he has, on every side? You have blessed the work of his hands, and his possessions have increased in the land. [11]But stretch out your hand and touch all that he has, and he will curse you to your face." . . .

[20]Then Job arose and tore his robe and shaved his head and fell on the ground and worshiped. [21]And he said, "Naked I came from my mother's womb, and naked shall I return. The LORD gave, and the LORD has taken away; blessed be the name of the LORD."

READ

Read the passage, noticing God's involvement in the story and circling *God* each time he is mentioned.

THINK

Notice the interaction between God and Satan. Does it bother you that God is bartering with Satan with Job's life? Is this the God you know?

Notice the words of Job, "Naked I came from my mother's womb, and naked shall I return. The LORD gave, and the LORD has taken away; blessed be the name of the LORD." If you lost everything — family, fortune, and eventually your health — would you be able to say such a thing? Why or why not? What would have to happen for you to utter similar words — and actually mean them?

PRAY

Spend time meditating on the gut-honest yet God-honoring words of Job. Let your emotions serve as a backdrop to your prayers. Invite the Holy Spirit to speak to you in the silence.

LIVE

Today as you use different objects (your car, computer, TV, and so on) and as you enter different places (your home, school, workplace, and so on), consider how you might respond if God instantly removed an item without explanation.

DAY 63

GOD ENCOUNTERS

On this seventh day, review and reflect on all you have read this week. Take the time to revel in the ways you've encountered God in the past six days.

GIVING COMFORT

JOB 5:17-21

¹⁷ Behold, blessed is the one whom God reproves;
    therefore despise not the discipline of the Almighty.
¹⁸ For he wounds, but he binds up;
    he shatters, but his hands heal.
¹⁹ He will deliver you from six troubles;
    in seven no evil shall touch you.
²⁰ In famine he will redeem you from death,
    and in war from the power of the sword.
²¹ You shall be hidden from the lash of the tongue,
    and shall not fear destruction when it comes.

READ

Read the passage aloud slowly, keeping in mind that Eliphaz from Teman is speaking to his friend Job, who has just experienced the death of his children and the loss of all he had.

THINK

Read the passage again and put yourself in the place of Job, who listened to these words. How do they fall on your ear?

Read the passage again and put yourself in the place of Eliphaz. What feelings and attitudes fill you as you speak these words?

1. What makes a comforter really helpful? Is telling the truth enough?
2. What did Job need from Eliphaz?
3. What might be in the heart of a person who preaches at someone who is so far down?

PRAY

Ask the Comforter, the Holy Spirit, to give you what is needed to truly comfort despairing people. If you want guidance for your prayer, ask the Comforter to give you tools to help people in trouble go to him. Ask him to give you tools to draw them out to say to him whatever they need to express. Plead with the Comforter to make you his messenger, to prevent you from moralizing and giving advice.

LIVE

Rest your mind on someone who is in deep trouble. Pray only the word *peace* for them — no suggestions, no fixing, no rescuing. Just trusting.

THE MYSTERY OF A MIGHTY GOD

JOB 9:2-4,14-23

2   Truly I know that it is so:
      But how can a man be in the right before God?
3   If one wished to contend with him,
      one could not answer him once in a thousand times.
4   He is wise in heart and mighty in strength
      — who has hardened himself against him, and succeeded? — . . .

14   How then can I answer him,
      choosing my words with him?
15   Though I am in the right, I cannot answer him;
      I must appeal for mercy to my accuser.
16   If I summoned him and he answered me,
      I would not believe that he was listening to my voice.
17   For he crushes me with a tempest
      and multiplies my wounds without cause;
18   he will not let me get my breath,
      but fills me with bitterness.
19   If it is a contest of strength, behold, he is mighty!
      If it is a matter of justice, who can summon him?
20   Though I am in the right, my own mouth would condemn me;
      though I am blameless, he would prove me perverse.
21   I am blameless; I regard not myself;
      I loathe my life.
22   It is all one; therefore I say,
      He destroys both the blameless and the wicked.
23   When disaster brings sudden death,
      he mocks at the calamity of the innocent.

READ

Read the passage. In Job's response to his recent tragedy, notice the powerful feelings that underlie his words: fear, anger, grief, and hope.

THINK

What phrase in Job's lament stands out to you? Spend time meditating on it. Mentally chew it the way you would chew a piece of gum — repeat it to yourself, pausing each time to see where it leads your mind and emotions.

PRAY

Keeping your phrase in mind, picture God in the room with you. How do you relate to his presence? Maybe you sit in reverence at his power, wisdom, and justice, realizing you've forgotten or minimized those qualities lately. Maybe you feel anguish like Job. Maybe you open up to your desire for a rescuer, for Christ's mercy.

At the end of this time, recall what this experience held for you. Write down for future reference anything that seemed significant.

LIVE

During the next week, before you begin your times of prayerful reading, recall your picture of God in the room. Recollect who he was to you and retain this image of him in your mind during each prayer time. Let that aspect of God mingle with the God you relate to during the week.

TALKING TRANSPARENTLY WITH GOD

JOB 19:13-27

¹³ He has put my brothers far from me,
  and those who knew me are wholly estranged from me.
¹⁴ My relatives have failed me,
  my close friends have forgotten me.
¹⁵ The guests in my house and my maidservants count me as a stranger;
  I have become a foreigner in their eyes.
¹⁶ I call to my servant, but he gives me no answer;
  I must plead with him with my mouth for mercy.
¹⁷ My breath is strange to my wife,
  and I am a stench to the children of my own mother.
¹⁸ Even young children despise me;
  when I rise they talk against me.
¹⁹ All my intimate friends abhor me,
  and those whom I loved have turned against me.
²⁰ My bones stick to my skin and to my flesh,
  and I have escaped by the skin of my teeth.
²¹ Have mercy on me, have mercy on me, O you my friends,
  for the hand of God has touched me!
²² Why do you, like God, pursue me?
  Why are you not satisfied with my flesh?

²³ Oh that my words were written!
  Oh that they were inscribed in a book!
²⁴ Oh that with an iron pen and lead
  they were engraved in the rock forever!
²⁵ For I know that my Redeemer lives,
  and at the last he will stand upon the earth.
²⁶ And after my skin has been thus destroyed,
  yet in my flesh I shall see God,
²⁷ whom I shall see for myself,
  and my eyes shall behold, and not another.

READ

Read the passage slowly, noticing the raw way Job communicates about God.

THINK

As you read Job's honest description of his situation — what it's really like — what word or phrase gives voice to some of your own thoughts, feelings, and desires? Perhaps one of Job's statements brings to mind something in your life that's weighing on you or confuses you.

PRAY

Talk to God about the feelings and thoughts that surface. Be as open as Job as you share them with him. You might write them out to him or just talk to him like a friend — one you're in conflict with, but one who wants to work through that conflict with you.

LIVE

As you go through the rest of your day, pay close attention to thoughts and feelings (similar to or different from those in your prayer time) that arise in relation to events, conversations, and experiences. Tell God about them as they come up, so you're carrying on an extended dialogue with him all day long.

At the end of the day, take a few moments to remember what happened, in particular what it was like to talk to God throughout the day's circumstances.

EMPTY COMFORT

JOB 22:1-11

¹ Then Eliphaz the Temanite answered and said:

² "Can a man be profitable to God?
   Surely he who is wise is profitable to himself.
³ Is it any pleasure to the Almighty if you are in the right,
   or is it gain to him if you make your ways blameless?
⁴ Is it for your fear of him that he reproves you
   and enters into judgment with you?
⁵ Is not your evil abundant?
   There is no end to your iniquities.
⁶ For you have exacted pledges of your brothers for nothing
   and stripped the naked of their clothing.
⁷ You have given no water to the weary to drink,
   and you have withheld bread from the hungry.
⁸ The man with power possessed the land,
   and the favored man lived in it.
⁹ You have sent widows away empty,
   and the arms of the fatherless were crushed.
¹⁰ Therefore snares are all around you,
   and sudden terror overwhelms you,
¹¹ or darkness, so that you cannot see,
   and a flood of water covers you."

READ

As you read the passage, consider what might have been comforting for Job and what might have left him more hurt than before.

THINK

Have there been times when you wished people would refrain from giving you perfectly packaged and Christian clichés in an attempt to console you? "Pray harder." "You'll have to persevere." "Oh, God's just working on you." "Search for the sin in your life and get rid of it." "Obey God." Maybe you didn't know what you wanted in your suffering, but that definitely wasn't it. Sometimes true comfort comes through silence and a hug.

Eliphaz, Bildad, and Zophar don't offer comfort, but instead attempt to convince Job of his sins. This time it's the social sin of neglecting the poor, the hungry, and the naked—none of which Job is guilty of.

Who are the people you interact with on a regular basis who are suffering emotional, mental, spiritual, or physical pain?

What are some ways you can appropriately comfort them in their pain?

PRAY

Who are hurting people in your life? Pray for them, submitting to God's guidance for how to best serve and minister to them.

LIVE

Consider a friend or acquaintance who needs comfort. Prayerfully approach the suffering individual, asking God to use you as a healing agent of comfort and hope. Also ask God to keep you from being someone who merely offers trite words that fall short.

THIRSTING FOR JUSTICE

JOB 24:1-10

1   Why are not times of judgment kept by the Almighty,
      and why do those who know him never see his days?
2   Some move landmarks;
      they seize flocks and pasture them.
3   They drive away the donkey of the fatherless;
      they take the widow's ox for a pledge.
4   They thrust the poor off the road;
      the poor of the earth all hide themselves.
5   Behold, like wild donkeys in the desert
        the poor go out to their toil, seeking game;
        the wasteland yields food for their children.
6   They gather their fodder in the field,
        and they glean the vineyard of the wicked man.
7   They lie all night naked, without clothing,
        and have no covering in the cold.
8   They are wet with the rain of the mountains
        and cling to the rock for lack of shelter.
9   (There are those who snatch the fatherless child from the breast,
        and they take a pledge against the poor.)
10   They go about naked, without clothing;
        hungry, they carry the sheaves.

READ

Read the passage aloud slowly.

THINK

Read the passage again, noting the words or phrases that touch you.

1. Why do these phrases touch you?
2. What is the heart of God like for these situations?

Though God stays hidden in order to let human beings be the autonomous beings he created them to be, he delights in bringing justice. Slowly read aloud Isaiah 51:5 twice:

> My righteousness draws near,
>> my salvation has gone out,
>> and my arms will judge the peoples;
> the coastlands hope for me,
>> and for my arm they wait.

Ponder your heart's response to this.

PRAY

Ask God to intervene in situations you think are unjust, small or big. If nothing comes to you, look at a newspaper or watch a newscast. Then come before God and ask for people to be treated with fairness and goodness and kindness.

LIVE

While you pray, hold in front of you a symbol of the world's troubles, perhaps a newspaper or newsmagazine, a globe or map. Hold it up for God's light to permeate.

GOD'S SILENCE

JOB 30:15-20

15   Terrors are turned upon me;
        my honor is pursued as by the wind,
        and my prosperity has passed away like a cloud.

16   And now my soul is poured out within me;
        days of affliction have taken hold of me.
17   The night racks my bones,
        and the pain that gnaws me takes no rest.
18   With great force my garment is disfigured;
        it binds me about like the collar of my tunic.
19   God has cast me into the mire,
        and I have become like dust and ashes.
20   I cry to you for help and you do not answer me;
        I stand, and you only look at me.

READ

Read the passage, attempting to identify in your own heart and mind with the expressions of the speaker.

THINK

Read the passage slowly again — until the words sink into your consciousness, becoming familiar to you and resonating with your present state of mind. Don't try to analyze Job's response or determine its validity. Simply open yourself to his experience.

PRAY

What goes on inside you when you hear Job talk about God's silence? Perhaps you feel irritated, or maybe you relate because you've experienced times when God seemed inaccessible. Talk to God about your reaction to this passage. To help clarify your reaction, write about it. Give yourself permission to be completely open and honest.

LIVE

Right now, practice resting in the knowledge that God is with you in both words and silence — whether you're doing things right or doing nothing at all, whether you feel he's near or you feel nothing. If this is especially tough for you to do, pray the prayer "Lord, I believe a little; help me believe more."

DAY 70

GOD ENCOUNTERS

On this seventh day, review and reflect on all you have read this week. Take the time to revel in the ways you've encountered God in the past six days.

CREATION MOVIE

JOB 38:4-11,24-27

⁴ Where were you when I laid the foundation of the earth?
  Tell me, if you have understanding.
⁵ Who determined its measurements — surely you know!
  Or who stretched the line upon it?
⁶ On what were its bases sunk,
  or who laid its cornerstone,
⁷ when the morning stars sang together
  and all the sons of God shouted for joy?

⁸ Or who shut in the sea with doors
  when it burst out from the womb,
⁹ when I made clouds its garment
  and thick darkness its swaddling band,
¹⁰ and prescribed limits for it
  and set bars and doors,
¹¹ and said, "Thus far shall you come, and no farther,
  and here shall your proud waves be stayed"?

²⁴ What is the way to the place where the light is distributed,
  or where the east wind is scattered upon the earth?

²⁵ Who has cleft a channel for the torrents of rain
  and a way for the thunderbolt,
²⁶ to bring rain on a land where no man is,
  on the desert in which there is no man,
²⁷ to satisfy the waste and desolate land,
  and to make the ground sprout with grass?

READ

Read the passage aloud slowly.

THINK

Read the passage again aloud, noticing that this is a poetic account of the Creation of the world in contrast to Genesis 1, which is a narrative account. Think about the following questions, remembering to consider the "why" behind each one.

1. What is your favorite moment in this Creation story?
2. Are you more fascinated by God as a measurements kind of being or as a tamer of waves?
3. How do you respond to God as a distributor of light or a scatterer of wind?
4. For what part of God's creation would you have wanted a front-row seat (for example, a daisy, a zebra, or a waterfall)?

PRAY

Tell God your responses to these questions. What do you think might be God's response to you?

LIVE

Go for a walk or hike or run in a beautiful place. Notice every single detail of nature that you can, and take pleasure in thinking about how God created it.

GOD CAN HANDLE YOU

JOB 42:7-13

⁷After the Lᴏʀᴅ had spoken these words to Job, the Lᴏʀᴅ said to Eliphaz the Temanite: "My anger burns against you and against your two friends, for you have not spoken of me what is right, as my servant Job has. ⁸Now therefore take seven bulls and seven rams and go to my servant Job and offer up a burnt offering for yourselves. And my servant Job shall pray for you, for I will accept his prayer not to deal with you according to your folly. For you have not spoken of me what is right, as my servant Job has." ⁹So Eliphaz the Temanite and Bildad the Shuhite and Zophar the Naamathite went and did what the Lᴏʀᴅ had told them, and the Lᴏʀᴅ accepted Job's prayer.

¹⁰And the Lᴏʀᴅ restored the fortunes of Job, when he had prayed for his friends. And the Lᴏʀᴅ gave Job twice as much as he had before. ¹¹Then came to him all his brothers and sisters and all who had known him before, and ate bread with him in his house. And they showed him sympathy and comforted him for all the evil that the Lᴏʀᴅ had brought upon him. And each of them gave him a piece of money and a ring of gold.

¹²And the Lᴏʀᴅ blessed the latter days of Job more than his beginning. And he had 14,000 sheep, 6,000 camels, 1,000 yoke of oxen, and 1,000 female donkeys. ¹³He had also seven sons and three daughters.

READ

As you read this passage aloud, picture the events taking place.

THINK

In the silence that follows your reading, continue to mentally engage with the scene. Focus on the part of the story that affects you most, the one that provokes an internal response. How do you relate to God as he appears in this passage? Share that with him.

PRAY

What do you feel or think when you see God affirming Job's honesty, even though that included sharing strong negative feelings like anger and grief? Is it surprising? Are you apprehensive? Is it a relief? Tell God about what you find inside.

LIVE

Peter Kreeft wrote, "[Job] is in a true relationship to God, as the three friends are not: a relationship of heart and soul, life-or-death passion. . . . God is infinite love, and the opposite of love is not hate but indifference. Job's love for God is infected with hate, but the three friends' love for God is infected with indifference. Job stays married to God and throws dishes at him; the three friends have a polite nonmarriage, with separate bedrooms and separate vacations. The family that fights together stays together."[6]

Ponder the idea that God can handle you, all of you, even your negative emotions. Do you really believe that God desires this honest intimacy with you? What would it look like for you to go one level deeper in intimacy with God?

A TREE PLANTED BY STREAMS

PSALM 1

1 Blessed is the man
     who walks not in the counsel of the wicked,
   nor stands in the way of sinners,
     nor sits in the seat of scoffers;
2 but his delight is in the law of the LORD,
     and on his law he meditates day and night.

3 He is like a tree
     planted by streams of water
   that yields its fruit in its season,
     and its leaf does not wither.
   In all that he does, he prospers.
4 The wicked are not so,
     but are like chaff that the wind drives away.

5 Therefore the wicked will not stand in the judgment,
     nor sinners in the congregation of the righteous;
6 for the LORD knows the way of the righteous,
     but the way of the wicked will perish.

READ

Go outside to your yard or a park. Once you find a healthy-looking tree, sit down and focus on it for a few moments. Look at the trunk and consider its strength. Focus on the leaves and admire their intricacies. Examine the roots that are above ground and consider the roots that are below ground.

After you do this, read the passage.

THINK

Contemplate the correlation between being in God's Word and the strength of a tree. Notice the difference between the wicked and the righteous in this psalm. What are the equivalents of "the counsel of the wicked," "the way of sinners," and "the seat of scoffers" in your life that should be avoided? Be specific. What will your life look like if it "yields its fruit in its season"?

PRAY

With your eyes open and looking at the tree, ask God to guide you in such a way that you will always be in blossom and bearing fruit. Pray that your roots will go down deep and find their place in the healthy soil of God's Word.

LIVE

Thank God for the gift of his Word. Let the metaphor of a healthy tree guide your decisions today. Plan a time later to spend some additional minutes in Scripture, living out the words of this psalm.

MAJESTIC IS YOUR NAME

PSALM 8

¹ O Lord, our Lord,
how majestic is your name in all the earth!
You have set your glory above the heavens.
²   Out of the mouth of babies and infants,
you have established strength because of your foes,
to still the enemy and the avenger.

³ When I look at your heavens, the work of your fingers,
the moon and the stars, which you have set in place,
⁴ what is man that you are mindful of him,
and the son of man that you care for him?

⁵ Yet you have made him a little lower than the heavenly beings
and crowned him with glory and honor.
⁶ You have given him dominion over the works of your hands;
you have put all things under his feet,
⁷ all sheep and oxen,
and also the beasts of the field,
⁸ the birds of the heavens, and the fish of the sea,
whatever passes along the paths of the seas.

⁹ O Lord, our Lord,
how majestic is your name in all the earth!

READ

Read the passage aloud slowly.

THINK

Read the passage aloud again, letting your mouth play with the phrases, connections, and comparisons that appeal to you. Perhaps one of these does:

- "established strength" and "still the enemy"
- "moon and stars" and "what is man"
- "works of your hands" and "all things under his feet"
- "your name in all the earth" and "majestic is your name"

One by one, hold in your mind the words that stood out to you. Imagine their physical representation, how they relate to each other. For example, hear the sounds of babies drowning out enemies, see God's name (and presence and power) known in all the earth but majestic as to echo around the world. What do these comparisons have to do with your life?

PRAY

Consider the exercise you just did. What does it make you want to say to God? Words of admiration? Requests to be a good caretaker of the earth? Offer it to him.

LIVE

In the evening or early morning when the sky is dark, take this book and a flashlight outside and read this psalm to God. Even if you have to whisper to avoid being heard, put your heart into it. Revel in the moment and enjoy God.

TELL GOD YOUR DESIRE

PSALM 13

¹   How long, O LORD? Will you forget me forever?
        How long will you hide your face from me?
²   How long must I take counsel in my soul
        and have sorrow in my heart all the day?
    How long shall my enemy be exalted over me?

³   Consider and answer me, O LORD my God;
        light up my eyes, lest I sleep the sleep of death,
⁴   lest my enemy say, "I have prevailed over him,"
        lest my foes rejoice because I am shaken.

⁵   But I have trusted in your steadfast love;
        my heart shall rejoice in your salvation.
⁶   I will sing to the LORD,
        because he has dealt bountifully with me.

READ

Read the passage with passion, experiencing for yourself the shift in emotion.

THINK

As you hear the psalmist's desire for God's attention, be aware of how you feel similarly. Search your awareness of what you want or need from God until you have a name for that desire. Desiring something practical, like a good grade on an exam, is fine. But pause to see what deeper desire might be behind it — perhaps a single word like *significance* or a phrase like "to know that you love me no matter what."

Now think about what name for God is most meaningful to you in light of the desire you just pinpointed. For example, if you desire a God who will radically alter a difficult circumstance, perhaps you will think of him as Powerful One. If you desire a God who will soothe your hurts and hold you close, perhaps you will think of him as Daddy.

PRAY

Consider that God is inviting you to express what you want. Tell him honestly and plainly. Combine your deeper desire with the name you chose for God. End up with a prayer that is six to nine syllables long, such as "Powerful One, give me justice." Use the next several minutes to pray this prayer to God, repeating it with each breath.

LIVE

Throughout the day, pray your phrase as often as possible — as you drive, as you wait in line, as you exercise. At times your prayer may be in the foreground of your thoughts; at others, in the background. At the end of the day, think about how God responded to your desire.

DAY 76
EXPANDED PASSAGE: PSALM 27

STAYING WITH GOD

PSALM 27:4-6

⁴ One thing have I asked of the LORD,
    that will I seek after:
that I may dwell in the house of the LORD
    all the days of my life,
to gaze upon the beauty of the LORD
    and to inquire in his temple.

⁵ For he will hide me in his shelter
    in the day of trouble;
he will conceal me under the cover of his tent;
    he will lift me high upon a rock.

⁶ And now my head shall be lifted up
    above my enemies all around me,
and I will offer in his tent
    sacrifices with shouts of joy;
I will sing and make melody to the LORD.

READ

Read the passage rhythmically. Sing it, if you wish. See if you can find a pattern to the words. Pay attention to the syllables of the words in each line.

THINK

The psalms are some of the most honest words to God ever put on paper. David's expression, though raw, shows his confidence that God will protect him when his enemies are trying to harm or kill him. What would have to happen for you to speak to God in the same honest way?

David's desire is that God will be his guiding light and life source. He wrote, "The LORD is the stronghold of my life; of whom shall I be afraid?" (verse 1). What would have to happen for you to say this same line . . . and mean it?

David sang, "I believe that I shall look upon the goodness of the LORD in the land of the living! Wait for the LORD; be strong, and let your heart take courage; wait for the LORD!" (verses 13-14). When are you tempted to quit on God? What encourages you to keep waiting for him?

PRAY/LIVE

Find an atlas or compass. Look at it and ponder the words of this psalm: "Teach me your way, O LORD, and lead me on a level path" (verse 11).

Ask God to guide you down his path and help you live the life he wants you to live.

DAY 77

GOD ENCOUNTERS

On this seventh day, review and reflect on all you have read this week. Take the time to revel in the ways you've encountered God in the past six days.

RESCUED FROM THE PIT

PSALM 28:1-2,6-9

1   To you, O Lord, I call;
    my rock, be not deaf to me,
    lest, if you be silent to me,
    I become like those who go down to the pit.
2   Hear the voice of my pleas for mercy,
       when I cry to you for help,
    when I lift up my hands
       toward your most holy sanctuary. . . .

6   Blessed be the Lord!
       For he has heard the voice of my pleas for mercy.
7   The Lord is my strength and my shield;
       in him my heart trusts, and I am helped;
    my heart exults,
       and with my song I give thanks to him.

8   The Lord is the strength of his people;
       he is the saving refuge of his anointed.
9   Oh, save your people and bless your heritage!
       Be their shepherd and carry them forever.

READ

Read the passage aloud slowly.

THINK

Read the passage again, whispering verses 1-2 as if in fear and then reading verses 6-9 in a louder, confident voice.

Put yourself in a cold, tar-black pit, silent except for the dripping of water. You call out to God and lift your arms to him, but at first there is no answer. Stay in this place for a few minutes. Imagine what you would do and think. What would you think about God? What would you say to him?

Feel in your body the moment when God shows up, when he takes your arms and pulls you out of the hole into the warm, bright light. You shiver and blink. Stay in this moment for a few minutes.

PRAY

Speak to God about what is most powerful for you in these verses. You might ask God to help you call out to him, to count on him, whenever you're close to the pit of life. If you are now in a pit, ask God to help you raise your hands in prayer and bless him. If you are not now in a pit, offer a prayer that someone jumping for joy might pray.

LIVE

Try it. Let your heart exult. Jump for joy and shout and sing.

CELEBRATING GOD

PSALM 34:1-9

1   I will bless the LORD at all times;
     his praise shall continually be in my mouth.
2   My soul makes its boast in the LORD;
     let the humble hear and be glad.
3   Oh, magnify the LORD with me,
     and let us exalt his name together!

4   I sought the LORD, and he answered me
     and delivered me from all my fears.
5   Those who look to him are radiant,
     and their faces shall never be ashamed.
6   This poor man cried, and the LORD heard him
     and saved him out of all his troubles.
7   The angel of the LORD encamps
     around those who fear him, and delivers them.

8   Oh, taste and see that the LORD is good!
     Blessed is the man who takes refuge in him!
9   Oh, fear the LORD, you his saints,
     for those who fear him have no lack!

READ

Read the passage aloud as many times as it takes for the words and thoughts to become familiar to you.

THINK/PRAY

Imagine the face and posture of the psalmist expressing this worship. Maybe you'd like to join him, or maybe you're annoyed. What posture does your body take on when you hear the speaker's enthusiasm? When you imagine the God he's speaking about? Move your body into this posture — be it bowing on the floor, clenching your fists, hugging your knees, folding your arms across your chest, dancing, or something else.

Now set aside your physical response and return to the text. Mull the words until you can determine your mental reaction to them. Can you put clear words to your thoughts? Tell God, and write them down.

Now return to the text one last time. Read it silently, listening for God's response to your posture and your words.

LIVE

In his book *Prayer*, Richard Foster speaks of stepping-stones along the path of learning to adore God. Ultimately, adoring God involves gratitude, magnifying him, and "foot-stomping celebration," but these must be grown into, and our hearts must be taught. A good first step is simply to make a habit of watching small things in nature: ducks, butterflies, fluttering leaves. This does not mean analyzing but rather discovering the pleasure in simply observing and participating in nature.[7]

Find a small part of God's creation and spend a few minutes enjoying and engaging with it.

A SAFE PLACE TO HIDE

PSALM 46:4-11

4   There is a river whose streams make glad the city of God,
         the holy habitation of the Most High.
5   God is in the midst of her; she shall not be moved;
         God will help her when morning dawns.
6   The nations rage, the kingdoms totter;
         he utters his voice, the earth melts.
7   The LORD of hosts is with us;
         the God of Jacob is our fortress.   *Selah*

8   Come, behold the works of the LORD,
         how he has brought desolations on the earth.
9   He makes wars cease to the end of the earth;
         he breaks the bow and shatters the spear;
         he burns the chariots with fire.
10   "Be still, and know that I am God.
         I will be exalted among the nations,
         I will be exalted in the earth!"
11   The LORD of hosts is with us;
         the God of Jacob is our fortress.   *Selah*

READ

Read the passage aloud.

THINK

When have you felt the safest in your lifetime? Why? Circle or underline every word in this passage that deals with the concept of safety and security. Consider your emotions that rise up in response to the words of this passage.

Why do you think the psalmist repeats this phrase "The LORD of hosts is with us; the God of Jacob is our fortress"?

What would your life look like if you lived this out: "Be still, and know that I am God"?

PRAY

Take several minutes to free your mind of every anxious thought, concern, or stress that you have. Ask God to release you from these thoughts that hold you captive and paralyze you.

After this time, ask God to fill you with the promises from this psalm concerning the safety and security found only in him.

LIVE

In the midst of your busy schedule today, live in the safety of God.

CLEANSE ME FROM MY SINS

PSALM 51:1-12

1 Have mercy on me, O God,
    according to your steadfast love;
  according to your abundant mercy
    blot out my transgressions.
2 Wash me thoroughly from my iniquity,
    and cleanse me from my sin!

3 For I know my transgressions,
    and my sin is ever before me.
4 Against you, you only, have I sinned
    and done what is evil in your sight,
  so that you may be justified in your words
    and blameless in your judgment.
5 Behold, I was brought forth in iniquity,
    and in sin did my mother conceive me.
6 Behold, you delight in truth in the inward being,
    and you teach me wisdom in the secret heart.

7 Purge me with hyssop, and I shall be clean;
    wash me, and I shall be whiter than snow.
8 Let me hear joy and gladness;
    let the bones that you have broken rejoice.
9 Hide your face from my sins,
    and blot out all my iniquities.
10 Create in me a clean heart, O God,
    and renew a right spirit within me.
11 Cast me not away from your presence,
    and take not your Holy Spirit from me.
12 Restore to me the joy of your salvation,
    and uphold me with a willing spirit.

READ
Read the passage aloud slowly.

THINK
Read the passage again, noting these items:

- the wrongs the psalmist confesses
- what the psalmist asks for from God

1. This psalm is an ideal psalm of confession because the psalmist not only confesses sins but also focuses on the way forward, noting the next positive steps to take. He asks for good things from God and does not get stuck in the past. Find where he does that.
2. The psalmist also understands that his sin is not just something he did, but a sin against God personally. Find the words *you* and *your.*
3. The biggest issue is not that he sinned but that he loves God. Why do you think we often make our sin the biggest issue instead?

PRAY
Pray the passage aloud, paraphrasing and embellishing the lines that fit your life today.

LIVE
Sit with your hands open in front of you with palms turned upward as a way of letting your confession bring you healing, cleansing, and renewal.

GOD RESTORES

PSALM 53:1-6

1 The fool says in his heart, "There is no God."
   They are corrupt, doing abominable iniquity;
   there is none who does good.

2 God looks down from heaven
      on the children of man
   to see if there are any who understand,
      who seek after God.

3 They have all fallen away;
      together they have become corrupt;
   there is none who does good,
      not even one.

4 Have those who work evil no knowledge,
      who eat up my people as they eat bread,
      and do not call upon God?

5 There they are, in great terror,
      where there is no terror!
   For God scatters the bones of him who encamps against you;
      you put them to shame, for God has rejected them.

6 Oh, that salvation for Israel would come out of Zion!
      When God restores the fortunes of his people,
      let Jacob rejoice, let Israel be glad.

PRAY

Spend several minutes in silence, examining your heart. What's in it today? Note what you find, but don't get too engrossed or sidetracked by any single thought or feeling. Simply acknowledge each item, as though you're gathering all your concerns and feelings into a basket.

READ

When you finish examining your heart, temporarily set aside the basket. Read the passage slowly and thoroughly, taking in the psalmist's experience. His energy is rising in response to a tough situation, and he is letting it drive him toward God.

THINK

What one aspect of the passage draws your attention? Maybe it is the psalmist's desire for justice, rather than a passive tolerance of wrongs. Or maybe it is his deep belief in God's concern for his welfare. Spend time pondering this.

Now return to your basket. Pick up each item and look at it through the filter of this passage. Again, don't get too absorbed in any one concern, but stay attuned to the psalm's message to you. How does it meet up with the items in your basket?

LIVE

Read the passage slowly again. To what action — whether emotional, mental, or physical — might God be calling you through these verses?

HE ONLY IS MY ROCK

PSALM 62:1-2

1 For God alone my soul waits in silence;
     from him comes my salvation.
2 He only is my rock and my salvation,
     my fortress; I shall not be greatly shaken.

READ

Take this book outside and read the passage.

THINK

In our Western mind-set, we describe God with intangible ideas, such as God is love, God is peace, or God is compassionate. But in the Eastern mind-set, thoughts are described in vivid imagery and word pictures. The Psalms in particular describe God with tangible ideas: God is Father, God is the wind, God is an eagle. In this psalm David describes God as a rock.

Outdoors, find a handful of rocks and look at them. Take a few moments to reflect on the specific characteristics of rocks and how they describe God's character. Write down your reflections.

PRAY

Thank God that he is like a rock, referring to your list to offer specific details. Thank him for what each of these aspects of his character means to you.

LIVE

Find a small stone and carry it with you today in your pocket or purse. Every time your hand closes on it, reflect on the fact that God is your rock.

DAY 84

GOD ENCOUNTERS

On this seventh day, review and reflect on all you have read this week. Take the time to revel in the ways you've encountered God in the past six days.

MY SOUL THIRSTS FOR YOU

PSALM 63:1-8

1   O God, you are my God; earnestly I seek you;
        my soul thirsts for you;
    my flesh faints for you,
        as in a dry and weary land where there is no water.
2   So I have looked upon you in the sanctuary,
        beholding your power and glory.
3   Because your steadfast love is better than life,
        my lips will praise you.
4   So I will bless you as long as I live;
        in your name I will lift up my hands.

5   My soul will be satisfied as with fat and rich food,
        and my mouth will praise you with joyful lips,
6   when I remember you upon my bed,
        and meditate on you in the watches of the night;
7   for you have been my help,
        and in the shadow of your wings I will sing for joy.
8   My soul clings to you;
        your right hand upholds me.

READ

Read the passage silently and slowly.

PRAY

Tell God how you honestly respond to this psalm.

Perhaps you don't have this drooling, lip-smacking desire for God. Maybe the idea even embarrasses you. Or maybe you'd like to be this way, but it sounds far too spiritual. Reveal your honest feelings to God.

Perhaps you do have these intense feelings for God. If so, which words in the psalm best describe that?

THINK

Read the passage again.

If one word or phrase describes your present state, say it aloud.

If one word or phrase describes how you would like to be, say it aloud.

LIVE

Consider this quotation from *The Cloud of Unknowing*: "Nourish in your heart a lively longing for God."[8] Bask in that idea, and try to see yourself doing it.

THE POSTURE OF GRATITUDE

PSALM 75:1-4

¹ We give thanks to you, O God;
    we give thanks, for your name is near.
We recount your wondrous deeds.

² "At the set time that I appoint
    I will judge with equity.
³ When the earth totters, and all its inhabitants,
    it is I who keep steady its pillars.   *Selah*
⁴ I say to the boastful, 'Do not boast,'
    and to the wicked, 'Do not lift up your horn.'"

LIVE

Take a clean sheet of paper and fill the page with all the things you are thankful for, big and small. Include items like names of people, elements of creation, God-orchestrated events and timing, and small things you often overlook. When you're finished, thank God for those blessings he is giving you today as well as those blessings he gave you months or even years ago.

READ/THINK

Now read the expanded passage. Notice the psalmist's reasons for thanking God. Make a list of these reasons on the back of your sheet of paper. This psalm highlights the fact that God is in complete and total control of the entire earth. Stop and ponder: Does that make you thankful or anxious or . . . ? Why?

PRAY

Based on the general outline of the expanded passage, take the list you made and prayerfully write your own psalm (poem) to God. Be creative and personal. (Nobody has to read what you write.) When you are finished, use your psalm to worship God. Read it aloud at least once.

I'LL WORSHIP YOU UNDIVIDED

PSALM 86:14-17

¹⁴ O God, insolent men have risen up against me;
    a band of ruthless men seeks my life,
    and they do not set you before them.
¹⁵ But you, O Lord, are a God merciful and gracious,
    slow to anger and abounding in steadfast love and faithfulness.
¹⁶ Turn to me and be gracious to me;
    give your strength to your servant,
    and save the son of your maidservant.
¹⁷ Show me a sign of your favor,
    that those who hate me may see and be put to shame
    because you, LORD, have helped me and comforted me.

READ

Stand up and read aloud the psalmist's proclamation of God's trust-worthiness. As you read the phrase "God, insolent men have risen up against me," kneel. Remain on your knees until you finish the passage, as the psalmist expresses the depth of his trust in God amid danger. Repeat slowly and attentively three times.

THINK

What do you notice about yourself as you do this exercise? In what ways do you experience the passage differently than you normally would? Perhaps your body's position helps your mind focus. Or perhaps you protest the position because it doesn't fit your mood or energy level. Meditate on the reasons for your reaction.

PRAY

Now read the passage again, this time silently, keeping in mind what you just learned about yourself. Let the Holy Spirit show you a word or phrase that touches what has arisen in you. Spend a few minutes repeating the word or phrase prayerfully. How is God speaking to you?

LIVE

Consider what it was like for you to let your body take the lead in prayer. In what ways did your body help or hinder you in engaging with God?

WHEN THE ROCKS CRY OUT

PSALM 96:7-10

7 Ascribe to the LORD, O families of the peoples,
   ascribe to the LORD glory and strength!
8 Ascribe to the LORD the glory due his name;
   bring an offering, and come into his courts!
9 Worship the LORD in the splendor of holiness;
   tremble before him, all the earth!

10 Say among the nations, "The LORD reigns!
   Yes, the world is established; it shall never be moved;
   he will judge the peoples with equity."

READ

Get in a comfortable position on your knees. As you are in this posture of submission, ask God to help your body be a symbolic expression of your heart during the next few moments. Admit to God that you want to be submissive to him — even if doing so is difficult — as you engage with his Word.

Keeping this position, read the passage.

THINK

The psalmist invites other people to join him in the praise of God. "Say among the nations, 'The LORD reigns!'" In what specific ways can we get the message out in our praise of God?

Consider this picture of worship: "Bring an offering, and come into his courts! Worship the LORD in the splendor of holiness." Is it hard to imagine that God likes it when his people celebrate in worship? Why or why not?

What is one attribute of God that you could celebrate right now? Why do you think that attribute comes to mind?

PRAY

While still on your knees, invite the Holy Spirit to come in and guide your prayers. Praise him for whatever comes to mind. If you feel comfortable, speak your praise aloud.

LIVE

Find a worship album or Christian radio station and spend the next several minutes listening to worship music. If you know the words to a song, join in and sing along, or invite friends to join you. If you know how to play an instrument, spend a few minutes playing it while singing praises to God.

BLESSING GOD

PSALM 103:1-14

[1] Bless the LORD, O my soul,
>   and all that is within me,
>   bless his holy name!

[2] Bless the LORD, O my soul,
>   and forget not all his benefits,

[3] who forgives all your iniquity,
>   who heals all your diseases,

[4] who redeems your life from the pit,
>   who crowns you with steadfast love and mercy,

[5] who satisfies you with good
>   so that your youth is renewed like the eagle's.

[6] The LORD works righteousness
>   and justice for all who are oppressed.

[7] He made known his ways to Moses,
>   his acts to the people of Israel.

[8] The LORD is merciful and gracious,
>   slow to anger and abounding in steadfast love.

[9] He will not always chide,
>   nor will he keep his anger forever.

[10] He does not deal with us according to our sins,
>   nor repay us according to our iniquities.

[11] For as high as the heavens are above the earth,
>   so great is his steadfast love toward those who fear him;

[12] as far as the east is from the west,
>   so far does he remove our transgressions from us.

[13] As a father shows compassion to his children,
>   so the LORD shows compassion to those who fear him.

[14] For he knows our frame;
>   he remembers that we are dust.

READ

Read the passage quietly to yourself.

THINK

The idea of blessing God may sound odd to us. We might think, *Who am I to bless God? Isn't God the only one to bless people?* But the literal meaning of the Hebrew word *bless* is "to kneel."[9] So when we bless God, our souls kneel to him, usually in worship or gratitude.

Read the passage again with your heart kneeling before God. If possible, physically kneel where you are and read aloud. As you do, notice the phrases that reflect what you are most eager to praise God for — perhaps that he isn't easily angered or doesn't endlessly nag.

PRAY

Stay kneeling and pray aloud those phrases about God that touched you most. As you pray, add to them other ideas about God that come to mind. Raise your hands if you wish.

LIVE

Quietly kneel before God in whatever posture and mood this psalm has brought you:

- resting peacefully on your heels with your hands in your lap
- rising onto your knees with your hands raised
- kneeling before a chair or bed and bringing your whole self forward onto it

Be with God this way for a few minutes.

SPIRITUAL HISTORY LESSONS

PSALM 106:1-4,6-12

1 Praise the LORD!
> Oh give thanks to the LORD, for he is good,
> > for his steadfast love endures forever!
2 Who can utter the mighty deeds of the LORD,
> > or declare all his praise?
3 Blessed are they who observe justice,
> > who do righteousness at all times!

4 Remember me, O LORD, when you show favor to your people;
> > help me when you save them. . . .

6 Both we and our fathers have sinned;
> > we have committed iniquity; we have done wickedness.
7 Our fathers, when they were in Egypt,
> > did not consider your wondrous works;
> they did not remember the abundance of your steadfast love,
> > but rebelled by the sea, at the Red Sea.
8 Yet he saved them for his name's sake,
> > that he might make known his mighty power.
9 He rebuked the Red Sea, and it became dry,
> > and he led them through the deep as through a desert.
10 So he saved them from the hand of the foe
> > and redeemed them from the power of the enemy.
11 And the waters covered their adversaries;
> > not one of them was left.
12 Then they believed his words;
> > they sang his praise.

READ

As you read this passage, listen for a word or phrase that says in some small way, "I am for you today."

THINK/PRAY

Let this word or phrase sink deeply into you by repeating it slowly to yourself several times. Bring your worries, thoughts, and memories to it, and see how it casts light on them. Talk to God about what's going through your mind and heart. Do you feel like he is "for you"?

LIVE

Ebenezer literally means "stone of help" in Hebrew. It can be used to refer to anything that reminds us of something spiritually significant. Today, create an Ebenezer for yourself.

First, think about how God spoke to you or what he did for you through today's passage. Second, write one sentence or a few words on a small piece of paper to describe that. Third, pick a symbol for it: Find a pebble from your yard, buy an inexpensive cross, or cut out a picture from a magazine. Fourth, fold up your note and attach it to the object. Fifth, put your Ebenezer somewhere you will see it often, as a visible reminder of what God said and did.

In the future, periodically reflect on your life (maybe two to four times a year) and create more Ebenezers, keeping them in a box, bowl, or bucket. Whenever you see them, recall who God has been to you.

DAY 91

GOD ENCOUNTERS

On this seventh day, review and reflect on all you have read this week. Take the time to revel in the ways you've encountered God in the past six days.

THE GIFT OF SCRIPTURE

PSALM 119:89-101,105

LAMEDH

⁸⁹ Forever, O LORD, your word
    is firmly fixed in the heavens.
⁹⁰ Your faithfulness endures to all generations;
    you have established the earth, and it stands fast.
⁹¹ By your appointment they stand this day,
    for all things are your servants.
⁹² If your law had not been my delight,
    I would have perished in my affliction.
⁹³ I will never forget your precepts,
    for by them you have given me life.
⁹⁴ I am yours; save me,
    for I have sought your precepts.
⁹⁵ The wicked lie in wait to destroy me,
    but I consider your testimonies.
⁹⁶ I have seen a limit to all perfection,
    but your commandment is exceedingly broad.

MEM

⁹⁷ Oh how I love your law!
    It is my meditation all the day.
⁹⁸ Your commandment makes me wiser than my enemies,
    for it is ever with me.
⁹⁹ I have more understanding than all my teachers,
    for your testimonies are my meditation.
¹⁰⁰ I understand more than the aged,
    for I keep your precepts.
¹⁰¹ I hold back my feet from every evil way,
    in order to keep your word. . . .

NUN

¹⁰⁵ Your word is a lamp to my feet
    and a light to my path.

READ

Read the passage very slowly. Then read it again, this time even slower.

THINK

You've probably heard people say, "The Lord spoke to me," or, "God told me x-y-z," and then been left feeling disbelief, confusion, frustration, or guilt. God does speak to us but not in a booming voice that sounds like actor James Earl Jones. God speaks to us through different means: creation, other people's words of guidance, promptings of the Holy Spirit, and "a low whisper" (1 Kings 19:12). But he also speaks to us through his Word.

Explore your attitudes or preconceived ideas about God's Word. Be brutally honest with yourself and God. Think of ways you could value God's Word more and find yourself more attentive to what it has to say.

Spend several minutes considering how God might be speaking to you through this passage concerning his Word.

PRAY

Pray through this passage of Scripture. Simply make the passage your very own, turning the words back to God (rephrased in your own words, if you wish) as a way to converse with him. Be assured that he is listening to you.

LIVE

Invite God to reveal general and specific elements of Scripture to guide your words, thoughts, and actions today.

CONFIDENCE IN GOD

PSALM 121

1 I lift up my eyes to the hills.
    From where does my help come?
2 My help comes from the LORD,
    who made heaven and earth.

3 _____ He will not let your foot be moved;
    he who keeps you will not slumber.
4 Behold, he who keeps Israel
    will neither slumber nor sleep.

5 The LORD is your keeper _____;
    the LORD is your shade on your right hand.
6 The sun shall not strike you by day, _____
    nor the moon by night.

7 The LORD will keep you _____ from all evil;
    he will keep your life.
8 The LORD will keep
    your going out and your coming in _____
    from this time forth and forevermore.

READ

Read the passage aloud slowly.

THINK

This psalm ranks as one of the greatest psalms of trust and confidence. As you read it aloud a second time, do something different from verse 3 on. Address yourself by name in the places where a blank appears.

As you read the passage a third time, notice the word or phrase that stands out most to you. Use that to create a mind-picture of yourself in a situation where you need to remember to trust. For example, picture yourself desperate for protection, and reread a phrase from verse 7 or 8. Or picture yourself in a situation where you need to know that God doesn't overlook or forget you, and reread a phrase from verse 3 or 4.

PRAY

Speak with God about how much you do or don't trust him. Tell him about your confidence level and ask him to give you grace to grow in it.

LIVE

Have a little fun here. Keep these ideas about confidence in mind and stand as confidently as you can. You might even want to gesture — put your hands on your hips or hold out your fists in front of you. Stay in this pose for several seconds, going over your selected phrase.

Now do this in front of a mirror. Imagine God standing next to you, protecting you in some way. For example, he could be shielding you from the side or standing behind you with arms wrapped around you.

A CALM AND QUIET SOUL

PSALM 131

1   O LORD, my heart is not lifted up;
        my eyes are not raised too high;
    I do not occupy myself with things
        too great and too marvelous for me.
2   But I have calmed and quieted my soul,
        like a weaned child with its mother;
        like a weaned child is my soul within me.

3   O Israel, hope in the LORD
        from this time forth and forevermore.

READ

After you read this psalm, wait patiently for your response to the material.

THINK/PRAY

How does the message of the psalm resonate with you? Maybe the reality of your life is different from the speaker's, but he gives voice to your desire. Or maybe his message challenges your attitude or perspective.

Read it a second time, then share your response with God through prayer. At first it will feel natural to pray in your own words, responding to what you're reading, but as you keep going, stretch beyond this and pray using the words of the passage. Although doing so might feel awkward at first, give yourself time to get used to it. You'll likely hear yourself praying statements you don't genuinely mean and then feel your heart protesting. But stay honest with God by acknowledging this to him. Don't be hard on yourself. Just recall that God accepts you and loves you, then continue.

When you read this psalm one more time, let your meditation go a bit deeper. Wait for deeper memories and thoughts. These mirror more about you and your life. Bring these insights into your prayer.

LIVE

Spend time in silence. Imagine your soul as "a weaned child with its mother." Even if you find your thoughts continuously running, practice silence. Achieving silence doesn't mean you have to focus on stopping your thoughts. Just let them pass through, then bring your mind back to the image of resting. Just enjoy being in the presence of God.

CHEWING ON THE CUD

PSALM 139:1-12

1 O Lord, you have searched me and known me!
2 You know when I sit down and when I rise up;
    you discern my thoughts from afar.
3 You search out my path and my lying down
    and are acquainted with all my ways.
4 Even before a word is on my tongue,
    behold, O Lord, you know it altogether.
5 You hem me in, behind and before,
    and lay your hand upon me.
6 Such knowledge is too wonderful for me;
    it is high; I cannot attain it.

7 Where shall I go from your Spirit?
    Or where shall I flee from your presence?
8 If I ascend to heaven, you are there!
    If I make my bed in Sheol, you are there!
9 If I take the wings of the morning
    and dwell in the uttermost parts of the sea,
10 even there your hand shall lead me,
    and your right hand shall hold me.
11 If I say, "Surely the darkness shall cover me,
    and the light about me be night,"
12 even the darkness is not dark to you;
    the night is bright as the day,
    for darkness is as light with you.

THINK

To ruminate literally means "to chew the cud." A cow will chew on one particular wad of cud for hours at a time, over and over again, swallowing it and bringing it back up from its stomach. Consider the metaphor of the cud as you think about the phrases "searched me and known me," "you discern my thoughts," and "you are there."

READ

Read the passage three times slowly, ruminating on it. Don't skim or speed-read; chew on each word. Hold the words in your mind until you feel you've considered every aspect of them.

PRAY

Spend time in silence, meditating on these phrases. Let them bounce around in your brain. Look at them from every direction. As you do that, explore the emotions and thoughts you are having. Specifically ask God, "Why am I feeling this way, God?" and put your heart in a posture of listening. Expect to hear from God.

LIVE

Spend a few more minutes listening to God and ask him, "What do you want me to do with what you have given to me?"

NO ONE IS LEFT OUT

PSALM 145:7-9,15-21

7   They shall pour forth the fame of your abundant goodness
      and shall sing aloud of your righteousness.

8   The LORD is gracious and merciful,
      slow to anger and abounding in steadfast love.
9   The LORD is good to all
      and his mercy is over all that he has made. . . .

15 The eyes of all look to you,
      and you give them their food in due season.
16 You open your hand;
      you satisfy the desire of every living thing.
17 The LORD is righteous in all his ways
      and kind in all his works.
18 The LORD is near to all who call on him,
      to all who call on him in truth.
19 He fulfills the desire of those who fear him;
      he also hears their cry and saves them.
20 The LORD preserves all who love him,
      but all the wicked he will destroy.

21 My mouth will speak the praise of the LORD,
      and let all flesh bless his holy name forever and ever.

READ

Read the passage aloud slowly.

THINK

This psalm celebrates God's goodness to all and his goodness through everything. Notice how often the words *all* and *every* appear. While many psalms emphasize God as "my God," this one shows God's mercy to all.

Read it again, either emphasizing or pausing after the words *all* and *every*.

1. Who might *all* include that you may not have thought about before? Maybe people you know, people far away, or objects foreign to you. As you do this, what pictures come to mind?
2. Notice the many phrases about God's goodness. Which ones resonate most with you?

PRAY

Thank God for his deep goodness toward all. Use phrases from the psalm that best express this theme from your point of view.

LIVE

Go for a walk or hike, taking this book with you. As you walk, stop at certain points and read a verse or two aloud. Listen to the echo of your voice. Enjoy God, who is enjoying hearing you pour forth these words.

PRAISE HIM, SUN AND MOON

PSALM 148:2-12

2 Praise him, all his angels;
  praise him, all his hosts!

3 Praise him, sun and moon,
  praise him, all you shining stars!
4 Praise him, you highest heavens,
  and you waters above the heavens!

5 Let them praise the name of the LORD!
  For he commanded and they were created.
6 And he established them forever and ever;
  he gave a decree, and it shall not pass away.

7 Praise the LORD from the earth,
  you great sea creatures and all deeps,
8 fire and hail, snow and mist,
  stormy wind fulfilling his word!

9 Mountains and all hills,
  fruit trees and all cedars!
10 Beasts and all livestock,
  creeping things and flying birds!

11 Kings of the earth and all peoples,
  princes and all rulers of the earth!
12 Young men and maidens together,
  old men and children!

READ

Read the passage a few times aloud, zeroing in on each image. Allow the words to wash over you in their vividness: See specific birds or wild beasts, sense the chill of the ice, hear the roaring of the ocean. Watch every action of the characters. Compare the way each created thing uniquely praises its Maker.

THINK

In the silence that follows the reading, meditate on what you've seen and heard. With all these pieces of creation in the background, praising God, how do you see him? What is he like? Spend time thinking about him.

PRAY

Pick the character attribute of God that seems the most powerful after your meditation. Envision God in this role, then see yourself entering his presence. How do you respond to him? How does he treat you? Rest in God's presence or talk to him or adore him — whatever fits the scene.

LIVE

As you go through your day, pay special attention to natural objects around you (rocks, trees, animals, hills) as well as people (individuals, crowds). Observe how they glorify their Creator by their existence. Don't be overcritical or get caught up in evaluating — just notice.

DAY 98

GOD ENCOUNTERS

On this seventh day, review and reflect on all you have read this week. Take the time to revel in the ways you've encountered God in the past six days.

WORTH FAR MORE THAN MONEY

PROVERBS 2:1-5

¹ If you receive my words
　　and treasure up my commandments with you
² . . . making your ear attentive to wisdom
　　and inclining your heart to understanding;
³ yes, if you call out for insight
　　and raise your voice for understanding,
⁴ if you seek it like silver
　　and search for it as for hidden treasures,
⁵ then you will understand the fear of the LORD
　　and find the knowledge of God.

READ

Read the passage, imagining a grandparent or an older, wiser friend saying these words to you.

THINK

Our culture rarely considers or values wisdom. People want many things, but wisdom isn't usually one of them, or it's not high on the priority list. And there seems to be a widespread assumption that a person simply grows into wisdom as he or she gets older. This is a passive approach to obtaining wisdom. But the writer of this proverb tells us not only that wisdom is worth pursuing but also that it should be pursued with much time and energy. This is a proactive approach to obtaining wisdom.

Read the passage again. What would pursuing wisdom with all your might look like? Do you believe that wisdom is "better than gain from silver and her profit better than gold" (3:14)? Is that hard to believe? Why or why not?

PRAY

Pause and ask God to give you wisdom. Ask him to help you raise the value and preciousness of wisdom in your life. Ask him to show you how to actively pursue wisdom. Listen for anything he might say now in response to your requests.

LIVE

Live wisely today, asking God to give you a spirit of discernment as you work, play, rest, eat, read, and sleep.

KEEP YOUR HEART WITH VIGILANCE

PROVERBS 4:20-23; 5:3,8-14

20 My son, be attentive to my words;
    incline your ear to my sayings.
21 Let them not escape from your sight;
    keep them within your heart.
22 For they are life to those who find them,
    and healing to all their flesh.
23 Keep your heart with all vigilance,
    for from it flow the springs of life. . . .

3 For the lips of a forbidden woman drip honey,
    and her speech is smoother than oil. . . .

8 Keep your way far from her,
    and do not go near the door of her house,
9 lest you give your honor to others
    and your years to the merciless,
10 lest strangers take their fill of your strength,
    and your labors go to the house of a foreigner,
11 and at the end of your life you groan,
    when your flesh and body are consumed,
12 and you say, "How I hated discipline,
    and my heart despised reproof!
13 I did not listen to the voice of my teachers
    or incline my ear to my instructors.
14 I am at the brink of utter ruin
    in the assembled congregation."

READ

Read the passage aloud slowly, keeping in mind that "a forbidden woman" refers to the things in your life that seduce you, meaning anything that sucks you in, lures you, misleads you, or even corrupts you.

THINK

1. Consider what has caused you to squander days of your life and left you full of regret. It might be patterns of relating to people, patterns of spending your time, or patterns of making decisions. Then read verses 8-14 again and wait for thoughts to rise to the surface of your mind.
2. Read verses 20-23 and see what comes to you about the ways you need to avoid such patterns. Do you need to listen? Be attentive to God's words? Keep a vigilant heart?
3. What would keeping your heart with all vigilance look like? Keeping watch might be different for you than for others. Avoid grabbing at the first thing that comes to mind. Wait in that.

PRAY

Begin by confessing your regrets about time and energy you've squandered. Don't rush through this. Allow enough time to fully describe these things and let them go. Then ask God to help you listen to him and keep your heart with vigilance.

LIVE

Leave this book open to this passage and underline the phrase in verses 20-23 that stands out to you. As you move through your day, allow this to remind you to listen and keep an alert heart.

DAY 101
EXPANDED PASSAGE: PROVERBS 7–8

LURED INTO AMBUSH

PROVERBS 7:7-8,13-23

7 I have seen among the simple,
    I have perceived among the youths,
    a young man lacking sense,
8 passing along the street near her corner,
    taking the road to her house. . . .

13 She seizes him and kisses him,
    and with bold face she says to him,
14 "I had to offer sacrifices,
    and today I have paid my vows;
15 so now I have come out to meet you,
    to seek you eagerly, and I have found you.
16 I have spread my couch with coverings,
    colored linens from Egyptian linen;
17 I have perfumed my bed with myrrh,
    aloes, and cinnamon.
18 Come, let us take our fill of love till morning;
    let us delight ourselves with love.
19 For my husband is not at home;
    he has gone on a long journey;
20 he took a bag of money with him;
    at full moon he will come home."

21 With much seductive speech she persuades him;
    with her smooth talk she compels him.
22 All at once he follows her,
    as an ox goes to the slaughter,
  or as a stag is caught fast
23   till an arrow pierces its liver;
  as a bird rushes into a snare;
    he does not know that it will cost him his life.

PRAY

Before you begin, ask the Holy Spirit to make his presence palpable as you pray. Ask him to make you open to whatever he gives, rather than taking charge of this time or trying to fix yourself. Even if a part of you disagrees, present yourself with the truth that opening to him is all you can really do.

READ/THINK

Read the passage once, slowly. Allow the story of the foolish man and the seductress to sink in until you understand its message. How do the words relate to your life? In what areas are you tempted—lured into ambush—to live foolishly? What are some things you know are right to do, but you drag your feet and don't do them? Don't try to fix yourself or be down on yourself. Instead, just let the reality settle in that this is who you are: someone very much in need of God's grace and mercy.

LIVE

Finish your devotion today by picturing God sitting with you. Tell him, "God, this is who I am." Remain open to whatever this might be, and if necessary, remind yourself that you don't want to fix yourself. If this seems difficult or if relaxing in his presence is challenging, take a few minutes to consider this truth: "The Lord is compassionate and merciful" (James 5:11). Then return to relaxing in God's presence. Write down anything significant from this time that you can refer to.

SELF-EXAMINATION

PROVERBS 10:22-32

22 The blessing of the LORD makes rich,
and he adds no sorrow with it.
23 Doing wrong is like a joke to a fool,
but wisdom is pleasure to a man of understanding.
24 What the wicked dreads will come upon him,
but the desire of the righteous will be granted.
25 When the tempest passes, the wicked is no more,
but the righteous is established forever.
26 Like vinegar to the teeth and smoke to the eyes,
so is the sluggard to those who send him.
27 The fear of the LORD prolongs life,
but the years of the wicked will be short.
28 The hope of the righteous brings joy,
but the expectation of the wicked will perish.
29 The way of the LORD is a stronghold to the blameless,
but destruction to evildoers.
30 The righteous will never be removed,
but the wicked will not dwell in the land.
31 The mouth of the righteous brings forth wisdom,
but the perverse tongue will be cut off.
32 The lips of the righteous know what is acceptable,
but the mouth of the wicked, what is perverse.

READ

Stand in front of a mirror and read the passage. When you're finished, stand motionless. Stare at yourself in the mirror.

THINK

When we read passages of God's Word that speak about the unrighteous or the evil or foolish person, we are often reminded of other individuals and think to ourselves, *That certainly isn't talking about me.* But we must be careful not to be blinded by the sin and pride in our own lives. Take a few minutes to perform a thorough self-examination. (This might be a difficult exercise for you; being willing to see our true selves is not easy.)

PRAY

Reread the passage. After each verse, pause, look in the mirror, and whisper, "God, is this me?" Allow time for God to prompt truths in your heart. Some of these thoughts may be hard to hear. If God brings to mind specific areas where you have failed, ask him to forgive you. If God brings to mind areas where you can grow, ask him to help you mature as you follow him. If God brings to mind ways in which you are living faithfully, thank him for his grace in your life.

LIVE

Whatever God-honoring quality was revealed to you today as you asked the question, "God, is this me?" go and live in that manner.

WISDOM OF THE PRUDENT

PROVERBS 14:2-13

2   Whoever walks in uprightness fears the LORD,
>   but he who is devious in his ways despises him.
3   By the mouth of a fool comes a rod for his back,
>   but the lips of the wise will preserve them.
4   Where there are no oxen, the manger is clean,
>   but abundant crops come by the strength of the ox.
5   A faithful witness does not lie,
>   but a false witness breathes out lies.
6   A scoffer seeks wisdom in vain,
>   but knowledge is easy for a man of understanding.
7   Leave the presence of a fool,
>   for there you do not meet words of knowledge.
8   The wisdom of the prudent is to discern his way,
>   but the folly of fools is deceiving.
9   Fools mock at the guilt offering,
>   but the upright enjoy acceptance.
10 The heart knows its own bitterness,
>   and no stranger shares its joy.
11 The house of the wicked will be destroyed,
>   but the tent of the upright will flourish.
12 There is a way that seems right to a man,
>   but its end is the way to death.
13 Even in laughter the heart may ache,
>   and the end of joy may be grief.

READ

Read through these wise observations about life, pausing after each to consider what it says. Pick the statement that seems particularly vivid to you today, and read through it several more times, silently and aloud, until you become familiar with its message.

THINK

Where do you see yourself and the way you act fitting into this observation about life's realities? Maybe the image of the ox makes you recognize the laziness you've been lounging in, or perhaps you're struck by how much energy you expend trying to fit in with people. As you absorb this reality check, what are you feeling?

PRAY

Allow your inner exploration to take you into dialogue with God. Tell him about your discoveries. Let yourself be led into thankfulness, humility, or need. Maybe you're grateful to see the danger of your laziness before you get burned, or maybe you want to tell God how much you desire validation, even when you understand the folly of measuring your worth by the acceptance of others. Whatever this passage offers you personally, continue exploring it with God. Return to the passage if you find yourself stuck.

LIVE

Maybe the words "walks in uprightness," "lips of the wise," or "faithful witness" mean something new to you after pondering this passage. In what area is God inviting you to turn your life around — with his help? Write down in a short statement what you sense God inviting you to do.

THE IMPORTANCE OF WORDS

PROVERBS 16:21-32

21 The wise of heart is called discerning,
    and sweetness of speech increases persuasiveness.
22 Good sense is a fountain of life to him who has it,
    but the instruction of fools is folly.
23 The heart of the wise makes his speech judicious
    and adds persuasiveness to his lips.
24 Gracious words are like a honeycomb,
    sweetness to the soul and health to the body.
25 There is a way that seems right to a man,
    but its end is the way to death.
26 A worker's appetite works for him;
    his mouth urges him on.
27 A worthless man plots evil,
    and his speech is like a scorching fire.
28 A dishonest man spreads strife,
    and a whisperer separates close friends.
29 A man of violence entices his neighbor
    and leads him in a way that is not good.
30 Whoever winks his eyes plans dishonest things;
    he who purses his lips brings evil to pass.
31 Gray hair is a crown of glory;
    it is gained in a righteous life.
32 Whoever is slow to anger is better than the mighty,
    and he who rules his spirit than he who takes a city.

READ

Read the passage. Underline the word or phrase that stands out to you the most. Read the passage again. Underline a different word or phrase that stands out to you.

THINK

You may have heard the saying that only two things cannot be taken back: time and our words. Think back over all the words you have said in conversation over the past twenty-four hours (conversations you have had with friends, comments you have made in passing, phone calls, jokes you have told, and so on). What percentage of your conversation would you say was positive, encouraging, and uplifting? What percentage was negative, discouraging, and sarcastic?

Consider the words you are glad you said. Consider the words you regret saying.

PRAY

For the words you regret, ask for forgiveness. For the positive words you spoke, thank God they were words that built up rather than tore down.

Ask God to bring to mind words of truth and healing that you could speak to others. Ask him to bring to mind specific people to whom you could speak these words in the next few days.

LIVE

Have the courage to seek out opportunities to speak words of truth and healing to people who need to hear them. Hold your tongue when you are upset or frustrated—when you are about to speak words you'll regret. Above all else, ask God to help you guard your mouth by thinking before speaking.

DAY 105

GOD ENCOUNTERS

On this seventh day, review and reflect on all you have read this week. Take the time to revel in the ways you've encountered God in the past six days.

HUMILITY

PROVERBS 18:10-15

¹⁰ The name of the LORD is a strong tower;
    the righteous man runs into it and is safe.
¹¹ A rich man's wealth is his strong city,
    and like a high wall in his imagination.
¹² Before destruction a man's heart is haughty,
    but humility comes before honor.
¹³ If one gives an answer before he hears,
    it is his folly and shame.
¹⁴ A man's spirit will endure sickness,
    but a crushed spirit who can bear?
¹⁵ An intelligent heart acquires knowledge,
    and the ear of the wise seeks knowledge.

READ
Read the passage aloud slowly.

THINK
Read the passage again slowly. Notice the different ways humility is expressed.

1. Which phrases describe who you have been and who you'd like to be?
2. What fears do you have about what might happen to you if you were humble? How might these fears be addressed by living in God's name, God's power, and God's presence as your place of protection?

Read the passage again.

3. What touches you most about this passage?
4. What is occurring in your life right now that this passage addresses?

PRAY
Ask God to show you more about living a richly humble life. Tell God what you need to learn from him about being his devoted, constant, listening student.

LIVE
Soak in the protection of God's name, presence, and power. Notice how this makes being humble easier.

WAIT FOR THE LORD

PROVERBS 20:22-30

²² Do not say, "I will repay evil";
   wait for the LORD, and he will deliver you.
²³ Unequal weights are an abomination to the LORD,
   and false scales are not good.
²⁴ A man's steps are from the LORD;
   how then can man understand his way?
²⁵ It is a snare to say rashly, "It is holy,"
   and to reflect only after making vows.
²⁶ A wise king winnows the wicked
   and drives the wheel over them.
²⁷ The spirit of man is the lamp of the LORD,
   searching all his innermost parts.
²⁸ Steadfast love and faithfulness preserve the king,
   and by steadfast love his throne is upheld.
²⁹ The glory of young men is their strength,
   but the splendor of old men is their gray hair.
³⁰ Blows that wound cleanse away evil;
   strokes make clean the innermost parts.

READ

Read this list of statements and instructions, pausing after each one to consider what it says. Does one stand out to you? Memorize it.

THINK

Why does this stand out to you? Let it lead you to ponder your own life. Try to avoid thinking about other people's actions or motives; think instead about only your own. Maybe you'll be reminded of making an impulsive promise, or perhaps you'll check your attitude toward "the splendor of old men is their gray hair" versus "the glory of young men is their strength."

PRAY

Invite God into your thoughts. Tell him what you have been discovering. Be aware of your feelings while you pray—maybe fear of emptiness at the thought of getting older, joy that God will deliver you someday, or sadness over a foolish decision and its consequences. Be yourself in God's presence.

LIVE

Explore your overall experience with this text so far. Why did you respond the way you did to the wise instruction God is communicating in this passage? If you didn't care much, this might tell you that you don't care much about doing the right thing. If you anxiously tried to think of ways to improve yourself, perhaps you feel uncomfortable exposing your weakness to God. Honestly recognize what's in your heart today—and what that tells you about how you see yourself and how you see God.

Remember that God knows all about you—even the parts of you that are rebellious and don't care about what's right—and yet he loves you deeply. If you struggle to believe this, read Isaiah 43:1-7.

107

DOLLARS AND CENTS

PROVERBS 22:22-23,26-27; 23:4-8

²² Do not rob the poor, because he is poor,
    or crush the afflicted at the gate,
²³ for the LORD will plead their cause
    and rob of life those who rob them. . . .
²⁶ Be not one of those who give pledges,
    who put up security for debts.
²⁷ If you have nothing with which to pay,
    why should your bed be taken from under you? . . .

⁴ Do not toil to acquire wealth;
    be discerning enough to desist.
⁵ When your eyes light on it, it is gone,
    for suddenly it sprouts wings,
    flying like an eagle toward heaven.
⁶ Do not eat the bread of a man who is stingy;
    do not desire his delicacies,
⁷ for he is like one who is inwardly calculating.
    "Eat and drink!" he says to you,
    but his heart is not with you.
⁸ You will vomit up the morsels that you have eaten,
    and waste your pleasant words.

READ

Read the passage. Make a note of every implication to finances and wealth that you find.

THINK

Scripture has a lot to say about how we deal with our finances. Wisdom will determine a lot about how we deal with money, and money will determine a lot about how we deal with wisdom. Proverbs speaks often of the importance of dealing with money, because it's not simply about dollars and cents. It's a deeper issue that involves what our heart is attached to.

Think back over the purchases you have made in the past week, big and small. What was your motive in making those purchases (practical purposes, reputation, comfort and pleasure, necessity)?

Which of those would you categorize as being wise purchases? Which would you categorize as being unwise?

As you think about the purchases you have made in the past week, what emotions are you feeling? Are they positive or negative? Full of freedom and joy or guilt and frustration? Why do you think you are feeling that way?

PRAY

Take out your wallet, purse, money clip, credit cards, checkbook, and key chain, and hold them in your hands. As you look at the pile in your hands, keep your eyes open and pray. Ask your heavenly Father to help you be a wise steward of all the money and possessions he has entrusted to you.

LIVE

108

Every time you pull out your wallet or purse to make a purchase, ask yourself the question, *Will this purchase be a wise one, and will it honor God?*

DAY 109
EXPANDED PASSAGE: PROVERBS 24

WISDOM WITH FEET ON IT

PROVERBS 24:3-4,15-21,28-29

³ By wisdom a house is built,
    and by understanding it is established;
⁴ by knowledge the rooms are filled
    with all precious and pleasant riches. . . .

¹⁵ Lie not in wait as a wicked man against the dwelling of the righteous;
    do no violence to his home;
¹⁶ for the righteous falls seven times and rises again,
    but the wicked stumble in times of calamity.

¹⁷ Do not rejoice when your enemy falls,
    and let not your heart be glad when he stumbles,
¹⁸ lest the LORD see it and be displeased,
    and turn away his anger from him.

¹⁹ Fret not yourself because of evildoers,
    and be not envious of the wicked,
²⁰ for the evil man has no future;
    the lamp of the wicked will be put out.

²¹ My son, fear the LORD and the king,
    and do not join with those who do otherwise. . . .

²⁸ Be not a witness against your neighbor without cause,
    and do not deceive with your lips.
²⁹ Do not say, "I will do to him as he has done to me;
    I will pay the man back for what he has done."

READ

Read the passage slowly. Now read the expanded passage.

THINK

Read the passage again, noticing that the first two verses introduce the importance of wisdom.

1. If you're wondering what wisdom is, notice the way the other verses describe how you can live out wisdom. Underline the practical descriptions of wisdom you find there.
2. Now read aloud the phrases you underlined. Which one resonates with you? Which one sounds like guidance you've been hearing God say to you for a while?
3. How does that phrase connect with you?

PRAY

Talk to God about what's been going on in your life and how the wise ideas in this passage shed light on your situation. Tell God why you would find it difficult or easy to do the wise thing. Thank God that he never finds it difficult — and that he can help you.

LIVE

Play with the idea that you're a truly wise person. Doodle a little in a journal, drawing a representation of yourself as wise. Consider why you drew what you did. Being wise doesn't mean you're a know-it-all or superior to other people so they don't want to hang out with you. Jesus was wise, but plenty of people liked to hang out with him.

WORD TO THE WISE

PROVERBS 28:4-12

4 Those who forsake the law praise the wicked,
    but those who keep the law strive against them.
5 Evil men do not understand justice,
    but those who seek the LORD understand it completely.
6 Better is a poor man who walks in his integrity
    than a rich man who is crooked in his ways.
7 The one who keeps the law is a son with understanding,
    but a companion of gluttons shames his father.
8 Whoever multiplies his wealth by interest and profit
    gathers it for him who is generous to the poor.
9 If one turns away his ear from hearing the law,
    even his prayer is an abomination.
10 Whoever misleads the upright into an evil way
    will fall into his own pit,
    but the blameless will have a goodly inheritance.
11 A rich man is wise in his own eyes,
    but a poor man who has understanding will find him out.
12 When the righteous triumph, there is great glory,
    but when the wicked rise, people hide themselves.

READ

Read the passage slowly, pausing for about thirty seconds after each verse to think about it.

THINK

There are many parts of Proverbs that carry a specific theme. But other parts of Proverbs deliver wise advice like machine-gun fire into the sky — wise sayings about various subjects in no particular order. Chapter 28 is one of these machine-gun-into-the-sky chapters. Yet no matter how they're fired, every bullet is precious.

This time, read the expanded passage, inviting the Holy Spirit to help you pick out two proverbs that speak to your specific condition this week.

PRAY

Ask the Holy Spirit to mold you and shape you so you become more and more like the two verses you have written down, so your life shows evidence of the change. Share these two verses with a close friend or family member, and invite him or her to help you work on these areas of your life.

LIVE

Write on an index card these verses the Holy Spirit brought to your attention. Carry the card with you. When you're sitting in traffic or have a few minutes between meetings or classes, pull out the card and consider the wise ways in which to live.

NOTICING THE NEEDY

PROVERBS 29:7,13-14,23,27

[7] A righteous man knows the rights of the poor;
a wicked man does not understand such knowledge. . . .

[13] The poor man and the oppressor meet together;
the LORD gives light to the eyes of both.

[14] If a king faithfully judges the poor,
his throne will be established forever. . . .

[23] One's pride will bring him low,
but he who is lowly in spirit will obtain honor. . . .

[27] An unjust man is an abomination to the righteous,
but one whose way is straight is an abomination to the wicked.

READ

Read the verses aloud slowly.

THINK

God is an advocate of the needy (see Proverbs 23:11). The biblical categories of the needy (the widow, the fatherless, and the alien or stranger) are "voiceless." Because their voices are not valued or heard, God commissions his people to become modern-day public defenders, so to speak, defending the causes of the needy, maintaining their rights and pleading their cases (see Deuteronomy 27:19; Psalm 82:3; Proverbs 23:10-11; Isaiah 1:17).

1. Read the verses again, noticing what God asks of you regarding the poor.
2. Read the verses one more time, asking God to show you what you need to know about your relationship to the have-nots in your society and neighborhood.

PRAY

Ask God to help you find ways to understand "the rights of the poor," to treat fairly those who are overlooked, and to live justly regarding the needy.

LIVE

Start seeing the have-nots in your world. You might find them riding buses, standing outside convenience stores, or riding their bikes. These people are present, but we usually overlook them. Really look at each person, especially his or her face. Acknowledge the person with a nod or a smile. Breathe in the deep good-heartedness of God, who asks you to understand "the rights of the poor."

DAY 112

GOD ENCOUNTERS

On this seventh day, review and reflect on all you have read this week. Take the time to revel in the ways you've encountered God in the past six days.

THE SKEPTIC AND THE BELIEVER

PROVERBS 30:1-9

1 The man declares, I am weary, O God;
   I am weary, O God, and worn out.
2 Surely I am too stupid to be a man.
   I have not the understanding of a man.
3 I have not learned wisdom,
   nor have I knowledge of the Holy One.
4 Who has ascended to heaven and come down?
   Who has gathered the wind in his fists?
Who has wrapped up the waters in a garment?
   Who has established all the ends of the earth?
What is his name, and what is his son's name?
   Surely you know!

5 Every word of God proves true;
   he is a shield to those who take refuge in him.
6 Do not add to his words,
   lest he rebuke you and you be found a liar.
7 Two things I ask of you;
   deny them not to me before I die:
8 Remove far from me falsehood and lying;
   give me neither poverty nor riches;
   feed me with the food that is needful for me,
9 lest I be full and deny you
   and say, "Who is the LORD?"
or lest I be poor and steal
   and profane the name of my God.

READ

As you read the words of this passage, be aware of the parts of your heart that are represented by the words. Perhaps under certain circumstances, you have intentionally ignored God's rules, while at other times you have run to God for protection, knowing he would help you.

THINK/PRAY

Read the passage a few more times. Each time you read, narrow your focus to the part that most deeply touches the reality of your life. Mull that over. Explore with God what he is saying to you through it, how he may want to lead, challenge, or refresh you.

LIVE

The prayer of verse 9 acknowledges the relationship between our physical and spiritual selves: When full of food, we may feel a false sense of security and disregard our need for God. When hungry, we may feel our need yet doubt that God will meet it.

Consider fasting today, for part or all of the day. Give up food or drink, or perhaps something you enjoy, such as reading or watching television. (Be sure to do this when you'll have time to replace your fasted activity with prayer. Also, check with your doctor before fasting from food or drink.) Let your fast help you get in touch with your heart's reaction to God.

When you would normally engage in the activity you're fasting from or when you feel an emptiness that you normally wouldn't notice, prayerfully read verse 9. In what ways does your fasting experience show you your need for God? Can you trust him to provide for your needs, or is your impulse to try to provide for yourself?

SEEKING PLEASURE

ECCLESIASTES 2:4-10

[4]I made great works. I built houses and planted vineyards for myself. [5]I made myself gardens and parks, and planted in them all kinds of fruit trees. [6]I made myself pools from which to water the forest of growing trees. [7]I bought male and female slaves, and had slaves who were born in my house. I had also great possessions of herds and flocks, more than any who had been before me in Jerusalem. [8]I also gathered for myself silver and gold and the treasure of kings and provinces. I got singers, both men and women, and many concubines, the delight of the sons of man.

[9]So I became great and surpassed all who were before me in Jerusalem. Also my wisdom remained with me. [10]And whatever my eyes desired I did not keep from them. I kept my heart from no pleasure, for my heart found pleasure in all my toil, and this was my reward for all my toil.

READ

Read the passage.

THINK

Nobody knows for certain who wrote Ecclesiastes — some have suggested King Solomon — but one thing is certain: The writer communicates with piercing honesty and urgent desperation about the condition of life. The writer has pursued every possible pleasure and has still come away empty.

Write down your prayerful answers to these questions:

1. What pleasures — big and small, evil and seemingly innocent — have you pursued in the past week?
2. What were your motives — good or bad — for pursuing and engaging in those pleasures? Dig deep and be honest: What meaning were you attempting to get?
3. What does it mean that you pursue pleasure? In other words, what lies does pleasure whisper in your ear?

PRAY

Choose the one pleasure you sought with the most effort. Write out a prayer to God that involves this pursuit and the pleasure itself. Maybe you need to ask God to forgive you because you sought the pleasure ultimately for meaning and significance. Now pray about the bigger picture. Take a hard look at the lifestyle you lead and the amount of pleasure you engage in on a regular basis. Lay everything before God and ask, "God, are these worth pursuing?"

LIVE

This week, with every pleasure you pursue, big and miniscule, consider what your motive is in approaching it.

114

DON'T GO IT ALONE

ECCLESIASTES 4:9-12

⁹Two are better than one, because they have a good reward for their toil. ¹⁰For if they fall, one will lift up his fellow. But woe to him who is alone when he falls and has not another to lift him up! ¹¹Again, if two lie together, they keep warm, but how can one keep warm alone? ¹²And though a man might prevail against one who is alone, two will withstand him — a threefold cord is not quickly broken.

READ

Read the passage aloud slowly.

THINK

Community is an important spiritual practice. The Trinity itself is a community of love. Here on earth we get to try that out! We were built for relationship—to help others and be helped by them. Read the passage again aloud, remembering that it's poetry and trying to read it with rhythm, emphasis, and pauses.

1. What words or phrases speak to you? Why?
2. What do these words or phrases tell you about how you've been helped? About how you're built to help others?

PRAY

Ask God to show you clearly how people have shared their work and their wealth with you, how they've picked you up when you've fallen down, how they've warmed you when you were alone, how they've protected you when you faced the worst. Take as long as you need.

LIVE

Hold a rope or anything braided in your hand. (If you don't have something braided, you can do this in a hardware store or by sketching a braid on a piece of paper.) Run your finger along one of the strands and identify that strand as yourself. Ponder who the other two strands might be in your life—perhaps people you have overlooked. Keep your eyes open for your other two strands today.

WHAT'S THE POINT?

ECCLESIASTES 6:1-9

¹There is an evil that I have seen under the sun, and it lies heavy on mankind: ²a man to whom God gives wealth, possessions, and honor, so that he lacks nothing of all that he desires, yet God does not give him power to enjoy them, but a stranger enjoys them. This is vanity; it is a grievous evil. ³If a man fathers a hundred children and lives many years, so that the days of his years are many, but his soul is not satisfied with life's good things, and he also has no burial, I say that a stillborn child is better off than he. ⁴For it comes in vanity and goes in darkness, and in darkness its name is covered. ⁵Moreover, it has not seen the sun or known anything, yet it finds rest rather than he. ⁶Even though he should live a thousand years twice over, yet enjoy no good — do not all go to the one place?

⁷All the toil of man is for his mouth, yet his appetite is not satisfied.⁸For what advantage has the wise man over the fool? And what does the poor man have who knows how to conduct himself before the living? ⁹Better is the sight of the eyes than the wandering of the appetite: this also is vanity and a striving after wind.

READ
Read the passage slowly.

THINK
In what ways do you relate to this point of view? Maybe you feel disillusioned with the promises of happiness made by each "new and improved" object, program, or adventure. Maybe you've felt so much pain you wish you'd never been born. Maybe you've been showered with good stuff that leaves you secure and comfortable, and you're left unsettled by the reality check in this passage. Look deep inside yourself and find out what's being stirred up there. What one image in the passage best encapsulates your thoughts?

PRAY
Sit with that image in your mind, and become aware of Jesus in the room with you now. Allow yourself to think more deeply about what he is saying through this passage about you and your life. Respond to him with an honest heart. Share with him exactly what you're feeling — the discontent and longing, the pain, the unsettling doubt, whatever it is. If you feel uncomfortable because you wish you could be doing something else, tell him that.

LIVE
Were you able to connect with Jesus in this time? If so, what was it like for you to relate to him? How would you describe the way Jesus was toward you during this time? If you weren't able to connect with him, what was that like for you? What would you have wanted from this time? Share your thoughts and feelings with Jesus.

PAIN

ECCLESIASTES 7:2-3

2 It is better to go to the house of mourning
　　than to go to the house of feasting,
　for this is the end of all mankind,
　　and the living will lay it to heart.
3 Sorrow is better than laughter,
　　for by sadness of face the heart is made glad.

READ

Spend five minutes slowly reading and rereading these two verses.

THINK

Why would the author of these words say such things? Do you relate to these verses? What feelings arise in response to them? Do you agree or disagree that "it is better to go to the house of mourning than to go to the house of feasting"? Why?

Consider a time when you experienced extreme sorrow. Looking back, what did you learn?

"Sorrow is better than laughter, for by sadness of face the heart is made glad." Do you agree or disagree with this statement? Why?

PRAY

If you are currently experiencing sorrow, request that the Lord give you a teachable spirit to learn valuable lessons during this time. If you are not experiencing sorrow, invite the Lord to prepare your heart for those times when you will.

LIVE

C. S. Lewis wrote, "God whispers to us in our joy and shouts to us in our pain."[10] Next time you hear about the death of someone you know or attend a funeral, journal your thoughts or process with a friend what you observed and what you learned. In the meantime, live a life that is teachable and moldable, especially during difficult times.

DO ALL TO THE GLORY OF GOD

ECCLESIASTES 9:7-10

[7]Go, eat your bread with joy, and drink your wine with a merry heart, for God has already approved what you do.

[8]Let your garments be always white. Let not oil be lacking on your head.

[9]Enjoy life with the wife whom you love, all the days of your vain life that he has given you under the sun, because that is your portion in life and in your toil at which you toil under the sun. [10]Whatever your hand finds to do, do it with your might, for there is no work or thought or knowledge or wisdom in Sheol, to which you are going.

READ

Read the passage aloud slowly.

THINK

This passage pictures what it looks like to do everything to the glory of God: "Whatever you do, in word or deed, do everything in the name of the Lord Jesus, giving thanks to God the Father through him" (Colossians 3:17).

1. In what ways does God "drink" or "enjoy"?
2. What pleasures do you enjoy that you think God might enjoy with you?

Read the passage aloud slowly again, noting the words or phrases that stand out to you.

3. What about life do you need to drink or enjoy?

PRAY

Respond to God regarding this idea of drinking or enjoying. Tell God if you're surprised to think of him this way. Talk to God about whether you need to do what this text says or cut back on doing too much of it. Be willing to hear from God about these things rather than coming up with your own answers, which might be based on what others have told you.

LIVE

Take a walk, preferably a hike. Move mentally and physically in the style of this passage. Seize every view open to you. Drink in the colors you see, the sounds you hear, and the aromas you smell. Enjoy a leaf or flower by rubbing it against your cheek.

118
119

DAY 119

GOD ENCOUNTERS

On this seventh day, review and reflect on all you have read this week. Take the time to revel in the ways you've encountered God in the past six days.

REJOICE IN YOUR YOUTH

ECCLESIASTES 11:9; 12:1-7

⁹Rejoice, O young man, in your youth, and let your heart cheer you in the days of your youth. Walk in the ways of your heart and the sight of your eyes. But know that for all these things God will bring you into judgment. . . .

¹Remember also your Creator in the days of your youth, before the evil days come and the years draw near of which you will say, "I have no pleasure in them"; ²before the sun and the light and the moon and the stars are darkened and the clouds return after the rain, ³in the day when the keepers of the house tremble, and the strong men are bent, and the grinders cease because they are few, and those who look through the windows are dimmed, ⁴and the doors on the street are shut—when the sound of the grinding is low, and one rises up at the sound of a bird, and all the daughters of song are brought low — ⁵they are afraid also of what is high, and terrors are in the way; the almond tree blossoms, the grasshopper drags itself along, and desire fails, because man is going to his eternal home, and the mourners go about the streets — ⁶before the silver cord is snapped, or the golden bowl is broken, or the pitcher is shattered at the fountain, or the wheel broken at the cistern, ⁷and the dust returns to the earth as it was, and the spirit returns to God who gave it.

READ

Read the passage.

THINK/LIVE

You are likely young, strong, healthy, and full of potential. But as you read this passage again, look deeply at the perspective it presents: old age. Mull over the images, putting yourself in that place as best you can. Think of the contact you've had with elderly people: the physical aspects, such as sights, sounds, textures, and smells; and the mental aspects, such as attitude, knowledge, and experience.

Now return to the present. Look down at your body. Examine your hands; feel your legs and stretch them out. Touch your hair and some of the muscles in your body. Look in a mirror at your eyes and face. Forget your standard checklist when you evaluate yourself. Instead see your youth, health, and strength. What does that feel like? What do you notice?

PRAY

Now read the first few lines of the passage again. When you are told to "let your heart cheer you in the days of your youth" and rejoice in it, what does that mean to you? What would being present to your life and enjoying it right now mean? Does being aware that you won't always be young change your view? Talk with God about what you think of youth and old age, and write down anything significant from this time.

ACCEPTED JUST AS YOU ARE

SONG OF SOLOMON 1:5-10

SHE

5 I am very dark, but lovely,
    O daughters of Jerusalem,
  like the tents of Kedar,
    like the curtains of Solomon.
6 Do not gaze at me because I am dark,
    because the sun has looked upon me.
  My mother's sons were angry with me;
    they made me keeper of the vineyards,
    but my own vineyard I have not kept!
7 Tell me, you whom my soul loves,
    where you pasture your flock,
    where you make it lie down at noon;
  for why should I be like one who veils herself
    beside the flocks of your companions?

HE

8 If you do not know,
    O most beautiful among women,
  follow in the tracks of the flock,
    and pasture your young goats
    beside the shepherds' tents.

9 I compare you, my love,
    to a mare among Pharaoh's chariots.
10 Your cheeks are lovely with ornaments,
    your neck with strings of jewels.

READ

Read the passage slowly.

THINK

Ask some questions of the text. Who are the speakers? What is the situation? What do you notice about the woman's fears? Do you have similar insecurities about your appearance or about what others think of you? Consider these questions, but don't let information gathering steal too much time from prayer.

PRAY

Read the passage again. As you listen to this couple's dialogue, watch for the quiet voice of a word or the subtle quality of an image through which God seems to be expressing his acceptance of you today. Mull this word or phrase over, letting it interplay with your concerns, ideas, and feelings. Remember not to be afraid of distracting memories or thoughts; they're part of the "you" that you bring to this experience.

Allow your mulling to turn into a conversation with this accepting God. If deeper memories or feelings arise, share them with him. Be open to how he may want to use the word or phrase he's given you as a means of blessing in the midst of your insecurities and fears.

LIVE

Take a while to let yourself relax in God's acceptance. If thoughts or feelings come, share them. If they do not, just enjoy the quietness, and experience what it's like to be accepted by God just as you are, without having to do anything or be anyone else.

DAY 122
EXPANDED PASSAGE: SONG OF SOLOMON 4

GOD HAS EYES FOR YOU

SONG OF SOLOMON 4:9-15

⁹ You have captivated my heart, my sister, my bride;
    you have captivated my heart with one glance of your eyes,
    with one jewel of your necklace.
¹⁰ How beautiful is your love, my sister, my bride!
    How much better is your love than wine,
    and the fragrance of your oils than any spice!
¹¹ Your lips drip nectar, my bride;
    honey and milk are under your tongue;
    the fragrance of your garments is like the fragrance of Lebanon.
¹² A garden locked is my sister, my bride,
    a spring locked, a fountain sealed.
¹³ Your shoots are an orchard of pomegranates
    with all choicest fruits,
    henna with nard,
¹⁴ nard and saffron, calamus and cinnamon,
    with all trees of frankincense,
myrrh and aloes,
    with all choice spices —
¹⁵ a garden fountain, a well of living water,
    and flowing streams from Lebanon.

READ

Read the passage slowly.

THINK

Read the passage again, but aloud this time. Consider this as God's love poem to you. Song of Songs illustrates how God treasures us — he can't take his eyes off us.

Which image do you prefer to be in God's sight?

☐ a bride
☐ one who captivates God's heart with a glance
☐ as pleasing as fine, rare wine
☐ as fragrant as an exotic spice
☐ one with kisses like honey
☐ one who speaks words like milk and honey
☐ one whose clothes smell like the outdoors
☐ a lover and friend
☐ a secret fountain
☐ a sparkling, splashing fountain

PRAY

Pray what you most need to pray — perhaps that:

- you would grasp how loved and treasured you are by God
- you would define your relationship with God in the way of this passage rather than seeing yourself as _____ (maybe "God's slave")
- you would begin to grasp what it means to treasure God

LIVE

Put yourself near one of the objects mentioned in this poem: a pleasing drink, an exotic spice, the fragrant outdoors, a fountain. Gaze at it and smell it, cherishing the idea that this is how God cherishes you.

LOVE IS INVINCIBLE

SONG OF SOLOMON 8:6-7,11-12

⁶ Set me as a seal upon your heart,
   as a seal upon your arm,
for love is strong as death,
   jealousy is fierce as the grave.
Its flashes are flashes of fire,
   the very flame of the LORD.
⁷ Many waters cannot quench love,
   neither can floods drown it.
If a man offered for love
   all the wealth of his house,
   he would be utterly despised. . . .

¹¹ Solomon had a vineyard at Baal-hamon;
   he let out the vineyard to keepers;
   each one was to bring for its fruit a thousand pieces of silver.
¹² My vineyard, my very own, is before me;
   you, O Solomon, may have the thousand,
   and the keepers of the fruit two hundred.

READ

Read the passage twice.

THINK

Direct your attention to the part of the text where you have the strongest reaction, either positive or negative. Maybe you'll consider the woman's statements about love. Do you agree or disagree with them? Or maybe you'll consider the man's promise to protect what is his. How do you respond to that promise?

PRAY

Start your prayer time by examining your feelings and beliefs about love — and not necessarily *romantic* love. Sift through these to see what in you is truly feeling and what is belief. For example, a feeling might be "I feel rejected." And a related belief might be "I believe no one could truly love me." Ask God what he thinks about your feelings and beliefs.

LIVE

Read the passage again, this time asking the Holy Spirit to show you a word or concept summing up something God is saying about love that you don't fully grasp or believe or that you don't yet accept or live out naturally. Ask God to teach you in the coming days and weeks, perhaps through further meditation, more about what he created love to be like.

BURNING OFF SIN

ISAIAH 6:1-8

¹In the year that King Uzziah died I saw the Lord sitting upon a throne, high and lifted up; and the train of his robe filled the temple. ²Above him stood the seraphim. Each had six wings: with two he covered his face, and with two he covered his feet, and with two he flew. ³And one called to another and said:

> Holy, holy, holy is the LORD of hosts;
> the whole earth is full of his glory!"

⁴And the foundations of the thresholds shook at the voice of him who called, and the house was filled with smoke. ⁵And I said: "Woe is me! For I am lost; for I am a man of unclean lips, and I dwell in the midst of a people of unclean lips; for my eyes have seen the King, the LORD of hosts!"

⁶Then one of the seraphim flew to me, having in his hand a burning coal that he had taken with tongs from the altar. ⁷And he touched my mouth and said: "Behold, this has touched your lips; your guilt is taken away, and your sin atoned for."

⁸And I heard the voice of the Lord saying, "Whom shall I send, and who will go for us?" Then I said, "Here am I! Send me."

READ

Read the passage, making special note of the dialogue between the angels and Isaiah.

THINK

As the Lord God's mouthpiece to the nations, Isaiah experiences this unforgettable encounter with the Lord at the outset of his ministry. A seraphim flies down to Isaiah and touches his mouth with a burning coal.

The mouth is one of the most sensitive parts of the body. Explore your spiritual life to identify sensitive areas that would hurt deeply at God's touch. Why are these areas the most sensitive? Consider what your relationship with God might look like, now and in the long term, if he purified these areas of your life.

PRAY

Invite God to burn these sensitive areas of your life so you can serve him more effectively. This is a scary prayer when offered sincerely and earnestly, but be encouraged by what happened in Isaiah's life as a result of his burned lips.

LIVE

Ask two people who are close to you what they believe to be areas of your life in need of refining by God's touch. Be prepared to consider answers that may be hard to hear but are beneficial.

THE PEACEABLE KINGDOM OF GOD

ISAIAH 11:6-9

⁶ The wolf shall dwell with the lamb,
    and the leopard shall lie down with the young goat,
and the calf and the lion and the fattened calf together;
    and a little child shall lead them.
⁷ The cow and the bear shall graze;
    their young shall lie down together;
    and the lion shall eat straw like the ox.
⁸ The nursing child shall play over the hole of the cobra,
    and the weaned child shall put his hand on the adder's den.
⁹ They shall not hurt or destroy
    in all my holy mountain;
for the earth shall be full of the knowledge of the LORD
    as the waters cover the sea.

READ

Read the passage aloud slowly, noting how natural enemies are coexisting side by side (wolf and lamb, cow and bear, child and cobra).

THINK

Read the passage again, noting which images are most powerful or amazing to you.

This passage gives us a vivid picture of the kingdom of God as it will exist in the future. What a different place it will be! Interact with this passage in one of these ways, depending on what stood out to you:

- Ponder what you would like best about such a peaceable world — one that is "full of the knowledge of the LORD as the waters cover the sea."
- Ponder what feelings would be present for these creatures to exist this way (for example, serenity).
- Name your own natural enemies and imagine them standing beside you, with you, for you. You might choose political enemies (for example, parties, opponents, countries, regions); family members, coworkers, or acquaintances you're at odds with; or an animal or a natural element that's difficult for you (for example, spiders, if you hate spiders).

PRAY

Share with God how you feel about such a peaceable world. Share with him what you think such a world shows you about him.

LIVE

Ponder the idea that this passage describes your future reality. You *will* experience this. This is what God is creating for you.

DAY 126

GOD ENCOUNTERS

On this seventh day, review and reflect on all you have read this week. Take the time to revel in the ways you've encountered God in the past six days.

A STRONG GOD

ISAIAH 27:1-5

¹In that day the LORD with his hard and great and strong sword will punish Leviathan the fleeing serpent, Leviathan the twisting serpent, and he will slay the dragon that is in the sea.

² In that day,
"A pleasant vineyard, sing of it!
³ I, the LORD, am its keeper;
every moment I water it.
Lest anyone punish it,
I keep it night and day;
⁴ I have no wrath.
Would that I had thorns and briers to battle!
I would march against them,
I would burn them up together.
⁵ Or let them lay hold of my protection,
let them make peace with me,
let them make peace with me."

READ

Read the passage slowly, letting your imagination play with the imagery. Picture everything vividly, as if you were a child reading a story with beautiful, lifelike illustrations.

THINK

Read the passage again. What do you notice about the way God interacts with "the dragon"? With "the vineyard"? What is he like? Now put yourself in the scene. What part do you play? How do you feel?

PRAY

Picture God turning to you and inviting you to talk with him about what you are feeling and thinking. Does he ever seem angry to you, or uncaring? What's it like for you to hear him say otherwise? Share with him your thoughts and feelings, and allow the conversation to unfold.

LIVE

Write about your experience of encountering the God who mercilessly kills the dragon, meanwhile mercifully letting the vine cling to him as it grows. Be sure to include what dialoguing with him was like for you. What will you take away from this time?

TRUSTING IN HORSES AND CHARIOTS

ISAIAH 31:1-3

1   Woe to those who go down to
    Egypt for help
        and rely on horses,
    who trust in chariots because they are many
        and in horsemen because they are very strong,
    but do not look to the Holy One of Israel
        or consult the LORD!
2   And yet he is wise and brings disaster;
        he does not call back his words,
    but will arise against the house of the evildoers
        and against the helpers of those who work iniquity.
3   The Egyptians are man, and not God,
        and their horses are flesh, and not spirit.
    When the LORD stretches out his hand,
        the helper will stumble, and he who is helped will fall,
        and they will all perish together.

READ

Read the passage at least six times. Don't rush through it. Get familiar with it.

THINK

In ancient times, Egypt was a prosperous and powerful nation. Horses and chariots were crucial for ensuring security, especially in times of war. We don't rely on horses and chariots to protect us today, but there are countless things we put our trust in.

Consider the circumstances in your life when you have depended on something or someone other than God. If God and God alone provides ultimate security and comfort, why do you think we turn to him for help only as a last resort? If we truly understood God's power and control — his sovereignty — how might that change how we live?

PRAY

Spend a few minutes in quiet and solitude. Use the time to seek out the dark corners of your life. Whisper, "What do I put my trust in?" Allow the Spirit to do his work. Don't rush the process, but simply wait for him to reveal the horses and chariots you depend on. When you see them clearly, confess them to God immediately. Be assured that he hears your prayers and forgives you graciously.

LIVE

Be constantly aware of the horses and chariots that seek your trust. Remind yourself of their lies — that they offer complete security and comfort — and the futility in believing those lies.

EXPANDED PASSAGE:
ISAIAH 34 (DESTRUCTION) AND 35 (RESTORATION)

PICTURES OF RESTORATION

ISAIAH 35:4-10

4 Say to those who have an anxious heart,
    "Be strong; fear not!
Behold, your God
    will come with vengeance,
with the recompense of God.
    He will come and save you."

5 Then the eyes of the blind shall be opened,
    and the ears of the deaf unstopped;
6 then shall the lame man leap like a deer,
    and the tongue of the mute sing for joy.
For waters break forth in the wilderness,
    and streams in the desert;
7 the burning sand shall become a pool,
    and the thirsty ground springs of water;
in the haunt of jackals, where they lie down,
    the grass shall become reeds and rushes.

8 And a highway shall be there,
    and it shall be called the Way of Holiness;
the unclean shall not pass over it.
    It shall belong to those who walk on the way;
    even if they are fools, they shall not go astray.
9 No lion shall be there,
    nor shall any ravenous beast come up on it;
they shall not be found there,
    but the redeemed shall walk there.
10 And the ransomed of the LORD shall return
    and come to Zion with singing;
everlasting joy shall be upon their heads;
    they shall obtain gladness and joy,
    and sorrow and sighing shall flee away.

READ

Read the first verse aloud and then read the rest silently.

THINK

Read the passage again, watching for its emphasis on restoration and healing.

1. What pictures of healing speak to you?

   ☐ God coming with vengeance
   ☐ blind eyes opening
   ☐ deaf ears hearing
   ☐ disabled people leaping
   ☐ voiceless people singing
   ☐ water flowing in the desert
   ☐ burning sand becoming a pool

2. What do you like best about the "Way of Holiness"?

   ☐ no unclean or sinful people
   ☐ no one can go astray
   ☐ no dangerous animals

3. What one phrase speaks to you most? Why do you think that is? What does your choice tell you about what you want from God?

PRAY

Tell God about the images you most resonate with. Tell him why. Ask God for the restoration or healing that you or others need.

LIVE

Choose a color that symbolizes you as a fully restored or healed person. Why did you choose it? Pick up something of that color and be glad you're holding it.

YOU ALONE ARE THE LORD

ISAIAH 37:9-11,14-20

⁹Now the king heard concerning Tirhakah king of Cush, "He has set out to fight against you." And when he heard it, he sent messengers to Hezekiah, saying, ¹⁰"Thus shall you speak to Hezekiah king of Judah: 'Do not let your God in whom you trust deceive you by promising that Jerusalem will not be given into the hand of the king of Assyria. ¹¹Behold, you have heard what the kings of Assyria have done to all lands, devoting them to destruction. And shall you be delivered?'"... ¹⁴Hezekiah received the letter from the hand of the messengers, and read it; and Hezekiah went up to the house of the LORD, and spread it before the LORD. ¹⁵And Hezekiah prayed to the LORD: ¹⁶"O LORD of hosts, God of Israel, enthroned above the cherubim, you are the God, you alone, of all the kingdoms of the earth; you have made heaven and earth. ¹⁷Incline your ear, O LORD, and hear; open your eyes, O LORD, and see; and hear all the words of Sennacherib, which he has sent to mock the living God. ¹⁸Truly, O LORD, the kings of Assyria have laid waste all the nations and their lands, ¹⁹and have cast their gods into the fire. For they were no gods, but the work of men's hands, wood and stone. Therefore they were destroyed. ²⁰So now, O LORD our God, save us from his hand, that all the kingdoms of the earth may know that you alone are the LORD."

READ

Read this passage a few times slowly. Picture what's going on, and imagine what Hezekiah, the king of Judah, might be feeling in this situation.

THINK

Notice the Assyrian king's reaction to the news that he's about to be attacked by an enemy: He tries to puff himself up by scoffing at Judah. What might have motivated him to do this at this specific time? In contrast, how does Hezekiah react to the message his enemy sends him? What stands out to you about these different attitudes? How do they relate to you?

PRAY

Think about an area in which you hold responsibility, such as being a group leader at school or a manager at work — or having responsibility to uphold your end of a friendship. What are some recent problems that you are responsible to help resolve? In what ways are you dealing (or not dealing) with them? Have a conversation with God about what it's like for you to have responsibility in this area; share your heart and mind with him.

LIVE

Now read the passage again, keeping in mind the specific situation. Try to bring the problem to God the way Hezekiah did. For help, write a description of the dilemma on a piece of paper and then follow Hezekiah's example, spreading it out before God and asking for his help. Ask him to guide you in how to resolve it. Be aware that God is your leader, even as you are a leader to others.

YOU ARE MINE

ISAIAH 43:1-4

[1] But now thus says the LORD,
    he who created you, O Jacob,
        he who formed you, O Israel:
    "Fear not, for I have redeemed you;
        I have called you by name, you are mine.
[2]   When you pass through the waters, I will be with you;
        and through the rivers, they shall not overwhelm you;
    when you walk through fire you shall not be burned,
        and the flame shall not consume you.
[3]   For I am the LORD your God,
        the Holy One of Israel, your Savior.
    I give Egypt as your ransom,
        Cush and Seba in exchange for you.
[4]   Because you are precious in my eyes,
        and honored, and I love you,
    I give men in return for you,
        peoples in exchange for your life."

READ

Read the passage aloud slowly, keeping in mind that God is the speaker.

THINK

Read the passage aloud again even more slowly, pausing between verses. Read it with the idea that God is saying these words directly to you.

1. Of God's words to you in this passage, what is your favorite?
2. Which phrase do you most need to hear from God?

Read the passage one more time. Rest in silence. Wait on God and hear him speaking directly to you.

PRAY

Respond to what God has said to you, perhaps with amazement or gratitude.

LIVE

Read the passage aloud one more time, and hear the echo of the words lingering in the air. Make up a song using a line from these verses. If you wish, use a tune you already know.

DEPENDABLE GODS?

ISAIAH 46:1-7

1   Bel bows down; Nebo stoops;
        their idols are on beasts and livestock;
    these things you carry are borne
        as burdens on weary beasts.
2   They stoop; they bow down together;
        they cannot save the burden,
            but themselves go into captivity.

3   "Listen to me, O house of Jacob,
        all the remnant of the house of Israel,
    who have been borne by me from before your birth,
        carried from the womb;
4   even to your old age I am he,
        and to gray hairs I will carry you.
    I have made, and I will bear;
        I will carry and will save.

5   "To whom will you liken me and make me equal,
        and compare me, that we may be alike?
6   Those who lavish gold from the purse,
        and weigh out silver in the scales,
    hire a goldsmith, and he makes it into a god;
        then they fall down and worship!
7   They lift it to their shoulders, they carry it,
        they set it in its place, and it stands there;
            it cannot move from its place.
    If one cries to it, it does not answer
        or save him from his trouble."

READ

Read the passage. Bel and Nebo were ancient false gods of the Israelites' neighbors. People would orient their lives around what they believed these gods were demanding or promising.

THINK

After you read how God addresses Israel's tendency to act like its neighbors — rather than trusting and obeying him — consider what gods might be in your culture and in your life. These don't have to be people or objects. They could be principles or beliefs that shape how we live, think, and feel every day. For example, "Having more money makes a person secure," or "If people just lost weight and worked out more, the opposite sex would be attracted to them."

Identify a god that tempts you personally. Are there aspects of the true God that you find difficult to accept (such as his holiness or the facts that he is invisible and sometimes silent)? In what ways do these idols capitalize on those doubts and make themselves appear more appealing than God? What do they promise you? Now consider: What do they really bring you?

PRAY/LIVE

Read God's plea to Israel once more. Tell him what you see in yourself and in this god you've identified. Be real. Now hear him ask you, "To whom will you 'compare me, that we may be alike?'" Don't answer immediately, but ponder the question. Ask him to help you stay committed to him and to working through the struggles you have with him. Watch today for when your idols are the most appealing to you, for when you are most likely to "worship" them or believe their message.

132
133

DAY 133

GOD ENCOUNTERS

On this seventh day, review and reflect on all you have read this week. Take the time to revel in the ways you've encountered God in the past six days.

DAY 134

EXPANDED PASSAGE: ISAIAH 48–50

THE (UN)FORGETFUL GOD OF HEAVEN

ISAIAH 49:13-18

13 Sing for joy, O heavens, and exult, O earth;
  break forth, O mountains, into singing!
For the Lord has comforted his people
  and will have compassion on his afflicted.

14 But Zion said, "The Lord has forsaken me;
  my Lord has forgotten me."

15 "Can a woman forget her nursing child,
  that she should have no compassion on the son of her womb?
Even these may forget,
  yet I will not forget you.
16 Behold, I have engraved you on the palms of my hands;
  your walls are continually before me.
17 Your builders make haste;
  your destroyers and those who laid you waste go out from you.
18 Lift up your eyes around and see;
  they all gather, they come to you.
As I live, declares the Lord,
  you shall put them all on as an ornament;
  you shall bind them on as a bride does."

READ

Read the passage, underlining or mentally noting each time the word *forget* is present.

THINK

Can you think of a specific moment when you were forgotten — either intentionally or unintentionally? How did that make you feel? Why?

What times in your life do you most desire to be remembered? Be specific. How does it feel for you to know that there is a God who will never forget you under any circumstance?

PRAY

Pour out your heart in gratitude before God for the fact that he "will not forget you."

LIVE

"Behold, I have engraved you on the palms of my hands." Take a pen and make a small mark on each of your hands. Every time you glance at one of the marks, remember God's character and rejoice in knowing that you are his child who will never be forgotten. If someone asks you about the marks, tell them about The God Who Remembers.

THE SUFFERING SERVANT

ISAIAH 53:2-5,11-12

2 For he grew up before him like a young plant,
      and like a root out of dry ground;
  he had no form or majesty that we should look at him,
      and no beauty that we should desire him.
3 He was despised and rejected by men;
      a man of sorrows, and acquainted with grief;
  and as one from whom men hide their faces
      he was despised, and we esteemed him not.

4 Surely he has borne our griefs
      and carried our sorrows;
  yet we esteemed him stricken,
      smitten by God, and afflicted.
5 But he was pierced for our transgressions;
      he was crushed for our iniquities;
  upon him was the chastisement that brought us peace,
      and with his wounds we are healed. . . .

11 Out of the anguish of his soul he shall see and be satisfied;
      by his knowledge shall the righteous one, my servant,
        make many to be accounted righteous,
        and he shall bear their iniquities.
12 Therefore I will divide him a portion with the many,
      and he shall divide the spoil with the strong,
  because he poured out his soul to death
      and was numbered with the transgressors;
  yet he bore the sin of many,
      and makes intercession for the transgressors.

READ

Read the passage aloud slowly, knowing that this "suffering servant" passage is a prophecy about Jesus. If possible, read the expanded passage as well.

THINK

Read the passage again. This time, consider who is speaking.

1. *We, our,* and *us* (verses 2-5) indicate that the speaker is Israel as a nation or a prophet of Israel (Isaiah). In this section, what words, phrases, or ideas are most personal for you?
2. *I* (verses 11-12) indicates God is the speaker. In this section, what most touches you about God's words about Jesus?
3. How will Jesus "make many to be accounted righteous" through what he experienced?

   ☐ his sacrifice of his life?
   ☐ his actions inspiring others?
   ☐ his person calling you?
   ☐ his praying for you? (see Romans 8:34)
   ☐ other:

PRAY

Respond to God about the words that touched you most. Talk also to God about how Jesus can make you righteous.

LIVE

Move through your day with this idea: Jesus died without a thought for his own welfare. If he died that way, how much more must he have lived that way? Try living that selflessly a few minutes at a time.

MY STEADFAST LOVE SHALL NOT DEPART

ISAIAH 54:4-10

⁴ "Fear not, for you will not be ashamed;
    be not confounded, for you will not be disgraced;
for you will forget the shame of your youth,
    and the reproach of your widowhood you will remember no more.
⁵ For your Maker is your husband,
    the LORD of hosts is his name;
and the Holy One of Israel is your Redeemer,
    the God of the whole earth he is called.
⁶ For the LORD has called you
    like a wife deserted and grieved in spirit,
like a wife of youth when she is cast off,
    says your God.
⁷ For a brief moment I deserted you,
    but with great compassion I will gather you.
⁸ In overflowing anger for a moment
    I hid my face from you,
but with everlasting love I will have compassion on you,"
    says the LORD, your Redeemer.

⁹ "This is like the days of Noah to me:
    as I swore that the waters of Noah
    should no more go over the earth,
so I have sworn that I will not be angry with you,
    and will not rebuke you.
¹⁰ For the mountains may depart
    and the hills be removed,
but my steadfast love shall not depart from you,
    and my covenant of peace shall not be removed,"
    says the LORD, who has compassion on you.

READ

Read this passage picturing God speaking to Israel after yet another problem in their relationship.

THINK/PRAY

When you hear God saying that he turned his back in anger only for a moment but was not giving up on the relationship, what is your reaction? When you try to picture a commitment that won't fall apart, what does this evoke in you? Share your response with God. Maybe you've never experienced a relationship like that, so you don't know what it would look like. Maybe you've had similar promises made to you but were betrayed. If this reminds you of someone in your life (past or present), talk with God about what you might be incorrectly assuming to be true of God based on your experience with that person. Recognize that God knows your past, and he knows the baggage you bring into your relationship with him. Trust that he "will have compassion on you" and will help you deal with that baggage.

LIVE

Make a note of the themes that emerged during your prayer time. Ask God to help you grow in trust that he is completely committed to you as one whose "steadfast love shall not depart from you" and one who "has compassion on you." Spend a few minutes sitting quietly in his presence, enjoying the tranquillity of that space before you move on to the rest of your day.

OUR TRANSGRESSIONS

ISAIAH 59:9-15

⁹ Therefore justice is far from us,
   and righteousness does not overtake us;
we hope for light, and behold, darkness,
   and for brightness, but we walk in gloom.
¹⁰ We grope for the wall like the blind;
   we grope like those who have no eyes;
we stumble at noon as in the twilight,
   among those in full vigor we are like dead men.
¹¹ We all growl like bears;
   we moan and moan like doves;
we hope for justice, but there is none;
   for salvation, but it is far from us.
¹² For our transgressions are multiplied before you,
   and our sins testify against us;
for our transgressions are with us,
   and we know our iniquities:
¹³ transgressing, and denying the Lord,
   and turning back from following our God,
speaking oppression and revolt,
   conceiving and uttering from the heart lying words.
¹⁴ Justice is turned back,
   and righteousness stands far away;
for truth has stumbled in the public squares,
   and uprightness cannot enter.
¹⁵ Truth is lacking,
   and he who departs from evil makes himself a prey.

READ

Read the passage aloud. Reflect the nature of the words by your tone and inflection. (That is, if these were your words, how might you sound if you said them?)

THINK

The subject of this passage may seem like a depressing one to explore. But so is our sin. We often attempt to live our lives with God while forgetting to acknowledge our transgressions before him. Yet confession of wrongdoing is a normal and expected part of life for followers of God. We regularly fall short of God's desires for us, and he wants to hear us acknowledge this and depend on him in every area of our lives.

Read the passage again aloud, but make it more personal. When you come to the word *we*, replace it with *I*, and when you come to the word *our*, replace it with *my*. What might God be thinking as he hears you read this?

PRAY

Now, make a list of sins — big and small — that you've committed in the past seven days. Perhaps include things you felt you were supposed to do but did not. In prayer, go through your list and, with each item, admit to God that you should not have participated in such wrongdoing. Do this with a humble and repentant heart.

LIVE

As you walk to class or drive to work or whenever you are between tasks, confess your sins to God. As you do this, be as specific as you can about your sins, acknowledging your desperation and futility in attempting to live apart from him.

RESCUE AND RELEASE

ISAIAH 61:1-3,10-11

¹ The Spirit of the Lord God is upon me,
   because the Lord has anointed me
to bring good news to the poor;
   he has sent me to bind up the brokenhearted,
to proclaim liberty to the captives,
   and the opening of the prison to those who are bound;
² to proclaim the year of the Lord's favor,
   and the day of vengeance of our God;
   to comfort all who mourn;
³ to grant to those who mourn in Zion —
   to give them a beautiful headdress instead of ashes,
the oil of gladness instead of mourning,
   the garment of praise instead of a faint spirit;
that they may be called oaks of righteousness,
   the planting of the Lord, that he may be glorified. . . .

¹⁰ I will greatly rejoice in the Lord;
   my soul shall exult in my God,
for he has clothed me with the garments of salvation;
   he has covered me with the robe of righteousness,
as a bridegroom decks himself like a priest with a beautiful headdress,
   and as a bride adorns herself with her jewels.
¹¹ For as the earth brings forth its sprouts,
   and as a garden causes what is sown in it to sprout up,
so the Lord God will cause righteousness and praise
   to sprout up before all the nations.

READ

Read the passage aloud slowly.

THINK

Read verses 1-3 aloud slowly.

1. What roles of deliverance, rescue, and release do you most admire in God (which Jesus also claimed)?
2. Consider what words or phrases in verses 1-3 stand out to you. What do they tell you about the work God is calling you to do alongside him?

Read verses 10-11 aloud slowly, keeping in mind that those who rescue and release others this way find great joy in it. When they work alongside God, they do not burn out.

3. Consider what words or phrases in verses 10-11 stand out to you. How are you being called to "rejoice in the LORD," especially as it comes through serving under God, partnering with him in what he is doing on this earth?

PRAY

Ask God for guidance in how you serve. You might pray about the avenues of service you are choosing. Or pray about serving with great rejoicing in the Lord instead of serving with joy in results or feelings of success.

LIVE

As you serve someone today, be present to the reality that you are doing this with God's hand, under his power. This is his work and you get to be a part of it!

THE LORD DELIGHTS IN YOU

ISAIAH 62:2-5

² The nations shall see your righteousness,
    and all the kings your glory,
and you shall be called by a new name
    that the mouth of the Lord will give.
³ You shall be a crown of beauty in the hand of the Lord,
    and a royal diadem in the hand of your God.
⁴ You shall no more be termed Forsaken,
    and your land shall no more be termed Desolate,
but you shall be called My Delight Is in Her,
    and your land Married;
for the Lord delights in you,
    and your land shall be married.
⁵ For as a young man marries a young woman,
    so shall your sons marry you,
and as the bridegroom rejoices over the bride,
    so shall your God rejoice over you.

READ

Read the passage aloud slowly.

THINK

Read the passage again. This time reverse all the *you* pronouns to *I* and *me* pronouns. For example, change

- "you shall be called by a new name" to "I shall be called by a new name"
- "for the LORD delights in you" to "for the LORD delights in me"
- "so shall your God rejoice over you" to "so shall my God rejoice over me.

Have fun reading it this way a few times.

1. If you were to ask God for a new name, what would it be?
2. Set aside the idea that these verses are fantasy, and ponder the idea that they describe reality — a reality of our universe that most people don't understand.

PRAY

Tell God how it makes you feel to know that he delights in you and is happy with you. Tell God what you would like your new name to be. Wait in this moment and see if other names come to you.

LIVE

Rest for a few minutes in the truth that God delights in you. If you wish, imagine situations in which you feel anything but special (for example, when you are hard on yourself, when someone puts you down, or when you get back a test, paper, or work review that isn't so great). See yourself responding to the situation by saying, "Yes, this is true, but God delights in me."

139
140

DAY 140

GOD ENCOUNTERS

On this seventh day, review and reflect on all you have read this week. Take the time to revel in the ways you've encountered God in the past six days.

ANTICIPATING THE WORKINGS OF GOD

ISAIAH 65:17-22

¹⁷ For behold, I create new heavens
  and a new earth,
and the former things shall not be remembered
  or come into mind.
¹⁸ But be glad and rejoice forever
  in that which I create;
for behold, I create Jerusalem to be a joy,
  and her people to be a gladness.
¹⁹ I will rejoice in Jerusalem
  and be glad in my people;
no more shall be heard in it the sound of weeping
  and the cry of distress.
²⁰ No more shall there be in it
  an infant who lives but a few days,
  or an old man who does not fill out his days,
for the young man shall die a hundred years old,
  and the sinner a hundred years old shall be accursed.
²¹ They shall build houses and inhabit them;
  they shall plant vineyards and eat their fruit.
²² They shall not build and another inhabit;
  they shall not plant and another eat;
for like the days of a tree shall the days of my people be,
  and my chosen shall long enjoy the work of their hands.

READ

Read the passage.

THINK

In this passage God speaks with great joy, and the people feel great excitement. Here we find, in the midst of judgment and sorrow, the promise of a bright future for those who love and trust the Lord. God makes statements about the future peace that will be among his people. He is sending out the old and bringing in the new. For followers of God, there is intense anticipation.

Think about your own future. What are those things, general and specific, that you believe God will use to bring hope into your life? Joy? Peace? How does God promise this will happen? How does the promise of hope and joy and peace influence the way you live?

PRAY

Pick some specific elements of how God will bring hope and joy and peace into your life. Share the details with him, including your excitement and anticipation.

LIVE

Live with the deep assurance of God's desire for you to possess hope and joy and peace today.

GOD'S KNOWLEDGE OF US

JEREMIAH 1:5

[5]Before I formed you in the womb I knew you,
and before you were born I consecrated you;
I appointed you a prophet to the nations.

READ

Write out Jeremiah 1:5 on an index card. Meditate on this verse.

THINK

God told Jeremiah that he had plans for Jeremiah's life before Jeremiah was even born. What a claim from God! Can you believe that God had plans for your life and knew everything about you before you were even conceived? Why or why not?

What emotions bubble to the surface when you consider that God knows you intimately? Are you excited? Comforted? Scared? Anxious? Indifferent? Why?

If God already knows everything about us, why does he desire that we pray to him?

PRAY

Meditate on this thought: The Creator of the universe, the living God, knows every possible thing about you. As you do so, tell God what you are feeling and why.

LIVE

Take the index card and put it where you will see it often (for example, on your bedside table, taped to the mirror in the bathroom, taped to the dashboard of your car, or in your purse or wallet). Whenever you look at it, read it and be reminded that God marked out a plan for your life long before you were born.

A TIME TO GRIEVE

JEREMIAH 8:18-21; 9:1-3

¹⁸ My joy is gone; grief is upon me;
    my heart is sick within me.
¹⁹ Behold, the cry of the daughter of my people
    from the length and breadth of the land:
"Is the LORD not in Zion?
    Is her King not in her?"
"Why have they provoked me to anger with their carved images
    and with their foreign idols?"
²⁰ "The harvest is past, the summer is ended,
    and we are not saved."
²¹ For the wound of the daughter of my people is my heart wounded;
    I mourn, and dismay has taken hold on me. . . .

¹ Oh that my head were waters,
    and my eyes a fountain of tears,
that I might weep day and night
    for the slain of the daughter of my people!
² Oh that I had in the desert
    a travelers' lodging place,
that I might leave my people
    and go away from them!
For they are all adulterers,
    a company of treacherous men.
³ They bend their tongue like a bow;
    falsehood and not truth has grown strong in the land;
for they proceed from evil to evil,
    and they do not know me, declares the LORD.

READ

Read the passage aloud slowly. Most of it describes Jeremiah's grieving over the way Judah ignores God. In 9:3, God interrupts and agrees.

THINK

What makes God grieve that also makes you grieve? What breaks your heart that breaks the heart of God? Perhaps it resembles the following: the wickedness of people (such as genocide or sex trafficking in the world), the lack of desire — even among professed believers — to know God, the diseases that terrorize people's bodies.

Read the passage aloud again, reflecting on the tragic circumstance that breaks your heart and also breaks the heart of God. What words or phrases in the passage best express your grief? What does it feel like to grieve over the things that grieve God? How do you respond to the idea that God often weeps throughout the prophetic portion of the Bible and that we need to honor that grief and join him?

PRAY

Grieve with God in prayer as a prophet (like Jeremiah), using the phrases in the passage that stood out to you. Don't feel that you have to tidy up your prayer with a positive ending, although "God, help!" would be appropriate.

LIVE

Read the newspaper, listening to the news for the evil and suffering in the world that God surely grieves over. Notice how different such listening is from detached curiosity. Hear about these events with the listening ears of God.

ROTTEN AS CLOTH

JEREMIAH 13:1-11

¹Thus says the Lord to me, "Go and buy a linen loincloth and put it around your waist, and do not dip it in water." ²So I bought a loincloth according to the word of the Lord, and put it around my waist. ³And the word of the Lord came to me a second time, ⁴"Take the loincloth that you have bought, which is around your waist, and arise, go to the Euphrates and hide it there in a cleft of the rock." ⁵So I went and hid it by the Euphrates, as the Lord commanded me. ⁶And after many days the Lord said to me, "Arise, go to the Euphrates, and take from there the loincloth that I commanded you to hide there." ⁷Then I went to the Euphrates, and dug, and I took the loincloth from the place where I had hidden it. And behold, the loincloth was spoiled; it was good for nothing.

⁸Then the word of the Lord came to me: ⁹"Thus says the Lord: Even so will I spoil the pride of Judah and the great pride of Jerusalem. ¹⁰This evil people, who refuse to hear my words, who stubbornly follow their own heart and have gone after other gods to serve them and worship them, shall be like this loincloth, which is good for nothing. ¹¹For as the loincloth clings to the waist of a man, so I made the whole house of Israel and the whole house of Judah cling to me, declares the Lord, that they might be for me a people, a name, a praise, and a glory, but they would not listen."

READ

As you read the passage, imaginatively put yourself in Jeremiah's place.

THINK

In your mind's eye, look down and see the linen loincloth you've been wearing for days or weeks. Set out on the journey to the Euphrates. Discover the cleft in the rock. Envision the long time that passes—what you do in the meantime, any particular events, the seasons that pass.

Now return to the rock and feel your own sweat as you dig out the loincloth again. How do you first detect it? By touch? Smell? Sight? As you unearth it, what thoughts go through your head? What is the smell like? What does it look like?

Next think about God's metaphor. Listen to his explanation of the Israelites' rotted hearts illustrated by this decaying loincloth. As you hear God's words, what are you thinking? What are you feeling?

PRAY

Set the text aside and explore your own heart honestly with God. When you think of God the Father rebuking you for something, what is your internal reaction? Do you perceive it as a positive thing, done in love? Or does his rebuke seem to say he is against you, doesn't care for you, or wants you to fix yourself? Talk this over with him.

LIVE

Read the passage again, listening for what God might be saying to you through Jeremiah. In what way is your Father challenging you? Make note of any action you feel he is leading you to.

TELLING GOD WHAT WE REALLY THINK

JEREMIAH 20:7-10

7   O Lord, you have deceived me,
         and I was deceived;
     you are stronger than I,
         and you have prevailed.
     I have become a laughingstock all the day;
         everyone mocks me.
8   For whenever I speak, I cry out,
         I shout, "Violence and destruction!"
     For the word of the Lord has become for me
         a reproach and derision all day long.
9   If I say, "I will not mention him,
         or speak any more in his name,"
     there is in my heart as it were a burning fire
         shut up in my bones,
     and I am weary with holding it in,
         and I cannot.
10   For I hear many whispering.
         Terror is on every side!
     "Denounce him! Let us denounce him!"
         say all my close friends,
         watching for my fall.
     "Perhaps he will be deceived;
         then we can overcome him
         and take our revenge on him."

READ

Read the passage twice very slowly.

THINK

Jeremiah was called by God to be a mouthpiece to the nation of Israel, but they rejected his message, scorning and mocking him. They even made death threats against him. And in this passage we read Jeremiah's complaint. He is not shy about telling God exactly what he feels. In fact, he has some choice words for the Creator concerning his situation.

Is it easy or hard for you to tell God exactly what you're thinking? Why? Do you think it's hard for God to hear our prayers when we are completely and blatantly honest with him?

LIVE

Write a letter to God, telling him what you think about him and how he is operating in the world. Include the good, the bad, and the ugly. Be thoughtful and honest and even raw if you need to be.

PRAY

After you finish writing the letter, find a room where you can shut the door and be alone. Read the letter aloud to God, speaking confidently because you know he hears your prayers.

CONSEQUENCES THAT BURN

JEREMIAH 28:10-17

[10]Then the prophet Hananiah took the yoke-bars from the neck of Jeremiah the prophet and broke them. [11]And Hananiah spoke in the presence of all the people, saying, "Thus says the LORD: Even so will I break the yoke of Nebuchadnezzar king of Babylon from the neck of all the nations within two years." But Jeremiah the prophet went his way.

[12]Sometime after the prophet Hananiah had broken the yoke-bars from off the neck of Jeremiah the prophet, the word of the LORD came to Jeremiah: [13]"Go, tell Hananiah, 'Thus says the LORD: You have broken wooden bars, but you have made in their place bars of iron. [14]For thus says the LORD of hosts, the God of Israel: I have put upon the neck of all these nations an iron yoke to serve Nebuchadnezzar king of Babylon, and they shall serve him, for I have given to him even the beasts of the field.' " [15]And Jeremiah the prophet said to the prophet Hananiah, "Listen, Hananiah, the LORD has not sent you, and you have made this people trust in a lie. [16]Therefore thus says the LORD: 'Behold, I will remove you from the face of the earth. This year you shall die, because you have uttered rebellion against the LORD.' "

[17]In that same year, in the seventh month, the prophet Hananiah died.

READ

Read the passage twice. (For more background, include the expanded passage.)

THINK

What does God seem to be addressing in Hananiah's underlying message or motive? Summarize in a sentence what you notice. What do you think about how God dealt with him? What do you, having read this story, feel toward God?

PRAY/LIVE

Take several minutes to think through your current situation. Where is God allowing you to feel the ache and consequence for something you've recently done (or not done)? Bring this openly before God and tell him how you feel about it. Ask him to help you see your heart clearly, to understand what drew you toward that action (or nonaction).

If you haven't let go of what you're doing wrong — despite the burning consequences — think about what rejecting this path might look like for you. What really keeps you from turning around? God is inviting you to live in a certain way in this area of your life. What are some small steps you could take toward receiving that invitation?

Take them.

DAY 147

GOD ENCOUNTERS

On this seventh day, review and reflect on all you have read this week. Take the time to revel in the ways you've encountered God in the past six days.

I WILL ANSWER YOU

JEREMIAH 33:2-3

²Thus says the LORD who made the earth, the LORD who formed it to establish it — the LORD is his name: ³Call to me and I will answer you, and will tell you great and hidden things that you have not known.

READ

Find a quiet place and read this passage slowly. Pause in the silence. Let these words wash over you. Make them personal. Claim them as God speaking specifically to you.

THINK

What sticks out to you? What word or phrase settles deeply in your soul? Why?

Deep down, do you really believe that God will answer you when you call to him? Why or why not? What does this passage say about his character?

As you hear God's personal message, spoken straight from his being, what do you feel? What words from this passage can you make your own?

PRAY

Ask God what he wants you to do with the word or phrase he has given you. Ask him how you can best live out this gift that the Holy Spirit has placed before you. Listen patiently in the silence for the response. You may be tempted to move on to some other thought or task, but resist, simply resting in the silence yet listening actively.

LIVE

Go and live out the answer of what the Holy Spirit instructed you to do today.

BAD THINGS HAPPEN TO VERY GOOD PEOPLE

JEREMIAH 38:1-6

¹Now Shephatiah the son of Mattan, Gedaliah the son of Pashhur, Jucal the son of Shelemiah, and Pashhur the son of Malchiah heard the words that Jeremiah was saying to all the people, ²"Thus says the LORD: He who stays in this city shall die by the sword, by famine, and by pestilence, but he who goes out to the Chaldeans shall live. He shall have his life as a prize of war, and live. ³Thus says the LORD: This city shall surely be given into the hand of the army of the king of Babylon and be taken." ⁴Then the officials said to the king, "Let this man be put to death, for he is weakening the hands of the soldiers who are left in this city, and the hands of all the people, by speaking such words to them. For this man is not seeking the welfare of this people, but their harm." ⁵King Zedekiah said, "Behold, he is in your hands, for the king can do nothing against you." ⁶So they took Jeremiah and cast him into the cistern of Malchiah, the king's son, which was in the court of the guard, letting Jeremiah down by ropes. And there was no water in the cistern, but only mud, and Jeremiah sank in the mud.

READ

Read the passage aloud slowly.

THINK

Even though Jeremiah was a faithful servant of God, circumstances weren't turning out well for him. Read the passage again and experience for yourself the feelings Jeremiah probably had. Feel yourself sinking in the mud.

1. How difficult is it for you to accept that bad things happen to people who love God and do good?
2. Pretend once again that you are Jeremiah sinking in the mud. All you have now is the companionship of God. How does that feel? How close is that to being enough for you? What do you (as Jeremiah) want to pray?
3. What does it mean to hope in God's own being instead of simply hoping God will rescue you?

PRAY

Talk to God about a situation in which you've been left behind in the mud. (This may be happening now or in the past, or it may be something you foresee happening in the future.)

LIVE

Sit with your palms open and turned upward toward God. Rest in the idea that some days we have the companionship of God when it appears we have nothing else. Is that enough?

Be on the lookout for people sinking in the mud whom you might be called to love and help.

GOD'S DEEP COMMITMENT

JEREMIAH 51:1-5

1 Thus says the LORD:
   "Behold, I will stir up the spirit of a destroyer
      against Babylon,
      against the inhabitants of Leb-kamai,
2 and I will send to Babylon winnowers,
      and they shall winnow her,
   and they shall empty her land,
      when they come against her from every side
      on the day of trouble.
3 Let not the archer bend his bow,
      and let him not stand up in his armor.
   Spare not her young men;
      devote to destruction all her army.
4 They shall fall down slain in the land of the Chaldeans,
      and wounded in her streets.
5 For Israel and Judah have not been forsaken
      by their God, the LORD of hosts,
   but the land of the Chaldeans is full of guilt
      against the Holy One of Israel."

READ

Read the passage, including the expanded passage, if possible.

THINK

Sense for yourself God's vigor and aggression in going after his enemy Babylon. Take a few minutes to imagine the images God uses to describe how he will treat them. What is your reaction?

Now focus your attention on God's final statement, regarding his commitment to Israel. What does this tell you about God's motives for the destruction he's planning for Babylon? Think about his regard for Israel: What does he feel toward them? What does he feel about their sin?

PRAY

Look back on what you noticed about God—both his aggression and his commitment. Is there a phrase from the passage that stands out to you? As you think about this phrase and repeat it to yourself a few times, meditate on this picture of who God is. If in doing so you feel drawn into dialogue with him, go ahead and enter in.

LIVE

Hold in your mind God's qualities of aggression and commitment, then consider your own life. Maybe you'll think about your relationships, your attitude at work or school, your hobbies, or what you enjoy doing on the weekends. What is God saying about an area of your life right now?

WHEN DISAPPOINTMENT COMES

LAMENTATIONS 3:19-30

¹⁹ Remember my affliction and my wanderings,
   the wormwood and the gall!
²⁰ My soul continually remembers it
   and is bowed down within me.
²¹ But this I call to mind,
   and therefore I have hope:
²² The steadfast love of the LORD never ceases;
   his mercies never come to an end;
²³ they are new every morning;
   great is your faithfulness.
²⁴ "The LORD is my portion," says my soul,
   "therefore I will hope in him."

²⁵ The LORD is good to those who wait for him,
   to the soul who seeks him.
²⁶ It is good that one should wait quietly
   for the salvation of the LORD.
²⁷ It is good for a man that he bear
   the yoke in his youth.

²⁸ Let him sit alone in silence
   when it is laid on him;
²⁹ let him put his mouth in the dust —
   there may yet be hope;
³⁰ let him give his cheek to the one who strikes,
   and let him be filled with insults.

THINK

Lamentations is one of the saddest books in the Bible, but just because it's chock-full of disappointment doesn't mean it's absent of hope. Jeremiah, writing this book as he mourns the utter destruction of the famous and once-splendid city of Jerusalem, speaks of pain and sadness and disappointment. But he also reflects on the undying goodness and faithfulness of God.

READ

Read the passage carefully. As you do so, note Jeremiah's complete honesty before God. Also note the change in Jeremiah's attitude toward the end of the chapter from extreme disappointment to an embrace of hope because of God's faithfulness.

PRAY

Take a few minutes to consider the disappointments you have experienced or are experiencing. Then follow the guidance of Jeremiah's words, starting with "Let him sit alone in silence." Just as he encourages, "there may yet be hope."

LIVE

Don't ever forget that despite disappointment and pain, God always remains faithful.

IN THE PIT

LAMENTATIONS 3:52-58

⁵² I have been hunted like a bird
    by those who were my enemies without cause;
⁵³ they flung me alive into the pit
    and cast stones on me;
⁵⁴ water closed over my head;
    I said, "I am lost."

⁵⁵ I called on your name, O LORD,
    from the depths of the pit;
⁵⁶ you heard my plea, "Do not close
    your ear to my cry for help!"
⁵⁷ You came near when I called on you;
    you said, "Do not fear!"

⁵⁸ You have taken up my cause, O Lord;
    you have redeemed my life.

READ

Read the passage aloud slowly. Jeremiah had been thrown into a cistern, where he sank in the mud (see Jeremiah 38:1-6). Here he may be telling us what he thought while he was down there.

THINK

Read verses 52-54 again and pause. Sit in that despair. Read verses 55-58. Grin with joy.

1. What words or phrases in each section resonate for you?
2. In what ways do you call out to God — or not? Do you numb out or shut yourself up instead? Why?
3. Have you ever sensed the closeness of God? If so, how? If not, what do you think it would be like?

PRAY

Talk to God about the times he has come close when you have called out. Or if this hasn't happened, talk with God about what you think it would be like.

LIVE

Be open to the closeness of God coming to you now — even if you're not in a pit. Store that closeness for the times when you'll need it.

REMEMBER, O LORD

LAMENTATIONS 5:1-12,17

1 Remember, O LORD, what has befallen us;
    look, and see our disgrace!
2 Our inheritance has been turned over to strangers,
    our homes to foreigners.
3 We have become orphans, fatherless;
    our mothers are like widows.
4 We must pay for the water we drink;
    the wood we get must be bought.
5 Our pursuers are at our necks;
    we are weary; we are given no rest.
6 We have given the hand to Egypt, and to Assyria,
    to get bread enough.
7 Our fathers sinned, and are no more;
    and we bear their iniquities.
8 Slaves rule over us;
    there is none to deliver us from their hand.
9 We get our bread at the peril of our lives,
    because of the sword in the wilderness.
10 Our skin is hot as an oven
    with the burning heat of famine.
11 Women are raped in Zion,
    young women in the towns of Judah.
12 Princes are hung up by their hands;
    no respect is shown to the elders. . . .
17 For this our heart has become sick,
    for these things our eyes have grown dim.

READ

Read the passage twice, keeping in mind other stories you've read about the Israelites' unreliable commitment to God and the times they walked away from him.

THINK

When you hold side by side this expression of Israel's humility with stories of their pride and hardheartedness, what is your response to their prayer in this passage? If you were God, how would you respond to them? Jot down some words that summarize your reaction.

PRAY

Read and absorb the following words spoken by Jesus many years later to the same people, when he came to give his life for them: "O Jerusalem, Jerusalem, the city that kills the prophets and stones those who are sent to it! How often would I have gathered your children together as a hen gathers her brood under her wings, and you were not willing!" (Luke 13:34). Set this book aside and sit with your eyes closed. Meditate on Jesus' words.

When you see this openhearted love that God continued to have for his people, despite their turning away, what do you feel? Ponder the reality that this is the God who rules the universe.

LIVE

What are the differences between your response to Israel and God's response? In what ways might your responses to yourself or others cloud your perception of how God responds? Ask him to help you learn to distinguish your reaction from his, so that you might know more clearly what he's like.

DAY 154

GOD ENCOUNTERS

On this seventh day, review and reflect on all you have read this week. Take the time to revel in the ways you've encountered God in the past six days.

A MOUTHFUL

EZEKIEL 3:1-11

¹And he said to me, "Son of man, eat whatever you find here. Eat this scroll, and go, speak to the house of Israel." ²So I opened my mouth, and he gave me this scroll to eat. ³And he said to me, "Son of man, feed your belly with this scroll that I give you and fill your stomach with it." Then I ate it, and it was in my mouth as sweet as honey.

⁴And he said to me, "Son of man, go to the house of Israel and speak with my words to them. ⁵For you are not sent to a people of foreign speech and a hard language, but to the house of Israel—⁶not to many peoples of foreign speech and a hard language, whose words you cannot understand. Surely, if I sent you to such, they would listen to you. ⁷But the house of Israel will not be willing to listen to you, for they are not willing to listen to me: because all the house of Israel have a hard forehead and a stubborn heart. ⁸Behold, I have made your face as hard as their faces, and your forehead as hard as their foreheads. ⁹Like emery harder than flint have I made your forehead. Fear them not, nor be dismayed at their looks, for they are a rebellious house." ¹⁰Moreover, he said to me, "Son of man, all my words that I shall speak to you receive in your heart, and hear with your ears. ¹¹And go to the exiles, to your people, and speak to them and say to them, 'Thus says the Lord GOD,' whether they hear or refuse to hear."

READ

Read the passage. Try to read as though you are far from God, have no understanding of who Jesus is, and have never read a Bible before.

THINK

In this book, God has many unique lessons to communicate to Ezekiel, which he desires Ezekiel to pass on to others. He gives him visions of spinning wheels, he has Ezekiel lie on his side for several days, he has him shave his beard and divide the hair into three parts — all in order to communicate an important message to others.

One of God's unique lessons has Ezekiel eating the sacred scroll of the Scriptures — literally eating the word-filled pages. And we read that Ezekiel says the Scriptures taste good, like honey.

Read the passage again, meditating particularly on the final portion starting with verse 10. Metaphorically speaking, what is the taste of God's word in your mouth?

PRAY/LIVE

What are two or three elements of Scripture that you are having a hard time digesting right now? Why? Tell God about it. Ask God to guide you in making the words your very own.

If you have honey, place a drop on your finger. Taste the honey slowly and attentively. Savor the sweetness in your mouth. As you do this, pray that God will give you such a desire for Scripture that it will taste like honey on your lips.

LEARN FROM THE WORST

EZEKIEL 18:14-17

[14]Now suppose this man fathers a son who sees all the sins that his father has done; he sees, and does not do likewise: [15]he does not eat upon the mountains or lift up his eyes to the idols of the house of Israel, does not defile his neighbor's wife, [16]does not oppress anyone, exacts no pledge, commits no robbery, but gives his bread to the hungry and covers the naked with a garment, [17]withholds his hand from iniquity, takes no interest or profit, obeys my rules, and walks in my statutes; he shall not die for his father's iniquity; he shall surely live.

READ

Read the passage aloud slowly.

THINK

Read the passage aloud again, noting all the things the child learned from the negative example of the parent.

1. What words or phrases or ideas particularly speak to you?
2. When have you learned important truths from watching someone else's negative example and then chosen to do otherwise?
3. Consider whether there is someone in your life now whose negative example can teach you something. (This could be someone you are close to and love deeply.)

PRAY

Ask God for wisdom to learn from the negative examples of people around you. Also ask God to help you avoid feeling morally superior to them — but instead be grateful for what you can learn. Pray for that person who is or was a negative example.

LIVE

Look at yourself in a mirror. See yourself as wholly different from the person who is a negative example — particularly if this person is a parent. Thank God that being wholly different is possible through him.

THE SHEPHERD AND ME

EZEKIEL 34:10-16

¹⁰Thus says the Lord GOD, Behold, I am against the shepherds, and I will require my sheep at their hand and put a stop to their feeding the sheep. No longer shall the shepherds feed themselves. I will rescue my sheep from their mouths, that they may not be food for them.

¹¹For thus says the Lord GOD: Behold, I, I myself will search for my sheep and will seek them out. ¹²As a shepherd seeks out his flock when he is among his sheep that have been scattered, so will I seek out my sheep, and I will rescue them from all places where they have been scattered on a day of clouds and thick darkness. ¹³And I will bring them out from the peoples and gather them from the countries, and will bring them into their own land. And I will feed them on the mountains of Israel, by the ravines, and in all the inhabited places of the country. ¹⁴I will feed them with good pasture, and on the mountain heights of Israel shall be their grazing land. There they shall lie down in good grazing land, and on rich pasture they shall feed on the mountains of Israel. ¹⁵I myself will be the shepherd of my sheep, and I myself will make them lie down, declares the Lord GOD. ¹⁶I will seek the lost, and I will bring back the strayed, and I will bind up the injured, and I will strengthen the weak, and the fat and the strong I will destroy. I will feed them in justice.

READ

Get a clean sheet of paper and something to draw with. Read the passage slowly, imagining the scene.

THINK

Read the passage again. As you do, let the images take vivid shape in your mind. You might read it a few times to get really familiar with the relationships, the experiences, the settings. In your mind, picture the pastures for grazing, the weak sheep and the strong, the way the shepherd interacts with them. Pick one thing that stands out to you and think about what it would look like or smell like or sound like and what it makes you feel.

PRAY

Consider whatever stood out to you and take several minutes to sketch whatever comes to mind. Avoid hurrying yourself or thinking that you can't draw. Just go with it. You might sketch many different things, or you might focus on one thing. As you draw, be aware of God's presence there with you. Don't force yourself to talk or think about anything in particular. Simply enjoy drawing with God.

LIVE

Think about approaching God as your Shepherd. What do you want to bring to him today? Are you injured or struggling? Are you feeling strong? Are you needing rest? Bring him your need and tell him about it. Receive the comfort he gives.

NOT A HAIR SINGED

DANIEL 3:19-27

¹⁹Then Nebuchadnezzar was filled with fury, and the expression of his face was changed against Shadrach, Meshach, and Abednego. He ordered the furnace heated seven times more than it was usually heated. ²⁰And he ordered some of the mighty men of his army to bind Shadrach, Meshach, and Abednego, and to cast them into the burning fiery furnace. ²¹Then these men were bound in their cloaks, their tunics, their hats, and their other garments, and they were thrown into the burning fiery furnace. ²²Because the king's order was urgent and the furnace overheated, the flame of the fire killed those men who took up Shadrach, Meshach, and Abednego. ²³And these three men, Shadrach, Meshach, and Abednego, fell bound into the burning fiery furnace.

²⁴Then King Nebuchadnezzar was astonished and rose up in haste. He declared to his counselors, "Did we not cast three men bound into the fire?" They answered and said to the king, "True, O king." ²⁵He answered and said, "But I see four men unbound, walking in the midst of the fire, and they are not hurt; and the appearance of the fourth is like a son of the gods."

²⁶Then Nebuchadnezzar came near to the door of the burning fiery furnace; he declared, "Shadrach, Meshach, and Abednego, servants of the Most High God, come out, and come here!" Then Shadrach, Meshach, and Abednego came out from the fire. ²⁷And the satraps, the prefects, the governors, and the king's counselors gathered together and saw that the fire had not had any power over the bodies of those men. The hair of their heads was not singed, their cloaks were not harmed, and no smell of fire had come upon them.

READ

Read the passage aloud slowly.

THINK

Read the passage aloud again, but this time read the dialogue as theatrically as possible. Catch the incredulous tones of the king in verses 24-25. And in verse 26, call out loudly as the king did.

Now read the passage silently and let yourself become someone in the passage: a bystander watching it all, the king, one of the three men, or even the mysterious fourth man. Imagine the thoughts and feelings of the person whose role you have assumed. If you had been this person, how would this experience have affected your relationship with God?

PRAY

Respond to God from what has come to you in this passage — particularly about trusting in him.

LIVE

Sit quietly before God with the palms of your hands open and turned upward. Receive from God. Be particularly open to receiving guidance, just as Shadrach, Meshach, and Abednego received from God. Receive the courage he gave them. Receive the power he gave them.

WHEN DOING THE RIGHT THING IS AGAINST THE LAW

DANIEL 6:6-10

⁶Then these high officials and satraps came by agreement to the king and said to him, "O King Darius, live forever! ⁷All the high officials of the kingdom, the prefects and the satraps, the counselors and the governors are agreed that the king should establish an ordinance and enforce an injunction, that whoever makes petition to any god or man for thirty days, except to you, O king, shall be cast into the den of lions. ⁸Now, O king, establish the injunction and sign the document, so that it cannot be changed, according to the law of the Medes and the Persians, which cannot be revoked." ⁹Therefore King Darius signed the document and injunction.

¹⁰When Daniel knew that the document had been signed, he went to his house where he had windows in his upper chamber open toward Jerusalem. He got down on his knees three times a day and prayed and gave thanks before his God, as he had done previously.

READ

The story of Daniel 6 is a familiar one, which means we often focus on Daniel inside the den of lions while missing what got him there in the first place. So before you read, pause and ask God to help you see this story with fresh eyes.

THINK

King Darius signs a deceptive decree that puts God-fearing Daniel in an interesting (to say the least) situation. But despite the new law and at great risk, Daniel maintains his routine of prayer. What does this story make you feel? Why?

Imagine yourself in the situation with Daniel. What do you see? What do you hear? If you were Daniel's friend, what would you say to him? What would you do? Would you kneel with him by the window? Would you kneel quietly in the corner so nobody could see you? Would you kneel at all? Would you stop praying to God?

Would these be difficult decisions for you? In what ways does this story speak to you about obedience?

PRAY

Allow the natural rhythm of your thoughts concerning Daniel's obedience to prompt you into conversation with God. (For example, you could pray after each category of thought or you could pray after your meditation is finished — whatever comes most naturally.)

Consider praying in a kneeling position by a window. As you pray, remember Daniel.

LIVE

Remember that God is worthy of your costly obedience.

KING OF THE UNIVERSE

DANIEL 7:11-14

[11]I looked then because of the sound of the great words that the horn was speaking. And as I looked, the beast was killed, and its body destroyed and given over to be burned with fire. [12]As for the rest of the beasts, their dominion was taken away, but their lives were prolonged for a season and a time.
[13] I saw in the night visions,

> and behold, with the clouds of heaven
>   there came one like a son of man,
> and he came to the Ancient of Days
>   and was presented before him.

[14] And to him was given dominion
>   and glory and a kingdom,
> that all peoples, nations, and languages
>   should serve him;
> his dominion is an everlasting dominion,
>   which shall not pass away,
> and his kingdom one
>   that shall not be destroyed.

READ

Read the passage as fast as you can. Then read it again at a normal pace. Finally read it aloud very slowly, focusing on and articulating each word.

THINK

The book of Daniel is full of radical stories of obedience, but it is also filled with strange and sensational dreams and visions. Chapter 7 includes a vision with four animals, plus the prophetic words found in verses 13-14.

Is God's kingly rule in the world evident to you? Do you believe he's really in charge? Think about God reigning as King over his people. Does that make you feel fear and dread or excitement and hope? Why?

If God is in control, we don't have to be. Does that thought induce anxiety or comfort? Why? Catastrophes, devastation, and suffering happen every day, yet God is ruling at this very moment. Do you believe that? How does believing that make you feel?

Not only is God in control today, but his reign lasts forever. In what ways does that fact impact your life?

PRAY

What are you worried about? Offer your concerns right now to the God who reigns over everything at this very moment and will continue to reign forever.

LIVE

Live freely and without worry as you focus on God's reign today.

DAY 161

GOD ENCOUNTERS

On this seventh day, review and reflect on all you have read this week. Take the time to revel in the ways you've encountered God in the past six days.

CONFESSING FOR YOUR GROUP

DANIEL 9:4-9,18

⁴I prayed to the LORD my God and made confession, saying, "O Lord, the great and awesome God, who keeps covenant and steadfast love with those who love him and keep his commandments, ⁵we have sinned and done wrong and acted wickedly and rebelled, turning aside from your commandments and rules. ⁶We have not listened to your servants the prophets, who spoke in your name to our kings, our princes, and our fathers, and to all the people of the land. ⁷To you, O Lord, belongs righteousness, but to us open shame, as at this day, to the men of Judah, to the inhabitants of Jerusalem, and to all Israel, those who are near and those who are far away, in all the lands to which you have driven them, because of the treachery that they have committed against you. ⁸To us, O LORD, belongs open shame, to our kings, to our princes, and to our fathers, because we have sinned against you. ⁹To the Lord our God belong mercy and forgiveness, for we have rebelled against him. . . .

¹⁸"O my God, incline your ear and hear. Open your eyes and see our desolations, and the city that is called by your name. For we do not present our pleas before you because of our righteousness, but because of your great mercy."

READ

Read the passage aloud slowly.

THINK

Consider a group you belong to for which you could confess. This might be your family, your church, your nation, or a circle of friends or colleagues.

Read the passage again silently, noting if certain words or phrases apply to your group situation. Notice these phrases especially:

- "turning aside from your commandments and rules"
- "but to us open shame"
- "have not listened to your servants the prophets"

Read the passage again silently, noting the qualities of God that are mentioned. Which qualities does your group most need? Perhaps:

- keeps covenant, steadfast love
- righteousness
- mercy

PRAY

Paraphrase verse 18 in a way that makes sense to your situation.

LIVE

Check your feelings regarding confession. Are you letting it be a time of release and rest in the presence of your Father or a time of beating yourself up? Rest in the release of it all.

TURNING MANY TO RIGHTEOUSNESS

DANIEL 12:1-3

¹At that time shall arise Michael, the great prince who has charge of your people. And there shall be a time of trouble, such as never has been since there was a nation till that time. But at that time your people shall be delivered, everyone whose name shall be found written in the book. ²And many of those who sleep in the dust of the earth shall awake, some to everlasting life, and some to shame and everlasting contempt. ³And those who are wise shall shine like the brightness of the sky above; and those who turn many to righteousness, like the stars forever and ever.

READ

Read today's expanded passage if possible. Lay your watch or a clock next to your Bible. As you read, consider how this passage affects time, both right now and in the future.

THINK

A great deal has been said and written about the end times — in radio talk shows, best-selling novels, Hollywood blockbusters, and conversations over coffee.

In light of these verses, what are you thinking about the end times? What are you feeling? Does talk like this about the future excite you or scare you?

Focus for a few minutes specifically on 12:1-3. How do we know if we are "those who are wise"? What does it mean to "turn many to righteousness"? What are the implications of these words in your life? Who do you have the opportunity to help get on the right path to life?

Do you think it's fair that God gives some people eternal life and banishes others to eternal shame? Is he being just when he does that? Why or why not?

PRAY

Tell God how you feel about the future — both your immediate future and the end of the world. Ask him to help you live wisely. Invite God to guide you in helping others turn to righteousness.

LIVE

Live with confidence today, knowing that God has already secured the future and will be victorious.

GOD AS LOVER

HOSEA 2:14-20

¹⁴ Therefore, behold, I will allure her,
    and bring her into the wilderness,
    and speak tenderly to her.
¹⁵ And there I will give her her vineyards
    and make the Valley of Achor a door of hope.
  And there she shall answer as in the days of her youth,
    as at the time when she came out of the land of Egypt.

¹⁶And in that day, declares the LORD, you will call me "My Husband," and no longer will you call me "My Baal." ¹⁷For I will remove the names of the Baals from her mouth, and they shall be remembered by name no more. ¹⁸And I will make for them a covenant on that day with the beasts of the field, the birds of the heavens, and the creeping things of the ground. And I will abolish the bow, the sword, and war from the land, and I will make you lie down in safety. ¹⁹And I will betroth you to me forever. I will betroth you to me in righteousness and in justice, in steadfast love and in mercy. ²⁰I will betroth you to me in faithfulness. And you shall know the LORD.

READ
Meditate on this passage.

THINK

When we think of love stories in the Bible, we usually think of the one narrated in Song of Songs, with all its steamy unpredictability. But Hosea offers us a love story too, one that's no less steamy, yet one that jolts us in a different way. In it Hosea actually lives out the heartbreaking metaphor of God's love for us . . . and our rejection of his love.

God commands Hosea to marry a prostitute named Gomer. Then God says that he is going to "allure her." Hosea had to pursue the woman again and again as a symbolic act of how God runs after us when we've been unfaithful.

We are the prostitute in this story. What does that feel like?

We are also God's beloved in this story. What does it feel like to be courted by such a lover, one who cares deeply about you despite your past? Is thinking of God as a lover — *your* lover — easy or difficult? Consider the possible reasons for your answer.

Read again the final words of this passage, starting with the line "And I will betroth you to me forever." What is your reaction?

PRAY

Make these words your prayer as you desire to know God intimately: "I will betroth you to me in faithfulness. And you shall know the LORD."

LIVE

Carry the image of God as lover in your mind today.

LOVE AGAIN

HOSEA 3:1-3

¹And the LORD said to me, "Go again, love a woman who is loved by another man and is an adulteress, even as the LORD loves the children of Israel, though they turn to other gods and love cakes of raisins." ²So I bought her for fifteen shekels of silver and a homer and a lethech of barley. ³And I said to her, "You must dwell as mine for many days. You shall not play the whore, or belong to another man; so will I also be to you."

READ
Read the passage slowly, whispering it.

THINK
Read the passage again slowly. Pause after verse 1 to consider how Hosea may have felt about doing what God instructed. Then read verses 2-3, noticing Hosea's firm resolution in restoring his wife.

1. What verses are most startling to you in this passage? Why?
2. How would you describe the way God loved the Israelite people (considering that they turned to other gods)?
3. Is there someone you need to love again? Reach out to? Simply stop criticizing and give that person a break?

PRAY
Ask God to help you love the person who came to mind in question 3 the way he loved the Israelites. (If this seems too difficult, include in your prayer your paraphrase of Romans 5:5: "God's love has been poured into our hearts through the Holy Spirit who has been given to us."

Ask God what that love might look like; it may look different from what you might automatically assume. Consider what this might cost you to love this person the way God shows you.

LIVE
Sit quietly before God, trying to sense what it was like for him to love the wayward Israelites no matter what.

LIP SERVICE

HOSEA 8:1-3

¹ Set the trumpet to your lips!
  One like a vulture is over the house of the LORD,
because they have transgressed my covenant
  and rebelled against my law.
² To me they cry,
  "My God, we — Israel — know you."
³ Israel has spurned the good;
  the enemy shall pursue him.

READ

Read the passage, focusing on the words *me* and *my*.

THINK

Despite our lover God pursuing us tenderly, we continue to reject his love. We treat him not with tenderness but with contempt, discarding all he has done with us. And we continue to live like whores.

Read the passage again. Israel claims to know God, but its actions don't match its words. When have you experienced a similar situation — family members, friends, significant others, or your spouse saying one thing to you but doing just the opposite? How does that feel?

Consider your actions over the past week, the times when you have been the one to say something and then do the opposite. Is your love for God displayed in your actions, or do your actions fly in the face of everything you say to him?

PRAY

Tell God your desire to fall deeper and deeper in love with him, praying and asking him to help your actions communicate that to him.

Confess recent circumstances when your actions toward God and people did not match your profession of love for God.

LIVE

Note whether your actions align with the love for God that you profess.

TIME TO SEEK THE LORD

HOSEA 10:11-12

¹¹ Ephraim was a trained calf
    that loved to thresh,
    and I spared her fair neck;
  but I will put Ephraim to the yoke;
    Judah must plow;
    Jacob must harrow for himself.
¹² Sow for yourselves righteousness;
    reap steadfast love; break up your fallow ground,
  for it is the time to seek the Lord,
    that he may come and rain righteousness upon you.

READ

Read the passage aloud slowly.

THINK

Read the passage aloud again. As you do, understand this to be God's dream for the northern tribes of Israel. Instead of doing these things, however, they rebelled.

Think of a time God used you to love someone or do something special for someone. In doing so, you were a well-trained calf!

1. What does this passage tell you about what a trained calf does?
2. Why is it a joy for a trained calf to "seek the LORD"?

Read the passage one more time. What words are attractive to your ears?

PRAY

Thank God for the times he has used you to do kingdom work — offering mercy, doing justice, or acting in faithfulness. Ask God to show you ways he wants to use you that you might not have noticed.

LIVE

Sit in the joy and satisfaction of seeking the Lord. If you have not experienced being used by God, imagine what that might feel like.

DAY 168

GOD ENCOUNTERS

On this seventh day, review and reflect on all you have read this week. Take the time to revel in the ways you've encountered God in the past six days.

HOW CAN I GIVE UP ON YOU?

HOSEA 11:1-5,7-9

1 When Israel was a child, I loved him,
    and out of Egypt I called my son.
2 The more they were called,
    the more they went away;
  they kept sacrificing to the Baals
    and burning offerings to idols.

3 Yet it was I who taught Ephraim to walk;
    I took them up by their arms,
    but they did not know that I healed them.
4 I led them with cords of kindness,
    with the bands of love,
  and I became to them as one who eases the yoke on their jaws,
    and I bent down to them and fed them.

5 They shall not return to the land of Egypt,
    but Assyria shall be their king,
    because they have refused to return to me. . . .
7 My people are bent on turning away from me,
    and though they call out to the Most High,
    he shall not raise them up at all.
8 How can I give you up, O Ephraim?
    How can I hand you over, O Israel?
  How can I make you like Admah?
    How can I treat you like Zeboiim?
  My heart recoils within me;
    my compassion grows warm and tender.

9 I will not execute my burning anger;
    I will not again destroy Ephraim;
  for I am God and not a man,
    the Holy One in your midst,
  and I will not come in wrath.

READ

Read the passage once to understand the situation. (Include the expanded passage for further information.) Read it again, but this time pause at each phrase or idea and linger there for a moment to really catch what is being said.

THINK

Quiet your mind. Read the passage a third time, aloud. This time notice the word or phrase that most vividly speaks to you of God's unrelenting faithfulness. Pause at this phrase, and hear yourself speak it. Then finish reading the passage.

PRAY

Spend time absorbing the word or phrase into yourself, as though your heart were a sponge slowly soaking up water. Memorize it. Let it intermingle with your concerns, memories, and feelings. Allow your meditation to grow into conversation with God. Notice God pointing out, through this illustration, how his devotedness frees you to experience life differently than you have before.

LIVE

Between now and your next time of prayer, plan at least three occasions throughout your day when you will pause and spend a few minutes mulling over the phrase that showed you the tenacity of God's love. Each time, you'll probably bring different emotions, attitudes, and experiences with you, and that's okay. Let them challenge God's message of commitment to you. Find out how his steadfast love responds to each challenge.

CORPORATE CONFESSION

JOEL 1:8-10

8 Lament like a virgin wearing sackcloth
   for the bridegroom of her youth.
9 The grain offering and the drink offering are cut off
   from the house of the LORD.
   The priests mourn,
      the ministers of the LORD.
10 The fields are destroyed,
      the ground mourns,
   because the grain is destroyed,
      the wine dries up,
      the oil languishes.

READ

Read the passage and, if possible, the expanded passage.

THINK

In the first chapter of Joel, the prophet speaks of a famine that has significance far beyond mere physical consequences. There are certain passages of Scripture that we love to read, passages of comfort and rest, hope and promise. But there are others — like this one — that confront us with the truth, as hard as it may be to hear.

American Christianity often emphasizes the importance of personal confession of sin. But the concept of corporate sin is rarely discussed. In contrast, confession of corporate sin was a regular occurrence in the ancient Jewish world. National sin grieved the heart of the God-fearing Hebrew, and confessing it was desired and expected.

Take out a piece of paper and write down the corporate sins that our communities, our government, our country, and even our churches need to confess. (Include what wrongdoing has been done and what good-doing has been left undone.)

PRAY

Spend time specifically acknowledging and confessing these corporate sins against God and others. Ask God for forgiveness.

LIVE

Live with the awareness of our collective sins, knowing that God desires repentance for us as a community, a country, and his people. Ask often for corporate forgiveness.

RETURN TO ME

JOEL 2:12-14

[12] "Yet even now," declares the Lord,
     "return to me with all your heart,
with fasting, with weeping, and with mourning;
[13]   and rend your hearts and not your garments."
Return to the Lord your God,
     for he is gracious and merciful,
slow to anger, and abounding in steadfast love;
     and he relents over disaster.
[14] Who knows whether he will not turn and relent,
     and leave a blessing behind him,
a grain offering and a drink offering
     for the Lord your God?

READ

Read the passage aloud slowly, noting that verse 12 includes words from God himself.

THINK

Read the passage aloud again, repeating God's words in verse 12 in the tone you think he would have said them.

God says the phrase "Return to me" many times through the prophets. God really does want his people, and he wants them back.

1. What does this passage tell you about what God is like?
2. How surprised are you that God wants his people (including you) to return to him? (Keep in mind that turning back doesn't have to mean you ever dramatically turned away; it might mean you've just been distracted.)

   ☐ Very surprised: You thought God would scold people who wander away or ignore him.
   ☐ Somewhat surprised: You figured God wouldn't turn away someone who returns, but he would never plead with them.
   ☐ Not surprised: You frequently sense God calling you back and know he's not mad at you.
   ☐ Other:

PRAY

Tell God how you feel about being (or becoming) someone who always returns to him. Do you always want to? Would you like to always want to? Talk to God about the blessings that come to you when you turn back to him.

LIVE

Picture this: If God had a body, how would he stand before people and plead for them to come back to him? What would he do with his hands? His arms? What would his face look like?

A REFUGE AND STRONGHOLD

JOEL 3:14-19

¹⁴ Multitudes, multitudes,
   in the valley of decision!
For the day of the LORD is near
   in the valley of decision.
¹⁵ The sun and the moon are darkened,
   and the stars withdraw their shining.

¹⁶ The LORD roars from Zion,
   and utters his voice from Jerusalem,
   and the heavens and the earth quake.
But the LORD is a refuge to his people,
   a stronghold to the people of Israel.
¹⁷ "So you shall know that I am the LORD your God,
   who dwells in Zion, my holy mountain.
And Jerusalem shall be holy,
   and strangers shall never again pass through it.

¹⁸ "And in that day
the mountains shall drip sweet wine,
   and the hills shall flow with milk,
and all the streambeds of Judah
   shall flow with water;
and a fountain shall come forth from the house of the LORD
   and water the Valley of Shittim.

¹⁹ "Egypt shall become a desolation
   and Edom a desolate wilderness,
for the violence done to the people of Judah,
   because they have shed innocent blood in their land."

READ

Read the passage, opening yourself up to the situation Joel is prophetically describing here. You might read it a few more times, allowing the words and images to become familiar.

THINK

Ponder the contrast between God as the terrifying roar amid chaos and God as a "stronghold to the people of Israel." Which words or images in particular catch your attention? Mull them over. Become aware of specific questions these verses raise for you.

PRAY

Let your questions and meditation lead you into conversation with God. You might think about facets of his character, like his terrifying might or his solid trustworthiness, or you might consider the reality of this future, even though we don't know exactly what it'll be like.

If your primary questions about the passage are intellectual, place them before God and ask him what he has for you. Stay honest with what you do and don't understand, sharing with God how this passage touches your life. Avoid getting lost in academic speculation or trying to force meaning out of the passage. Just ask God how he would like to use this experience of your limitedness today.

LIVE

As you look once more at the two vastly different perspectives on God presented in this passage, which side of God are you most in need of today: his fierce ability to bring justice or his safe protection from harm? Spend time now quietly resting in the presence of this God.

THE GOD OF JUSTICE

AMOS 2:6-8

⁶ Thus says the LORD:

"For three transgressions of Israel,
and for four, I will not revoke the punishment,
because they sell the righteous for silver,
and the needy for a pair of sandals—
⁷ those who trample the head of the poor into the dust of the earth
and turn aside the way of the afflicted;
a man and his father go in to the same girl,
so that my holy name is profaned;
⁸ they lay themselves down beside every altar
on garments taken in pledge,
and in the house of their God they drink
the wine of those who have been fined."

READ

Read the words of God in these verses with the tone of voice you think God might have had when speaking these words.

THINK

The book of Amos communicates clearly and compellingly that God cares deeply about social justice — and he dislikes it when his people turn their heads from doing right. God is truly a God of mercy, yet he is also a God of justice. That means he treats injustice harshly.

What injustices exist around you — among your friends and in your city, state, country, and the entire world? What are we to do about injustice specifically?

Thinking *I'm not a part of an injustice* is easy. But take a hard look around you. In what ways might you be contributing — directly or indirectly — to injustice in the world? In what ways might you get involved — directly or indirectly — to facilitate justice that would reveal the heart of God?

If injustice makes God sick to his stomach, what should the presence of injustice do to you? Does it?

PRAY

Ask God to make injustice in the world as repulsive to you as it is to him. Ask him for wisdom to address injustice in a way that honors him with a godly balance of boldness and tenderness.

LIVE

Read some of the articles in today's news. As you absorb the accounts of atrocity, war, and corruption, pray for each situation. Pray that the God of justice will intervene.

SEEKING GOOD

AMOS 5:7,11-15

⁷ O you who turn justice to wormwood
     and cast down righteousness to the earth! . . .

¹¹ Therefore because you trample on the poor
     and you exact taxes of grain from him,
   you have built houses of hewn stone,
     but you shall not dwell in them;
   you have planted pleasant vineyards,
     but you shall not drink their wine.
¹² For I know how many are your transgressions
     and how great are your sins —
   you who afflict the righteous, who take a bribe,
     and turn aside the needy in the gate.
¹³ Therefore he who is prudent will keep silent in such a time,
     for it is an evil time.

¹⁴ Seek good, and not evil,
     that you may live;
   and so the LORD, the God of hosts, will be with you,
     as you have said.
¹⁵ Hate evil, and love good,
     and establish justice in the gate;
   it may be that the LORD, the God of hosts,
     will be gracious to the remnant of Joseph.

READ
Read the passage aloud slowly.

THINK
Read the passage again silently, noticing the pictures in the passage. Which do you find most dreadful?

Pictures of how those who have enough treat those who don't:	
cast down righteousness to the earth	trample on the poor
take taxes of grain from people	afflict the righteous
taking bribes	turn aside the needy
Pictures of the consequences to those who have enough but don't share:	
houses you won't dwell in	vineyards but won't drink the wine

Read verses 14-15 again aloud. What is God saying to you about seeking good and helping others live?

PRAY
Talk to the Lord about what it would look like for you to seek good.

LIVE
Be alert for situations of injustice in which you can speak up or help someone. If you don't find any, ask someone else to give you ideas.

DAY 175

GOD ENCOUNTERS
On this seventh day, review and reflect on all you have read this week. Take the time to revel in the ways you've encountered God in the past six days.

PLUMB LINE

AMOS 7:1-9

¹This is what the Lord God showed me: behold, he was forming locusts when the latter growth was just beginning to sprout, and behold, it was the latter growth after the king's mowings. ²When they had finished eating the grass of the land, I said,

> "O Lord God, please forgive!
>   How can Jacob stand?
>   He is so small!"
> ³ The Lord relented concerning this:
>   "It shall not be," said the Lord.

⁴This is what the Lord God showed me: behold, the Lord God was calling for a judgment by fire, and it devoured the great deep and was eating up the land. ⁵Then I said,

> "O Lord God, please cease!
>   How can Jacob stand?
>   He is so small!"
> ⁶ The Lord relented concerning this:
>   "This also shall not be," said the Lord God.

⁷This is what he showed me: behold, the Lord was standing beside a wall built with a plumb line, with a plumb line in his hand. ⁸And the Lord said to me, "Amos, what do you see?" And I said, "A plumb line." Then the Lord said,

> "Behold, I am setting a plumb line
>   in the midst of my people Israel;
>   I will never again pass by them;
> ⁹ the high places of Isaac shall be made desolate,
>   and the sanctuaries of Israel shall be laid waste,
>   and I will rise against the house of Jeroboam with the sword."

READ
Read the passage carefully.

THINK
What theme do you see emerging? Write it down in one sentence. Be aware of what thinking might have motivated God to use the plumb line.

LIVE
Take a small, heavy object, like a key, a ring, or a pendant, and hang it from a string. As the object hangs straight toward the ground, the string is your plumb line by which you can measure the uprightness of other items. Take time to ponder this. Play with your plumb line and observe how it works. What do you notice?

PRAY
Setting the text and your plumb line aside, sit with your eyes closed. What are you feeling? What are your concerns and needs? Who are you as the person who is approaching this text today?

Now read the passage again. In what ways do you see the theme you already noted intersecting with your life today? Is there a message God is speaking to you? How does the plumb line hang in the midst of your own life? If you have trouble seeing a connection, read the passage again, pausing in the place that affects you most and leads you into prayer. Write down anything that seems significant.

GOD, THE RADICAL POLITICIAN

OBADIAH 12-14

¹² But do not gloat over the day of your brother
    in the day of his misfortune;
  do not rejoice over the people of Judah
    in the day of their ruin;
  do not boast
    in the day of distress.
¹³ Do not enter the gate of my people
    in the day of their calamity;
  do not gloat over his disaster
    in the day of his calamity;
  do not loot his wealth
    in the day of his calamity.
¹⁴ Do not stand at the crossroads
    to cut off his fugitives;
  do not hand over his survivors
    in the day of distress.

READ

Read the passage aloud slowly. Understand that the prophet Obadiah is speaking to the nation of Edom who enjoyed watching the nation of Judah experience troubles.

THINK

Put yourself in the place of the nation of Edom. You've had an ancient feud with the Israelites, and they are your bitter enemies. Politics are politics — enemy nations do *not* help each other. Right? Now read the passage again, with its very different viewpoint. Hear God's radical response to Edom's very normal behavior.

God's odd stance has been stated another way in 1 Corinthians 13:6: "[Love] does not rejoice at wrongdoing, but rejoices with the truth." What role does the love of God play in political affairs? What role does the love of God play in how nations treat the peoples of the world whom God loves?

PRAY

Ask God to help the nations of the world consider how they treat one another, especially nations who are ancient enemies. Pray for Christians who are active in inserting God's radical love into international politics (for example, Christian Peacemaker Teams).

LIVE

Stand in front of a world map or globe. Put your hand on a nation who has been an enemy of your nation. Pray for the people of that country. Pray for its leaders.

RESISTANT OR OBEDIENT?

JONAH 1:1-3

¹Now the word of the LORD came to Jonah the son of Amittai, saying, ²"Arise, go to Nineveh, that great city, and call out against it, for their evil has come up before me." ³But Jonah rose to flee to Tarshish from the presence of the LORD. He went down to Joppa and found a ship going to Tarshish. So he paid the fare and went down into it, to go with them to Tarshish, away from the presence of the LORD.

READ

Pray and ask God to give you fresh eyes to see this familiar story in a new way. Then read the passage and chapters 1–2, if possible.

THINK

We might summarize this familiar story by saying that Jonah's resistance to being obedient to God's ways meant his learning a lesson the hard way. But there's more to it than that. In fact, the text tells us that Jonah was "flee[ing] the presence of the LORD." We run away from God too, even if only in subtle ways. When do you run from God?

PRAY

Try praying while holding out your hands, palms up, in front of you. Use this posture as a way to release your desires to God, to receive what he has for you, and to communicate your openness and willingness to obey him.

Ask the Holy Spirit to search your heart and reveal areas of your life where you resist what God desires. Invite him to illuminate your unwillingness to obey, and give him permission to do whatever it takes to show you that he cares deeply for you.

Request forgiveness for those times you have run from God, for your rebellion.

When you are finished, keeping your hands out, listen carefully in the silence.

LIVE

Go and live courageously and obediently in God's purposes for your life.

IN A SULK

JONAH 4:5-11

⁵Jonah went out of the city and sat to the east of the city and made a booth for himself there. He sat under it in the shade, till he should see what would become of the city. ⁶Now the Lᴏʀᴅ God appointed a plant and made it come up over Jonah, that it might be a shade over his head, to save him from his discomfort. So Jonah was exceedingly glad because of the plant. ⁷But when dawn came up the next day, God appointed a worm that attacked the plant, so that it withered. ⁸When the sun rose, God appointed a scorching east wind, and the sun beat down on the head of Jonah so that he was faint. And he asked that he might die and said, "It is better for me to die than to live." ⁹But God said to Jonah, "Do you do well to be angry for the plant?" And he said, "Yes, I do well to be angry, angry enough to die." ¹⁰And the Lᴏʀᴅ said, "You pity the plant, for which you did not labor, nor did you make it grow, which came into being in a night and perished in a night. ¹¹And should not I pity Nineveh, that great city, in which there are more than 120,000 persons who do not know their right hand from their left, and also much cattle?"

READ

Allow the words and events of this passage to become familiar to you as you read. Let yourself sink into the scene described.

THINK

As you hear God's conversation with Jonah, think about how you would describe his reaction to Jonah's anger. Now read God's words again, and pay attention to the tone of voice you imagine God using. Is it condemning? Mocking? How might your perception of God shift if the same words were said in a tender but firm voice?

PRAY

What do you feel when you hear Jonah express his anger? When you see him walk away? Perhaps it makes you nervous or uncomfortable, or maybe there are times when you, too, want to yell at God. Talk to God about what you notice in your response, or write about it in a journal. Give yourself permission to be open and honest.

LIVE

Take some time to consider this statement: "God will love you [even] if you never pray."[11] Do you believe it? Talk to God about your reaction.

Recall your first, instinctive perception of God's response to Jonah. What does this show about what you believe to be God's feelings toward you when you are resentful or disobedient? Ask him to help you understand over the coming months what his love for you is like and to help you take it in and receive it.

IDOL MAKING

MICAH 1:3-7

3 For behold, the LORD is coming out of his place,
    and will come down and tread upon the high places of the earth.
4 And the mountains will melt under him,
    and the valleys will split open,
  like wax before the fire,
    like waters poured down a steep place.
5 All this is for the transgression of Jacob
    and for the sins of the house of Israel.
  What is the transgression of Jacob?
    Is it not Samaria?
  And what is the high place of Judah?
    Is it not Jerusalem?
6 Therefore I will make Samaria a heap in the open country,
    a place for planting vineyards,
  and I will pour down her stones into the valley
    and uncover her foundations.
7 All her carved images shall be beaten to pieces,
    all her wages shall be burned with fire,
    and all her idols I will lay waste,
  for from the fee of a prostitute she gathered them,
    and to the fee of a prostitute they shall return.

READ

Pause and request that God give you an open heart for what you are about to read. Give him permission to speak to you specifically about what he wants you to hear. Acknowledge that you desire to hear him speak to you and will listen attentively.

Now read the passage with listening ears and an open heart.

THINK

Sometimes we let ourselves believe that idols are mere physical objects that people made hundreds, even thousands, of years ago. But theologically speaking, an idol is anything that eclipses our worship of God. And with this definition, *everybody* makes idols today, whether material or immaterial.

What gets between you and a heartfelt, humble, and thankful response to God? To what shrines and idols, gods and goddesses are you tempted to give your allegiance? Make a mental list (or write it on paper, if it helps).

Why do you think you are drawn to believe that certain things will give you more significance, purpose, and meaning than God himself? Why does God hate those things that take your worship, attention, and devotion? Is God's jealousy selfish? Why or why not?

PRAY

Bring your list of idols before God. Be utterly transparent with him, acknowledging and confessing the people, places, thoughts, ideas, emotions, and so on that have come between you and God. Invite him to fight alongside you against these temptations that divert your soul from the truth.

LIVE

When an idol lures you, simply whisper, "God, help me worship you and you alone."

TEACH US HIS WAYS

MICAH 4:1-4

¹ It shall come to pass in the latter days
    that the mountain of the house of the Lord
shall be established as the highest of the mountains,
    and it shall be lifted up above the hills;
and peoples shall flow to it,
²   and many nations shall come, and say:
"Come, let us go up to the mountain of the Lord,
    to the house of the God of Jacob,
that he may teach us his ways
    and that we may walk in his paths."
For out of Zion shall go forth the law,
    and the word of the Lord from Jerusalem.
³ He shall judge between many peoples,
    and shall decide for strong nations far away;
and they shall beat their swords into plowshares,
    and their spears into pruning hooks;
nation shall not lift up sword against nation,
    neither shall they learn war anymore;
⁴ but they shall sit every man under his vine and under his fig tree,
    and no one shall make them afraid,
    for the mouth of the Lord of hosts has spoken.

READ
Read the passage aloud slowly.

THINK
Read the passage again, noting what it says about the law and the word of the Lord going forth — how it's found, what it says, and what it results in.

1. What words or ideas touch you in the passage? Perhaps

    - nations streaming to hear God
    - people wanting to live God's way
    - people giving up their swords and spears to do their work quietly
    - other:

2. Why do you think those words or ideas touch you? How does this connect with what you want in life?

PRAY
Pray for God's true teaching to prevail in troubled places — within troubled people, within troubled relationships, within troubled groups, between troubled nations.

LIVE
Sit quietly before God, mentally rehearsing the sort of person you need to be to bring true teaching that results in such peace.

DAY 182
GOD ENCOUNTERS
On this seventh day, review and reflect on all you have read this week. Take the time to revel in the ways you've encountered God in the past six days.

OUR GOD

MICAH 7:15-20

15 As in the days when you came out of the land of Egypt,
　　I will show them marvelous things.
16 The nations shall see and be ashamed of all their might;
　　they shall lay their hands on their mouths;
　　　their ears shall be deaf;
17 they shall lick the dust like a serpent,
　　like the crawling things of the earth;
　　they shall come trembling out of their strongholds;
　　　they shall turn in dread to the LORD our God,
　　　and they shall be in fear of you.

18 Who is a God like you, pardoning iniquity
　　and passing over transgression
　　　for the remnant of his inheritance?
　　He does not retain his anger forever,
　　　because he delights in steadfast love.
19 He will again have compassion on us;
　　he will tread our iniquities underfoot.
　　You will cast all our sins
　　　into the depths of the sea.
20 You will show faithfulness to Jacob
　　and steadfast love to Abraham,
　　as you have sworn to our fathers
　　　from the days of old.

PRAY

Before you read, pray about what's on your heart today. Is there something you want to talk to God about? Maybe it's a vague sense of shame or irritation, or maybe something specific is happening. Whatever it is, share your heart with God. Try writing your prayer in a journal. Ask God to speak to you right where you are through today's excerpt.

READ/THINK

As much as you can, set aside what you've been thinking about for a few minutes, trusting that God will hold it for you. Read today's passage, noticing what's happening in Micah's situation and the kinds of problems that God, through him, is addressing in Israel. If you have time, read the expanded passage too, observing in particular what God is like.

Write down what you notice about God and the attributes he displays in this passage.

LIVE

Look at what you wrote about yourself and about God. How do you think God is responding to you and the issues you shared earlier through this passage from Micah? What angers God? What touches his heart? When does he show tenderness, and when does he show firmness?

How do these traits compare to the way you normally perceive God? Where do you think your idea of him came from? Can you identify elements of your perception that are not of God but are rather reflections of you or other people you know?

Talk to God about what you notice.

PATIENT POWER

NAHUM 1:1-6

¹ An oracle concerning Nineveh. The book of the vision of Nahum of Elkosh.

² The LORD is a jealous and avenging God;
    the LORD is avenging and wrathful;
the LORD takes vengeance on his adversaries
    and keeps wrath for his enemies.
³ The LORD is slow to anger and great in power,
    and the LORD will by no means clear the guilty.
His way is in whirlwind and storm,
    and the clouds are the dust of his feet.
⁴ He rebukes the sea and makes it dry;
    he dries up all the rivers;
Bashan and Carmel wither;
    the bloom of Lebanon withers.
⁵ The mountains quake before him;
        the hills melt;
the earth heaves before him,
        the world and all who dwell in it.

⁶ Who can stand before his indignation?
    Who can endure the heat of his anger?
His wrath is poured out like fire,
    and the rocks are broken into pieces by him.

READ

Read the passage.

THINK

Ponder this passage: "The Lord is slow to anger and great in power."

When you consider the word *power,* what comes to mind? Do you think of *power* as a positive or negative concept? Why?

When you consider God as powerful, is that positive or negative to you? Why? What's the difference between his being powerful and his being slow to anger, or patient? Does the "patient" factor change your feelings about his power? If so, in what way? What would the world be like if God were powerful and *impatient*?

Why is it important that God is patiently powerful?

PRAY

Spend a few minutes letting the idea of a God who is patient yet powerful rest in your mind. Then ask God what he wants you to know about his power today, right now.

Thank him for his patience.

Thank him for his power.

LIVE

Rest today in the midst of your schedule, comforted that the God you serve is both powerful and patient.

WHAT ARE YOU COUNTING ON?

NAHUM 3:14-17

¹⁴ Draw water for the siege;
   strengthen your forts;
go into the clay;
   tread the mortar;
   take hold of the brick mold!
¹⁵ There will the fire devour you;
   the sword will cut you off.
   It will devour you like the locust.
Multiply yourselves like the locust;
   multiply like the grasshopper!
¹⁶ You increased your merchants
   more than the stars of the heavens.
   The locust spreads its wings and flies away.

¹⁷ Your princes are like grasshoppers,
   your scribes like clouds of locusts
settling on the fences
   in a day of cold —
when the sun rises, they fly away;
   no one knows where they are.

READ

Read the passage slowly to yourself. Be aware that this sad passage describes the ancient city of Nineveh, which is doomed. Everything Nineveh counted on has fallen through.

THINK

Read the passage again, noting what Nineveh counted on to keep itself out of trouble.

Why is it so tempting to rely on economic prosperity (merchants) and the government (princes)? (We even use phrases such as "having faith in" the stock market or "having faith in" government officials.)

What would your life look like if you relied on God for your future and your safety instead of on the economy or the government?

PRAY

Examine what you have that comes from the economy or the government, such as a job, streetlights, or a public library. Ask God to show you how much you count on these things and what counting on him in a deeper way would mean.

LIVE

Imagine yourself living in a place where the economy and the government have fallen apart. What might you feel like if you relied totally on God?

SPEAKING OUR MINDS AND HEARTS

HABAKKUK 1:12-17

¹² Are you not from everlasting,
    O Lord my God, my Holy One?
    We shall not die.
  O Lord, you have ordained them as a judgment,
    and you, O Rock, have established them for reproof.
¹³ You who are of purer eyes than to see evil
    and cannot look at wrong,
  why do you idly look at traitors
    and remain silent when the wicked swallows up
    the man more righteous than he?
¹⁴ You make mankind like the fish of the sea,
    like crawling things that have no ruler.
¹⁵ He brings all of them up with a hook;
    he drags them out with his net;
  he gathers them in his dragnet;
    so he rejoices and is glad.
¹⁶ Therefore he sacrifices to his net
    and makes offerings to his dragnet;
  for by them he lives in luxury,
    and his food is rich.
¹⁷ Is he then to keep on emptying his net
    and mercilessly killing nations forever?

READ
Read Habakkuk 1:12-17.

THINK
Sometimes we have a hard time being completely honest with God. But when we read certain passages of Scripture, such as in the Psalms and here in Habakkuk, we are encouraged to know that not only is God okay with our honesty, but he even invites it. Most prophets speak on behalf of God to us; Habakkuk speaks on behalf of us to God — and he does it with honesty that might make some people blush.

When you read Habakkuk's bold words — "Why do you idly look at traitors and remain silent when the wicked swallows up the man more righteous than he?" — how do you feel?

Does the same level of honesty in Habakkuk's words show up in you when you talk to God? Why or why not? Is that good or bad? What might happen in your life if you could speak to God with such honesty?

PRAY
Consider your life — your friendships, place in life, expectations, dreams, goals, hopes, job, school situation, and so on. About which of these areas do you wish you could speak honestly with God?

Take the risk and tell God exactly what's on your mind. Resist censoring yourself. Speak honestly and openly, assured that God is capable enough to handle your honesty.

LIVE
Know that God invites your honest communication with him at all times because, above all, he wants your heart.

186

LIVE BY FAITH

HABAKKUK 2:1-4

1 I will take my stand at my watchpost
     and station myself on the tower,
and look out to see what he will say to me,
     and what I will answer concerning my complaint.
2 And the LORD answered me:

"Write the vision;
     make it plain on tablets,
     so he may run who reads it.
3 For still the vision awaits its appointed time;
     it hastens to the end — it will not lie.
If it seems slow, wait for it;
     it will surely come; it will not delay.

4 "Behold, his soul is puffed up; it is not upright within him,
     but the righteous shall live by his faith."

READ

Read the passage aloud slowly, noting that this is a conversation between God and the prophet Habakkuk.

THINK

Habakkuk has just complained to God about the degraded life of Judah and asked God when he will act. In verse 1, Habakkuk insists on an answer, and verses 2-4 are the core of God's answer. Read the passage again with all this in mind.

1. What do you think of Habakkuk's questioning attitude? What does God seem to think of it?
2. In verses 2-4, God speaks to Habakkuk. What does God want Habakkuk to know or do?
3. Which of the words in this passage resonate most with you? Why do you think that is?

PRAY

Respond to God's statement "The righteous shall live by his faith." What does this make you want to say to God? To ask God?

LIVE

Rest in Habakkuk 2:20: "But the LORD is in his holy temple; let all the earth keep silence before him."

O LORD, REMEMBER MERCY

HABAKKUK 3:1-6

¹ A prayer of Habakkuk the prophet, according to Shigionoth.

² O LORD, I have heard the report of you,
  and your work, O LORD, do I fear.
In the midst of the years revive it;
  in the midst of the years make it known;
  in wrath remember mercy.
³ God came from Teman,
  and the Holy One from Mount Paran.   *Selah*
His splendor covered the heavens,
  and the earth was full of his praise.
⁴ His brightness was like the light;
  rays flashed from his hand;
  and there he veiled his power.
⁵ Before him went pestilence,
  and plague followed at his heels.
⁶ He stood and measured the earth;
  he looked and shook the nations;
then the eternal mountains were scattered;
  the everlasting hills sank low.
  His wcre the everlasting ways.

READ

Read Habakkuk's description of God's activities. As you do, let them remind you of actions and characteristics of God that have stood out to you as you've read stories of the Israelites in his Word.

THINK

Think about what it means to ask God to "in the midst of the years revive [your work]," referring to his work in Israel. What was he like with Israel? How did he deal with them? What characterized his relationship with them?

PRAY

Picture Habakkuk inviting you to join him in his prayer that God would act toward you as he did toward Israel. What rises up in you when you consider this? Fear? Frustration? Hope? Explore this with God. What does it show you about your internal picture of him? Of yourself?

LIVE

Sit silently with God and slowly reexamine what has taken place during your time with him today. Close with the following prayer: *Merciful God, shine your light of truth into me in the coming weeks and months, that I might more clearly understand what you're like and how you see me. Let my fears and pride be exposed for what they are, and keep them from distorting my picture of who you are. Give me courage, that I might face my true self, and hope, that I might face you. Help me see in you what Habakkuk saw, that "in wrath remember mercy." Amen.*

DAY 189

GOD ENCOUNTERS

On this seventh day, review and reflect on all you have read this week. Take the time to revel in the ways you've encountered God in the past six days.

THE BALANCE BETWEEN BEING JUST AND BEING MERCIFUL

ZEPHANIAH 1:7-11

⁷ Be silent before the Lord GOD!
 For the day of the LORD is near;
the LORD has prepared a sacrifice
 and consecrated his guests.
⁸ And on the day of the LORD's sacrifice —
 "I will punish the officials and the king's sons
 and all who array themselves in foreign attire.
⁹ On that day I will punish
 everyone who leaps over the threshold,
and those who fill their master's house
 with violence and fraud.

¹⁰ "On that day," declares the LORD,
 "a cry will be heard from the Fish Gate,
a wail from the Second Quarter,
 a loud crash from the hills.
¹¹ Wail, O inhabitants of the Mortar!
 For all the traders are no more;
 all who weigh out silver are cut off."

READ

Read these verses in a place that is absolutely quiet.

THINK

Many people see God as a God of comfort, guidance, and love. This image is not wrong, but it is incomplete. God is also a God of justice, one who becomes angry with our complacent and arrogant sin when we dump him altogether.

How does the fact that God is a God of justice balance in your mind with the fact that God is also a God of mercy (as we know from other places of Scripture)?

Pause and consider areas of complacency and rebellion in your life. Wait and listen for the Holy Spirit to show you. In light of these areas, what do you feel about this God who says he loves you?

PRAY

In the midst of silence, continue searching your heart for recent thoughts and actions that have gone in a direct opposition to what God desires for your life. Tell God how you are feeling deep within. He wants to hear from you. Verbalize specifically your rebellion against him. Ask for his mercy. Ask him to give you the proper understanding of the balance between his justice and his mercy in the world.

LIVE

When you are tempted to sin today, be aware of how your rebellion angers the heart of God.

GOD SHOWS UP

ZEPHANIAH 2:3,6-10

³ Seek the LORD, all you humble of the land,
  who do his just commands;
seek righteousness; seek humility;
  perhaps you may be hidden
  on the day of the anger of the LORD. . . .

⁶ And you, O seacoast, shall be pastures,
  with meadows for shepherds
  and folds for flocks.
⁷ The seacoast shall become the possession
  of the remnant of the house of Judah,
  on which they shall graze,
and in the houses of Ashkelon
  they shall lie down at evening.
For the LORD their God will be mindful of them
  and restore their fortunes.

⁸ "I have heard the taunts of Moab
  and the revilings of the Ammonites,
how they have taunted my people
  and made boasts against their territory.
⁹ Therefore, as I live," declares the LORD of hosts,
  the God of Israel,
"Moab shall become like Sodom,
  and the Ammonites like Gomorrah,
a land possessed by nettles and salt pits,
  and a waste forever.
The remnant of my people shall plunder them,
  and the survivors of my nation shall possess them."
¹⁰ This shall be their lot in return for their pride,
  because they taunted and boasted
  against the people of the LORD of hosts.

READ

Read the passage aloud slowly and silently.

You've probably experienced the wrath of a bully. The nation of Moab had been bullying the nation of Judah. In this passage God says that he plans to sweep in and save Judah. The encouraging words in verses 6-7 are spoken of Judah; verses 8-10 are indictments of Moab to defend Judah.

THINK

Read the passage again, noting the primary sins of Moab. As you read, grieve over them:

- boasting, revilings, and taunts
- put-downs and pride

In what ways do these two sets of sins feed off each other?

When have you experienced such treatment? In what way did God intervene to rescue you? If you don't feel that God did so, take this rescue of Judah and appropriate it for yourself. This isn't fantasy—God did rescue you in some way, even if you didn't realize it.

PRAY

Thank God for rescuing you and providing moments of pastureland in your life. Ask God if he wants to use you to rescue someone. Listen for his guidance in doing so.

LIVE

Sit quietly before God. Feel in your gut the sensation of humiliation at someone else's prideful taunts. Then feel in your gut the sensations of safety and rescue. Understand that you are reliving Judah's experience.

AT HOME IN GOD

ZEPHANIAH 3:9-13

⁹ For at that time I will change the speech of the peoples
    to a pure speech,
that all of them may call upon the name of the Lᴏʀᴅ
    and serve him with one accord.
¹⁰ From beyond the rivers of Cush
    my worshipers, the daughter of my dispersed ones,
    shall bring my offering.

¹¹ On that day you shall not be put to shame
    because of the deeds by which you have rebelled against me;
for then I will remove from your midst
    your proudly exultant ones,
and you shall no longer be haughty
    in my holy mountain.
¹² But I will leave in your midst
    a people humble and lowly.
They shall seek refuge in the name of the Lᴏʀᴅ,
¹³   those who are left in Israel;
they shall do no injustice
    and speak no lies,
nor shall there be found in their mouth
    a deceitful tongue.
For they shall graze and lie down,
    and none shall make them afraid.

READ

Read this passage, carefully listening for what it tells you about sin's impact on our lives.

THINK

How does this passage fill out your perspective on sin — what it's like to live with it, and what it's like to live without it? How does our sin affect us? From Zephaniah's point of view, why does God want us not to sin?

PRAY

Reread Zephaniah's description of a life that is cleared of sin. How does it make you feel? Timid? Hopeful? Sad? Does it feel foreign and unfamiliar? Become aware of God's presence with you now, and expose to him your response to this vision of life. Explore with him why the passage makes you feel the way you do.

LIVE

Consider how God is responding to what you just shared with him. Return to the question, Why does God want us not to sin? Again ponder Zephaniah's answer to this, and let it form your understanding of God's response to you now. What does God desire for you? What kind of life does he want you to have?

TURNAROUND NEEDED

HAGGAI 1:3-6,8-11

³Then the word of the LORD came by the hand of Haggai the prophet, ⁴"Is it a time for you yourselves to dwell in your paneled houses, while this house lies in ruins? ⁵Now, therefore, thus says the LORD of hosts: Consider your ways. ⁶You have sown much, and harvested little. You eat, but you never have enough; you drink, but you never have your fill. You clothe yourselves, but no one is warm. And he who earns wages does so to put them into a bag with holes. . . .

⁸"Go up to the hills and bring wood and build the house, that I may take pleasure in it and that I may be glorified, says the LORD. ⁹You looked for much, and behold, it came to little. And when you brought it home, I blew it away. Why? declares the LORD of hosts. Because of my house that lies in ruins, while each of you busies himself with his own house. ¹⁰Therefore the heavens above you have withheld the dew, and the earth has withheld its produce. ¹¹And I have called for a drought on the land and the hills, on the grain, the new wine, the oil, on what the ground brings forth, on man and beast, and on all their labors."

READ

Read the passage aloud slowly. God isn't demanding that the returned exiles (the Jews) change a thing or two. Their entire lives need a turnaround.

THINK

Read the passage aloud again.

1. How would you describe the turnaround God wants from the returned exiles?
2. How does stinginess affect one's mind so that a life of misery is inevitable?
3. How does this passage speak to you today?

PRAY

Talk to God about any stinginess in your soul. If you find none, look at any misery in your life and ask God to show you if it relates to a stingy, grudging attitude.

LIVE

Sit in the feeling of generosity. Imagine yourself joyously cutting timber, building walls, and honoring God. See yourself living your life this way.

HANDING OUT GLORY AND PEACE

HAGGAI 2:1-9

¹In the seventh month, on the twenty-first day of the month, the word of the LORD came by the hand of Haggai the prophet, ²"Speak now to Zerubbabel the son of Shealtiel, governor of Judah, and to Joshua the son of Jehozadak, the high priest, and to all the remnant of the people, and say, ³'Who is left among you who saw this house in its former glory? How do you see it now? Is it not as nothing in your eyes? ⁴Yet now be strong, O Zerubbabel, declares the LORD. Be strong, O Joshua, son of Jehozadak, the high priest. Be strong, all you people of the land, declares the LORD. Work, for I am with you, declares the LORD of hosts, ⁵according to the covenant that I made with you when you came out of Egypt. My Spirit remains in your midst. Fear not. ⁶For thus says the LORD of hosts: Yet once more, in a little while, I will shake the heavens and the earth and the sea and the dry land. ⁷And I will shake all nations, so that the treasures of all nations shall come in, and I will fill this house with glory, says the LORD of hosts. ⁸The silver is mine, and the gold is mine, declares the LORD of hosts. ⁹The latter glory of this house shall be greater than the former, says the LORD of hosts. And in this place I will give peace, declares the LORD of hosts.'"

READ

Read the passage aloud, injecting the emotion of the characters as much as possible.

THINK

What stands out to you from the words of the Lord of Hosts? Perhaps it's God shaking all nations so that treasures come in, the words "fear not," or the recurring "be strong!" What does this draw your attention to about yourself, about God, and about the glory and peace God desires his people to have?

PRAY/LIVE

Let your heart get caught up in pondering this insight for a while, as though you are playing with Play-Doh. Reshape two or three experiences (past or current) by the mold of this perspective, and see what they look like. Specifically, what in your life might be helped by this glory and peace?

Now listen for God's input on your current situation(s), remaining in the mold of glory and peace. In what areas might he want you to change your mind-set or take a particular action?

THE PROACTIVE NATURE OF GOD

ZECHARIAH 2:1-5,10-13

¹And I lifted my eyes and saw, and behold, a man with a measuring line in his hand! ²Then I said, "Where are you going?" And he said to me, "To measure Jerusalem, to see what is its width and what is its length." ³And behold, the angel who talked with me came forward, and another angel came forward to meet him ⁴and said to him, "Run, say to that young man, 'Jerusalem shall be inhabited as villages without walls, because of the multitude of people and livestock in it. ⁵And I will be to her a wall of fire all around, declares the LORD, and I will be the glory in her midst.' " . . .

¹⁰Sing and rejoice, O daughter of Zion, for behold, I come and I will dwell in your midst, declares the LORD. ¹¹And many nations shall join themselves to the LORD in that day, and shall be my people. And I will dwell in your midst, and you shall know that the LORD of hosts has sent me to you. ¹²And the LORD will inherit Judah as his portion in the holy land, and will again choose Jerusalem."

¹³Be silent, all flesh, before the LORD, for he has roused himself from his holy dwelling.

READ
Read the passage.

THINK
The prophet Zechariah receives several visions from God and writes about them in detail at the beginning of his book. Take the next several minutes to ponder this vision. In the interaction God says, "Sing and rejoice, O daughter of Zion, for behold, I come and I will dwell in your midst" (verse 10). Consider God's incredible plan to send his Son, Jesus, to live among us. What comes to mind as you think about God's pursuing his people enough to dwell in their midst?

"Be silent, all flesh, before the LORD, for he has roused himself from his holy dwelling" (verse 13). What fills your mind as you consider that God is active in human history? How is that reality different from what other people, the media, and our culture say about God's involvement in the world?

What does God's activity say about his character? How do you respond to this type of God?

PRAY
Allow the reality of a loving God pursuing his people, on the move and moving into your neighborhood, guide your prayers right now.

What would your world be like if God moved into the house, apartment, or building next door to you? Allow your communication with God to flow out of your thoughts.

LIVE
As you walk or drive in your neighborhood, consider the implications for your life of having God residing in your — our! — midst. And thank God for the fact that he actively pursues you.

DAY 196

GOD ENCOUNTERS
On this seventh day, review and reflect on all you have read this week. Take the time to revel in the ways you've encountered God in the past six days.

SHOW KINDNESS AND MERCY

ZECHARIAH 7:4-10

[4]Then the word of the LORD of hosts came to me: [5]"Say to all the people of the land and the priests, When you fasted and mourned in the fifth month and in the seventh, for these seventy years, was it for me that you fasted? [6]And when you eat and when you drink, do you not eat for yourselves and drink for yourselves? [7]Were not these the words that the LORD proclaimed by the former prophets, when Jerusalem was inhabited and prosperous, with her cities around her, and the South and the lowland were inhabited?"

[8]And the word of the LORD came to Zechariah, saying, [9]"Thus says the LORD of hosts, Render true judgments, show kindness and mercy to one another, [10]do not oppress the widow, the fatherless, the sojourner, or the poor, and let none of you devise evil against another in your heart."

READ

Read the passage aloud slowly.

THINK

Read the passage aloud again.

1. If God were looking directly at you and saying these verses, what would he mean by the phrase, "Was it for me that you fasted?"
2. Who do you know needing justice, love, and compassion?
3. Which of your religious activities do you think might merely be meeting your own selfish needs? Examine them.

PRAY

Thank God for being interested in people. Admit any ideas you have that God is mostly interested in church programs and what church people are supposed to do.

LIVE

Imagine God being interested in you just because you're you. Now imagine God being interested in someone you don't find interesting. Wonder at that.

ANNULLING THE COVENANT

ZECHARIAH 11:4-11

⁴Thus said the LORD my God: "Become shepherd of the flock doomed to slaughter. ⁵Those who buy them slaughter them and go unpunished, and those who sell them say, 'Blessed be the LORD, I have become rich,' and their own shepherds have no pity on them. ⁶For I will no longer have pity on the inhabitants of this land, declares the LORD. Behold, I will cause each of them to fall into the hand of his neighbor, and each into the hand of his king, and they shall crush the land, and I will deliver none from their hand."

⁷So I became the shepherd of the flock doomed to be slaughtered by the sheep traders. And I took two staffs, one I named Favor, the other I named Union. And I tended the sheep. ⁸In one month I destroyed the three shepherds. But I became impatient with them, and they also detested me. ⁹So I said, "I will not be your shepherd. What is to die, let it die. What is to be destroyed, let it be destroyed. And let those who are left devour the flesh of one another." ¹⁰And I took my staff Favor, and I broke it, annulling the covenant that I had made with all the peoples. ¹¹So it was annulled on that day, and the sheep traders, who were watching me, knew that it was the word of the LORD.

READ

Read the passage several times slowly, until you begin to grasp the symbolism and what's going on.

THINK

When you consider the consequences God allows to come to Israel for their continual disobedience to him, what stands out to you? Why do you think God would allow such horrible things to happen to them? What does this have to do with you?

PRAY

Read the passage again, prayerfully. What about God does it highlight? What words or actions especially draw your attention when you consider your life in light of this passage?

LIVE

Consider the following extract from Jan Karon's *These High, Green Hills:*

> "There's something I've been wanting to ask you, Father," said Nurse Kennedy, walking with him along the hall.
> "Shoot."
> "Why is it God so often breaks our hearts?"
> "Well, sometimes He does it to increase our faith. That's the way He stretches us. But there's another reason, I think, why our hearts get broken."
> She looked at him.
> "Usually," he said, "what breaks is what's brittle."[12]

In what area has your heart become brittle toward God? Have you been trying to protect your heart from him? If so, why? Don't put pressure on yourself to change this: There is probably some reason you have felt the need to protect yourself. But today, with God's help, become aware of it, and explore with him what might happen if you trust him with that area of your heart.

DAY 199
EXPANDED PASSAGE: MALACHI 1

A REMINDER OF GOD'S MESSAGE OF LOVE

MALACHI 1:1-5

¹The oracle of the word of the LORD to Israel by Malachi.

²"I have loved you," says the LORD. But you say, "How have you loved us?" "Is not Esau Jacob's brother?" declares the LORD. "Yet I have loved Jacob ³but Esau I have hated. I have laid waste his hill country and left his heritage to jackals of the desert." ⁴If Edom says, "We are shattered but we will rebuild the ruins," the LORD of hosts says, "They may build, but I will tear down, and they will be called 'the wicked country,' and 'the people with whom the LORD is angry forever.'" ⁵Your own eyes shall see this, and you shall say, "Great is the LORD beyond the border of Israel!"

READ

Before reading, close your eyes and pay attention to your breathing. After a few minutes of this silence, whisper, "God, I'm ready to hear from you now. Speak and I will listen."

Then turn to the book of Malachi and read the first five verses.

THINK

God's overriding message to his people, evident throughout all the books of Scripture, is this: "I love you." But our muddled and complex lives blur that Message, and we forget the power of it. We need constant reminders of what's important in life, and history is an important reminder of God's incredible love for us. Looking back on the past can help provide the clarity and focus we've lost and give us back a God-minded perspective.

LIVE

Write out the ways God has been faithful to you in the past — big and small — through your relationships, your circumstances, your family, the blessings he has provided, important events, and so on.

Take as much time as you need.

PRAY

Reread verse 5: "Your own eyes shall see this, and you shall say, 'Great is the LORD beyond the border of Israel!'" Follow these instructions. Pray through your list line by line. Pour out your heart to God in unabashed gratefulness. Thank him for his faithfulness throughout your life and throughout the lives of many others.

GIVE LIFE AND PEACE

MALACHI 2:5-10

⁵"My covenant with him was one of life and peace, and I gave them to him. It was a covenant of fear, and he feared me. He stood in awe of my name. ⁶True instruction was in his mouth, and no wrong was found on his lips. He walked with me in peace and uprightness, and he turned many from iniquity. ⁷For the lips of a priest should guard knowledge, and people should seek instruction from his mouth, for he is the messenger of the Lord of hosts. ⁸But you have turned aside from the way. You have caused many to stumble by your instruction. You have corrupted the covenant of Levi, says the Lord of hosts, ⁹and so I make you despised and abased before all the people, inasmuch as you do not keep my ways but show partiality in your instruction."

¹⁰Have we not all one Father? Has not one God created us? Why then are we faithless to one another, profaning the covenant of our fathers?

READ

Read the passage aloud slowly.

THINK

Read the passage aloud again, but this time substitute the word *Christian* everywhere the word *priest* appears, because Peter said, as he spoke to Christians, "But you are a chosen race, a royal priesthood, a holy nation, a people for his own possession that you may proclaim the excellencies of him who called you out of darkness into his marvelous light. Once you were not a people, but now you are God's people; once you had not received mercy, but now you have received mercy" (1 Peter 2:9-10).

1. In what ways do you enjoy the work of a priest?

   ☐ giving life and peace
   ☐ keeping covenant with God
   ☐ honoring God and standing in reverent awe before God
   ☐ teaching truth and not lies
   ☐ walking with God in peace and uprightness
   ☐ turning people from iniquity
   ☐ other:

2. In what ways do Christians mess up many lives and make people despise them, not living as God says and not teaching God's truth impartially?

3. In what areas of your life do you need more of God's help to be a priest for him?

PRAY

Tell God how you feel about being chosen to be a "royal priesthood." Admit your faults and doubts. Feel the joy of being used by God, even if you don't do it perfectly.

LIVE

Imagine God anointing you anew as a priest to give others "life and peace" from God.

FIT FOR GOD

MALACHI 3:1-5

¹Behold, I send my messenger, and he will prepare the way before me. And the Lord whom you seek will suddenly come to his temple; and the messenger of the covenant in whom you delight, behold, he is coming, says the LORD of hosts. ²But who can endure the day of his coming, and who can stand when he appears? For he is like a refiner's fire and like fullers' soap. ³He will sit as a refiner and purifier of silver, and he will purify the sons of Levi and refine them like gold and silver, and they will bring offerings in righteousness to the LORD. ⁴Then the offering of Judah and Jerusalem will be pleasing to the LORD as in the days of old and as in former years.

⁵Then I will draw near to you for judgment. I will be a swift witness against the sorcerers, against the adulterers, against those who swear falsely, against those who oppress the hired worker in his wages, the widow and the fatherless, against those who thrust aside the sojourner, and do not fear me, says the LORD of hosts.

THINK

Saint Irenaeus once said, "The glory of God is man fully alive." For a few minutes, isolate the second half of this statement and think about what it means to be "fully alive." Have you ever felt this way? When? What were you doing?

READ

Now read the passage (including the expanded passage for background). Do the words *purify* and *pleasing* have positive or negative implications to you? How do they intermingle with your idea of being fully alive? Do they act like pins to a balloon? Or do they mesh organically into the bigger picture?

PRAY

With your understanding of being fully alive in one hand and your awareness of God's desire for your purity in the other, explore how much you do or do not see the two connecting. Maybe you can easily see God's presence with you in your picture of yourself fully alive, or maybe that's hard to do; maybe you think living fully must be done behind God's back. Be honest — even if you recognize that your beliefs are not true, tell the truth of what's in your heart.

LIVE

Sit quietly with God, opening yourself to what he might want to say in response to what you've shared with him today. You might look back at the passage or reconsider Irenaeus's words. Wonder at the freedom intrinsic in someone who is fully alive *and* pure before God.

THE TESTAMENTS, OLD AND NEW

MATTHEW 2:1-6

¹Now after Jesus was born in Bethlehem of Judea in the days of Herod the king, behold, wise men from the east came to Jerusalem, ²saying, "Where is he who has been born king of the Jews? For we saw his star when it rose and have come to worship him." ³When Herod the king heard this, he was troubled, and all Jerusalem with him; ⁴and assembling all the chief priests and scribes of the people, he inquired of them where the Christ was to be born. ⁵They told him, "In Bethlehem of Judea, for so it is written by the prophet:

6   "'And you, O Bethlehem, in the land of Judah,
        are by no means least among the rulers of Judah;
    for from you shall come a ruler
        who will shepherd my people Israel.'"

READ

Read the passage, trying to absorb the words from the perspective of a Jew who has never heard of Jesus before.

THINK

In his gospel, Matthew emphasizes the number of Old Testament prophecies fulfilled in the person of Jesus. The Jewish people longed to see the Messiah, the Anointed One, whom they had been expecting for several hundred years. Jesus, Matthew writes, is the one they had been waiting for.

Read the passage again, and note the Old Testament quotation. How do you feel, knowing that God orchestrated these happenings to point to Jesus?

What promises has God made to you, in Scripture or personally, that have yet to come to fruition? Do you wonder if they will ever be fulfilled?

How does Matthew's focus on Old Testament prophecies affect your situation? What implication does it have on your daily life?

PRAY

Take time to thank God for the promises he has kept in your life. Ask God to give you an extra measure of faith to trust him when you feel he may never keep his other promises to you. Admit the specific areas where you have a hard time trusting that he will be faithful.

LIVE

God keeps his promises. Live in the truth that he is a promise keeper.

DAY 203

GOD ENCOUNTERS

On this seventh day, review and reflect on all you have read this week. Take the time to revel in the ways you've encountered God in the past six days.

DAY 204

EXPANDED PASSAGE: MATTHEW 5

LIVE BEFORE GOD

MATTHEW 5:27-29,33-37

²⁷You have heard that it was said, "You shall not commit adultery." ²⁸But I say to you that everyone who looks at a woman with lustful intent has already committed adultery with her in his heart. ²⁹If your right eye causes you to sin, tear it out and throw it away. For it is better that you lose one of your members than that your whole body be thrown into hell. . . .

³³Again you have heard that it was said to those of old, "You shall not swear falsely, but shall perform to the Lord what you have sworn." ³⁴But I say to you, Do not take an oath at all, either by heaven, for it is the throne of God, ³⁵or by the earth, for it is his footstool, or by Jerusalem, for it is the city of the great King. ³⁶And do not take an oath by your head, for you cannot make one hair white or black. ³⁷Let what you say be simply "Yes" or "No"; anything more than this comes from evil.

READ

Read the passage aloud slowly.

THINK

Imagine yourself going to the mailbox today and finding in it a letter addressed to you, containing the words of this passage. Think of yourself opening the letter. Then read the passage aloud again, and as you do, see yourself walking back from the mailbox.

1. What meaning do the words have for you? What is Jesus getting at?
2. How do you pretend having a pure thought life or meaning what you say is easier than it is?
3. How do these commands speak to the deepest part of you, the part Jesus wants?

PRAY

Ask Jesus to show you situations in which you are likely to say something you don't mean. Ask him to help you discover what that's about — perhaps impressing people or pretending to be better than you are.

LIVE

Jesus understands how difficult his words are for us. Sense yourself being pulled along with love and grace by Jesus.

PRAY WITH SIMPLICITY

MATTHEW 6:5-13

[5]And when you pray, you must not be like the hypocrites. For they love to stand and pray in the synagogues and at the street corners, that they may be seen by others. Truly, I say to you, they have received their reward. [6]But when you pray, go into your room and shut the door and pray to your Father who is in secret. And your Father who sees in secret will reward you.

[7]And when you pray, do not heap up empty phrases as the Gentiles do, for they think that they will be heard for their many words. [8]Do not be like them, for your Father knows what you need before you ask him. [9]Pray then like this:

> Our Father in heaven,
> hallowed be your name.
> [10] Your kingdom come,
> your will be done,
> on earth as it is in heaven.
> [11] Give us this day our daily bread,
> [12] and forgive us our debts,
> as we also have forgiven our debtors.
> [13] And lead us not into temptation,
> but deliver us from evil.

READ

Read the passage aloud slowly, noticing what it says about simple prayer versus complex, showy prayer. What is the most important issue for you listed below? Be honest.

Simple Prayer	Complex, Showy Prayer
finding a private place	turning prayer into a public production
pray to the Father in secret	praying to be seen by others
being with God as simply and honestly as you can	using empty phrases and many words
watching the focus shift from you to God	using techniques to get what you want from God

THINK

Read the passage again. This time, picture yourself sitting with other people about six feet from Jesus and listening as he says these words. When does Jesus look directly at you as he teaches? What words is he saying because he knows you need them? Why are those words meant for you?

PRAY

Paraphrase the Lord's Prayer (verses 9-13). In other words, add to or change each phrase in a way that makes the prayer specific to you.

LIVE

Sit quietly before God, praying the Lord's Prayer if you wish, or just being silent. Feel the focus shift from you to God. Enjoy that.

AN INVITATION

MATTHEW 9:9-13

[9]As Jesus passed on from there, he saw a man called Matthew sitting at the tax booth, and he said to him, "Follow me." And he rose and followed him.

[10]And as Jesus reclined at table in the house, behold, many tax collectors and sinners came and were reclining with Jesus and his disciples. [11]And when the Pharisees saw this, they said to his disciples, "Why does your teacher eat with tax collectors and sinners?" [12]But when he heard it, he said, "Those who are well have no need of a physician, but those who are sick. [13]Go and learn what this means, 'I desire mercy, and not sacrifice.' For I came not to call the righteous, but sinners."

READ

Once you are in a quiet place, thank God for the gift of his Word. Then read the passage.

THINK

When have you felt like the outsider? When have people scrutinized and criticized you for the people you associated with? Do you think their judgment was fair? Why or why not?

Ponder these words from Jesus: "'I desire mercy, and not sacrifice.' For I came not to call the righteous, but sinners." Where do you think Jesus was going with this statement?

If you were present that day, how might have you responded?

PRAY

Hold your hands open in front of you. Sit in silence for several moments, staring at them. Invite the Holy Spirit to guide your life today. Pray that your hands will be a physical representation of what you desire your heart to be. Acknowledge that you are a physical open invitation to the Holy Spirit for his guidance toward paths of mercy, not religiosity. Ask him to bring to mind outsiders to whom you can show mercy today.

LIVE

As you are reminded of God's mercy on your life, take the risk of showing mercy to outsiders.

JESUS THE HEALER

MATTHEW 9:18-26

[18]While he was saying these things to them, behold, a ruler came in and knelt before him, saying, "My daughter has just died, but come and lay your hand on her, and she will live." [19]And Jesus rose and followed him, with his disciples. [20]And behold, a woman who had suffered from a discharge of blood for twelve years came up behind him and touched the fringe of his garment, [21]for she said to herself, "If I only touch his garment, I will be made well." [22]Jesus turned, and seeing her he said, "Take heart, daughter; your faith has made you well." And instantly the woman was made well. [23]And when Jesus came to the ruler's house and saw the flute players and the crowd making a commotion, [24]he said, "Go away, for the girl is not dead but sleeping." And they laughed at him. [25]But when the crowd had been put outside, he went in and took her by the hand, and the girl arose. [26]And the report of this went through all that district.

READ

Read the passage.

THINK/PRAY

Pick the episode that is more striking to you — either the healing of the hemorrhaging woman or the raising of the ruler's daughter. (If you choose the first story, read Leviticus 15:25-30 now to better understand her situation.)

Read the passage again, carefully. Immerse yourself in the story as though you are a character in it — an observer or one named in the passage. Use every sense to enter the scene; take part in each moment. Where are you in relation to others? To Jesus? What is it like for you to be there? How are you feeling?

After you exit the scene, talk with Jesus about what you saw and experienced.

LIVE

Think about your experience in the scene, as well as your discussion with Jesus, and jot down anything you want to remember.

Put your pen aside and sit quietly for a few minutes. Listen to the sound of your own breathing and the silence.

End by saying the Lord's Prayer aloud: "Our Father in heaven, hallowed be your name. Your kingdom come, your will be done, on earth as it is in heaven. Give us this day our daily bread, and forgive us our debts, as we also have forgiven our debtors. And lead us not into temptation, but deliver us from evil" (Matthew 6:9-13).

COME TO ME

MATTHEW 11:28-30

[28]Come to me, all who labor and are heavy laden, and I will give you rest. [29]Take my yoke upon you, and learn from me, for I am gentle and lowly in heart, and you will find rest for your souls. [30]For my yoke is easy, and my burden is light.

READ
Read the passage slowly.

THINK
Read the passage again, listening for the words or phrases that stand out to you, such as:

- "come to me"
- "I will give you rest"
- "real rest"
- "take my yoke upon you"
- "I am gentle and lowly in heart"
- "my burden is light"

Notice the many different ways Jesus says, "Hang out with me." Which one do you find most inviting? Why?

What would it feel like to walk with Jesus and work with him? It's okay to be honest; "easy" and "light" may not describe what you think it would really be like. Instead you might think it would be forced and difficult. If so, what would you *desire* for it to be like?

Have you feared that a walk with Jesus might require heavy or ill-fitting things? What are they?

PRAY
Jesus speaks very personally and conversationally in this passage, using phrases like "Come to me." In fact, *I, my* or *me* occurs seven times, and *you* or *your* occurs four times. So consider that Jesus has been talking to *you*. What is your reply? What do you need to discuss with Jesus today?

LIVE
Walk with Jesus, either in your mind or on an actual walk. As you do, turn these words from Jesus over in your mind: *rest, gently, learn from me, easy, light*.

SEEING AND HEARING

MATTHEW 13:10-17

¹⁰Then the disciples came and said to him, "Why do you speak to them in parables?" ¹¹And he answered them, "To you it has been given to know the secrets of the kingdom of heaven, but to them it has not been given. ¹²For to the one who has, more will be given, and he will have an abundance, but from the one who has not, even what he has will be taken away. ¹³This is why I speak to them in parables, because seeing they do not see, and hearing they do not hear, nor do they understand. ¹⁴Indeed, in their case the prophecy of Isaiah is fulfilled that says:

> " 'You will indeed hear but never understand,
>   and you will indeed see but never perceive.
> ¹⁵ For this people's heart has grown dull,
>   and with their ears they can barely hear,
>   and their eyes they have closed,
> lest they should see with their eyes
>   and hear with their ears
> and understand with their heart
>   and turn, and I would heal them.'

¹⁶But blessed are your eyes, for they see, and your ears, for they hear. ¹⁷For truly, I say to you, many prophets and righteous people longed to see what you see, and did not see it, and to hear what you hear, and did not hear it."

READ

Read the passage carefully.

THINK

Notice what Jesus says about human hearts. What does he draw attention to about our receptivity to his message? How does he deal with our resistance? What does he want for us?

Now read Jesus' words again, and hear them as if he is saying them to you personally. Meditate on his words until the message becomes familiar. What stands out that relates to your life?

PRAY

Tell Jesus about your meditation — your thoughts and feelings. Listen for his response.

LIVE

Search your memory (or your journal) for any insights God has given you in recent weeks as you have interacted with his Word. What have those truths led you to do? Were there times when God invited you to act on or think about something, but you ignored the request or put it off? Why? Revisit that experience with Jesus. Remember that his greatest desire is not to get you to act a certain way but to engage with you in relationship.

DAY 210

GOD ENCOUNTERS

On this seventh day, review and reflect on all you have read this week. Take the time to revel in the ways you've encountered God in the past six days.

A MATTER OF THE HEART

MATTHEW 15:1-14

¹Then Pharisees and scribes came to Jesus from Jerusalem and said, ²"Why do your disciples break the tradition of the elders? For they do not wash their hands when they eat." ³He answered them, "And why do you break the commandment of God for the sake of your tradition? ⁴For God commanded, 'Honor your father and your mother,' and, 'Whoever reviles father or mother must surely die.' ⁵But you say, 'If anyone tells his father or his mother, "What you would have gained from me is given to God," ⁶he need not honor his father.' So for the sake of your tradition you have made void the word of God. ⁷You hypocrites! Well did Isaiah prophesy of you, when he said:

⁸ "'This people honors me with their lips,
       but their heart is far from me;
⁹   in vain do they worship me,
       teaching as doctrines the commandments of men.'"

¹⁰And he called the people to him and said to them, "Hear and understand: ¹¹it is not what goes into the mouth that defiles a person, but what comes out of the mouth; this defiles a person." ¹²Then the disciples came and said to him, "Do you know that the Pharisees were offended when they heard this saying?" ¹³He answered, "Every plant that my heavenly Father has not planted will be rooted up. ¹⁴Let them alone; they are blind guides. And if the blind lead the blind, both will fall into a pit."

READ

Sit at a table with this devotional. Read this passage with your palms open as a way of communicating that you are open to hear from God.

THINK

Jesus seems to spend a lot of time provoking the Pharisees by speaking harshly to them. Of all the religious groups in Israel, Jesus rebukes the Pharisees the most. And yet, these are supposed to be the most devout leaders in the entire nation. Joining Jesus in bashing the Pharisees is tempting. Thinking *I'm glad I'm not like them* is easy. But we often resemble the Pharisees more than we'd like to admit.

Think back and identify a time when your heart responded to Jesus the way the Pharisees responded to him. What might help you identify the moments when your heart is more Pharisee-like than Jesus-like? Who can you invite to help keep your heart in check?

Ponder the words Matthew quotes from Isaiah (verses 8-9). Under what circumstances does this describe you? What do you think God wants you to do about it?

PRAY

Ask God to give you a Jesus-like heart, one that is humble, transparent, and genuine.

LIVE

Invite others to help you keep your heart in check by giving them permission to ask you tough heart questions.

THE SOFTENED HEART

MATTHEW 19:3-9

³And Pharisees came up to him and tested him by asking, "Is it lawful to divorce one's wife for any cause?" ⁴He answered, "Have you not read that he who created them from the beginning made them male and female, ⁵and said, 'Therefore a man shall leave his father and his mother and hold fast to his wife, and the two shall become one flesh'? ⁶So they are no longer two but one flesh. What therefore God has joined together, let not man separate." ⁷They said to him, "Why then did Moses command one to give a certificate of divorce and to send her away?" ⁸He said to them, "Because of your hardness of heart Moses allowed you to divorce your wives, but from the beginning it was not so. ⁹And I say to you: whoever divorces his wife, except for sexual immorality, and marries another, commits adultery."

READ

Read the passage aloud slowly. Consider that this teaching is an example Jesus gave from a longer teaching about forgiveness.

THINK

Matthew recorded this to come just after Jesus tells the parable about the servant who is forgiven a great deal and cannot forgive someone who has harmed him only slightly.

Imagine that you are there as Jesus is teaching. You've heard his parable about the unforgiving servant, and now he speaks of people being hardhearted. As you read the passage again, consider that we divorce ourselves from people in many ways — leaving a church, leaving a project, leaving a friendship. (If you wish, read Matthew 18:23-35 or try to recall the parable of the unforgiving servant. Try to feel for yourself that servant's incredible hardheartedness.)

1. What is hardheartedness really about?
2. How does hardheartedness toward others violate God's will for all of us?
3. Where in your life is hardheartedness a problem?
4. What is God urging you to do to cultivate a softened heart?

PRAY

Ask God to bring to mind those who might want to plead with you, "Have patience with me" (see Matthew 18:26,29). Try to picture yourself having mercy on this person. If it seems impossible, ask God to pour out his love into your heart.

LIVE

Sit quietly before God. Become hardhearted — how does this feel in your body? Become softhearted — how does that feel in your body? Stay with the softheartedness for several minutes.

JESUS DROVE THEM OUT

MATTHEW 21:12-17

¹²And Jesus entered the temple and drove out all who sold and bought in the temple, and he overturned the tables of the money-changers and the seats of those who sold pigeons. ¹³He said to them, "It is written, 'My house shall be called a house of prayer,' but you make it a den of robbers."

¹⁴And the blind and the lame came to him in the temple, and he healed them. ¹⁵But when the chief priests and the scribes saw the wonderful things that he did, and the children crying out in the temple, "Hosanna to the Son of David!" they were indignant, ¹⁶and they said to him, "Do you hear what these are saying?" And Jesus said to them, "Yes; have you never read,

"'Out of the mouth of infants and nursing babies
   you have prepared praise'?"

¹⁷And leaving them, he went out of the city to Bethany and lodged there.

READ

Read the passage aloud.

THINK/PRAY

Imagine you are there when Jesus comes in the temple and cleanses it. To get your imagination going, read the passage a second time, but then set this book aside, close your eyes, and see yourself as a part of the scene.

Who are you? Where are you? Smell the incense and the scent of burning, sacrificed animal flesh. Jump at the loud crash of the tables and the fury in Jesus' voice as the sounds echo in the stunned silence. What are the expressions on the faces around you?

Now let the blind and crippled come into your view. Watch Jesus healing them. Listen to the voices of the children as they play and shout, "Hosanna!" What's your reaction to them? To Jesus' interaction with the disabled? To the indignation of the religious leaders? (Include not only your mental reaction but your physical reaction too, if any.)

Now follow Jesus as he walks out of the city, still fuming. Picture him initiating a conversation with you about the events of the day. Imagine that he asks you what it was like. Tell him.

LIVE

In C. S. Lewis's *The Lion, the Witch and the Wardrobe,* the lion, Aslan, "isn't safe. But he's good."[13]

Consider this statement in light of what you've just read about Jesus. How does this view of Jesus—that he sometimes does things that are painful to us—alter your perception of who he is? In what ways does this affect how you relate to him?

THE LEAST OF THESE

MATTHEW 25:31-40

[31]When the Son of Man comes in his glory, and all the angels with him, then he will sit on his glorious throne. [32]Before him will be gathered all the nations, and he will separate people one from another as a shepherd separates the sheep from the goats. [33]And he will place the sheep on his right, but the goats on the left. [34]Then the King will say to those on his right, "Come, you who are blessed by my Father, inherit the kingdom prepared for you from the foundation of the world. [35]For I was hungry and you gave me food, I was thirsty and you gave me drink, I was a stranger and you welcomed me, [36]I was naked and you clothed me, I was sick and you visited me, I was in prison and you came to me." [37]Then the righteous will answer him, saying, "Lord, when did we see you hungry and feed you, or thirsty and give you drink? [38]And when did we see you a stranger and welcome you, or naked and clothe you? [39]And when did we see you sick or in prison and visit you?" [40]And the King will answer them, "Truly, I say to you, as you did it to one of the least of these my brothers, you did it to me."

READ

Read the passage aloud slowly. As you read it, understand that Jesus said these words aloud too. They are his words.

THINK

This is a part of an entire sermon (or thematic sermon series) on watchfulness (see Matthew 23–25). The people in this passage were watching for the needy, but they didn't know it was Jesus they were watching. Read the passage again silently and slowly.

1. What words or phrases stand out to you?
2. Who are the least of these in your life?
3. Imagine yourself overlooked and ignored. What do you now have in common with Jesus?
4. In what ways is God asking you to give someone food, drink, a room, clothes; to stop and visit someone; to go to a person locked away physically, emotionally, or mentally?

PRAY

Ask Jesus how he exists in the overlooked and ignored, or the "least of these." Ponder this mystery. Ask him to show you your next step in grasping some part of this.

LIVE

As you serve people who are overlooked and ignored, be mindful of the presence of Jesus. See if you can spot him.

MY GOD, WHY?

MATTHEW 27:45-54

⁴⁵Now from the sixth hour there was darkness over all the land until the ninth hour. ⁴⁶And about the ninth hour Jesus cried out with a loud voice, saying, "Eli, Eli, lema sabachthani?" that is, "My God, my God, why have you forsaken me?" ⁴⁷And some of the bystanders, hearing it, said, "This man is calling Elijah." ⁴⁸And one of them at once ran and took a sponge, filled it with sour wine, and put it on a reed and gave it to him to drink. ⁴⁹But the others said, "Wait, let us see whether Elijah will come to save him." ⁵⁰And Jesus cried out again with a loud voice and yielded up his spirit.

⁵¹And behold, the curtain of the temple was torn in two, from top to bottom. And the earth shook, and the rocks were split. ⁵²The tombs also were opened. And many bodies of the saints who had fallen asleep were raised, ⁵³and coming out of the tombs after his resurrection they went into the holy city and appeared to many. ⁵⁴When the centurion and those who were with him, keeping watch over Jesus, saw the earthquake and what took place, they were filled with awe and said, "Truly this was the Son of God!"

READ

If you have time, read Matthew 26:31–27:56. If not, read the shorter passage.

THINK

Church historian Bruce Shelley wrote, "Christianity is the only major religion to have as its central event the humiliation of its God."[14] Consider not only that Jesus' humiliation is immense, but his anguish is deeper than we can imagine. His own people wildly demanded his death. His friends deserted him. And now even his intimately loving Father has turned away.

Spend time wrestling heart and mind with why the Almighty would choose such a path. Reread Jesus' own words a few times to get closer to his experience.

PRAY

What wells up inside you as you spend time with the paradox of Jesus' death? Wonder? Grief? Distractedness? Tell Jesus about what surfaces. Then gently pull your thoughts back to his sacrifice and death, reading the passage again if you need to. Allow yourself to sink into the event deeply, again being aware of your reaction and talking to Jesus about it.

LIVE

Find a new place to be silent. For example, walk in a quiet place or sit in an empty church sanctuary. Bring your wristwatch or cell phone and set the alarm so you can forget the time until it reminds you. Meditate on Jesus' sacrifice for you, then wait for what he would have you receive from him.

PARALYZED AND DESPERATE

MARK 2:1-12

[1]And when he returned to Capernaum after some days, it was reported that he was at home. [2]And many were gathered together, so that there was no more room, not even at the door. And he was preaching the word to them. [3]And they came, bringing to him a paralytic carried by four men. [4]And when they could not get near him because of the crowd, they removed the roof above him, and when they had made an opening, they let down the bed on which the paralytic lay. [5]And when Jesus saw their faith, he said to the paralytic, "Son, your sins are forgiven." [6]Now some of the scribes were sitting there, questioning in their hearts, [7]"Why does this man speak like that? He is blaspheming! Who can forgive sins but God alone?" [8]And immediately Jesus, perceiving in his spirit that they thus questioned within themselves, said to them, "Why do you question these things in your hearts? [9]Which is easier, to say to the paralytic, 'Your sins are forgiven,' or to say, 'Rise, take up your bed and walk'? [10]But that you may know that the Son of Man has authority on earth to forgive sins"—he said to the paralytic—[11]"I say to you, rise, pick up your bed, and go home." [12]And he rose and immediately picked up his bed and went out before them all, so that they were all amazed and glorified God, saying, "We never saw anything like this!"

READ

Ask a friend or family member to read the verses aloud to you. Close your eyes and listen intently.

THINK

Imagine yourself in the story, referring to the text again as much as you need to. For a few minutes each, place yourself in the skins of the different individuals. Consider yourself on the roof with the four friends and the paralytic. Become the crippled man on the mat. Think of yourself as one of the four friends. Imagine yourself as someone standing in the crowded room of the house, able to easily see and hear the Pharisees. And consider yourself the owner of the house.

With which person in the story do you identify the most? Why?

PRAY

Imagine yourself again as the paralytic lying on his stretcher. Jesus looks at you and says, "Son, your sins are forgiven." What is the expression on his face? What is the tone of his voice? What are you feeling when you hear those words?

Talk to Jesus about his actions and your reactions — mental, emotional, physical, spiritual.

LIVE

Consider those people around you who need a life-altering interaction with Jesus. What might you need to do to bring them to the feet of Jesus, even if it means making a big sacrifice for them?

DAY 217

GOD ENCOUNTERS

On this seventh day, review and reflect on all you have read this week. Take the time to revel in the ways you've encountered God in the past six days.

TELLING YOUR WHOLE TRUTH

MARK 5:25-34

²⁵And there was a woman who had had a discharge of blood for twelve years, ²⁶and who had suffered much under many physicians, and had spent all that she had, and was no better but rather grew worse. ²⁷She had heard the reports about Jesus and came up behind him in the crowd and touched his garment. ²⁸For she said, "If I touch even his garments, I will be made well." ²⁹And immediately the flow of blood dried up, and she felt in her body that she was healed of her disease. ³⁰And Jesus, perceiving in himself that power had gone out from him, immediately turned about in the crowd and said, "Who touched my garments?" ³¹And his disciples said to him, "You see the crowd pressing around you, and yet you say, 'Who touched me?'" ³²And he looked around to see who had done it. ³³But the woman, knowing what had happened to her, came in fear and trembling and fell down before him and told him the whole truth. ³⁴And he said to her, "Daughter, your faith has made you well; go in peace, and be healed of your disease."

READ

Read the passage aloud slowly.

THINK

Read the passage again, putting yourself in the place of the woman. (If it helps to imagine yourself instead as a man with an oozing sore, that's fine.)

1. From where did you get the courage to come behind Jesus and touch his clothes?
2. When Jesus looks at you, how do you feel?
3. How does it feel for you to tell Jesus your whole truth — and for him to listen so well? (Read in the expanded passage how he also listens well when he has a little girl to heal.)
4. How does it feel to be complimented publicly by this holy man?

PRAY

Tell Jesus the "whole truth" about something that's troubling you. Kneel as the woman did. Let the eyes of Jesus rest on you and bless you.

LIVE

Get up from your kneeling position and then sit or stand. Close your eyes and sense that you are healed and going in peace.

FALLING AT HIS FEET

MARK 7:24-30

²⁴And from there he arose and went away to the region of Tyre and Sidon. And he entered a house and did not want anyone to know, yet he could not be hidden. ²⁵But immediately a woman whose little daughter had an unclean spirit heard of him and came and fell down at his feet. ²⁶Now the woman was a Gentile, a Syrophoenician by birth. And she begged him to cast the demon out of her daughter. ²⁷And he said to her, "Let the children be fed first, for it is not right to take the children's bread and throw it to the dogs." ²⁸But she answered him, "Yes, Lord; yet even the dogs under the table eat the children's crumbs." ²⁹And he said to her, "For this statement you may go your way; the demon has left your daughter." ³⁰And she went home and found the child lying in bed and the demon gone.

READ

Read the expanded passage to get the big picture in which this incident occurs. As you do, identify with Jesus' disciples: Witness his amazing miracles. Feel the exhaustion of not even having time to eat. See the people constantly pressing in on all sides.

Now reread the shorter passage. What is your reaction to the Greek woman's request? How do you feel when Jesus initially turns her down? When he changes his mind?

THINK

Pause to allow the Holy Spirit to help you understand what your initial reactions tell you about your heart.

Then take a moment to look more closely at this woman. What tensions, concerns, and frustrations fill her daily life? What do you see in her face when she's told to "let the children be fed first"? When she replies? What does she feel when she sees her healed daughter?

Maybe at the end of this meditation you see things in a new light. In what ways does your new perspective mingle with your first reaction?

PRAY/LIVE

Become aware of Jesus in the room with you now, inviting you to talk with him about what today's passage was like for you. Don't hide feelings and thoughts that have surfaced within you, but openly share with him any questions, frustrations, or concerns you have. What does Jesus want you to see today? What does he want you to know? Spend several minutes in silence considering what you've experienced.

HEARTSTRINGS

MARK 10:17-22

[17]And as he was setting out on his journey, a man ran up and knelt before him and asked him, "Good Teacher, what must I do to inherit eternal life?" [18]And Jesus said to him, "Why do you call me good? No one is good except God alone. [19]You know the commandments: 'Do not murder, Do not commit adultery, Do not steal, Do not bear false witness, Do not defraud, Honor your father and mother.'" [20]And he said to him, "Teacher, all these I have kept from my youth." [21]And Jesus, looking at him, loved him, and said to him, "You lack one thing: go, sell all that you have and give to the poor, and you will have treasure in heaven; and come, follow me." [22]Disheartened by the saying, he went away sorrowful, for he had great possessions.

READ

Pick a pace and read this passage quickly. Read it again at a different pace. Did you notice anything different the second time?

THINK

Write down your thoughts about this story. How are you similar to the rich man? How are you different?

Jesus knows that, though the rich man is morally good, he still has strings attached to his heart that will keep him from being a devoted follower.

Take an internal inventory of your heart. What things are deeply attached to your heart that must be relinquished for you to be a whole-hearted follower of Jesus? They may be possessions, but they may also be thoughts, relationships, activities, and so on.

Later in the passage, Jesus says this about anyone's chance of getting into God's kingdom: "With man it is impossible, but not with God. For all things are possible with God" (verse 27). Based on these words from Jesus, write in your own words a description of the grace God offers to each one of us.

PRAY

Reflect on God's grace. Thank God for the grace he extends to you. Confess the times when you have abused his grace. Offer God the strings of your heart, those that keep you from completely following Jesus. Ask God to help you sever those strings and replace them with fray-proof connections to him.

LIVE

Live in freedom and follow Jesus.

THE BIG PICTURE

MARK 12:28-34

²⁸And one of the scribes came up and heard them disputing with one another, and seeing that he answered them well, asked him, "Which commandment is the most important of all?" ²⁹Jesus answered, "The most important is, 'Hear, O Israel: The Lord our God, the Lord is one. ³⁰And you shall love the Lord your God with all your heart and with all your soul and with all your mind and with all your strength.' ³¹The second is this: 'You shall love your neighbor as yourself.' There is no other commandment greater than these." ³²And the scribe said to him, "You are right, Teacher. You have truly said that he is one, and there is no other besides him. ³³And to love him with all the heart and with all the understanding and with all the strength, and to love one's neighbor as oneself, is much more than all whole burnt offerings and sacrifices." ³⁴And when Jesus saw that he answered wisely, he said to him, "You are not far from the kingdom of God." And after that no one dared to ask him any more questions.

READ

Read the passage aloud slowly.

THINK

Put yourself in the place of the religion scholar. You have studied theology and can explain its intricate details. You are weary with how most scholars argue over minor issues. You've come to Jesus to ask him to give you the big picture. Read the passage again, letting Jesus answer you directly.

Be impressed with Jesus' answer: He has combined part of the often-repeated *Shema Israel* (see Deuteronomy 6:4-9) and the last part of a much less quoted command: "You shall not take vengeance or bear a grudge against the sons of your own people, but you shall love your neighbor as yourself: I am the LORD" (Leviticus 19:18).

Consider an issue you've been puzzling over, a decision you need to make, or an approach you need to take with a difficult person. How does Jesus' simple but majestic summary help you?

PRAY

Ask God to help you love him "with all your heart and with all your soul and with all your mind and with all your strength." Take one at a time, if you wish. Then consider someone you know. Ask God to help you love that person the way you already love yourself. (You feed yourself, you clothe yourself, you give yourself a place to live — that's love.)

LIVE

Picture Jesus saying to you, "Love the Lord your God with all your heart and with all your soul and with all your mind and with all your strength. . . . Love your neighbor as yourself." Don't take this as a scolding but as the best, wisest thing any person could do.

PETER'S FAILURE

MARK 14:66-72

⁶⁶And as Peter was below in the courtyard, one of the servant girls of the high priest came, ⁶⁷and seeing Peter warming himself, she looked at him and said, "You also were with the Nazarene, Jesus." ⁶⁸But he denied it, saying, "I neither know nor understand what you mean." And he went out into the gateway and the rooster crowed. ⁶⁹And the servant girl saw him and began again to say to the bystanders, "This man is one of them." ⁷⁰But again he denied it. And after a little while the bystanders again said to Peter, "Certainly you are one of them, for you are a Galilean." ⁷¹But he began to invoke a curse on himself and to swear, "I do not know this man of whom you speak." ⁷²And immediately the rooster crowed a second time. And Peter remembered how Jesus had said to him, "Before the rooster crows twice, you will deny me three times." And he broke down and wept.

READ

As you read the passage, put yourself in Peter's sandals. To get a more vivid picture of what is happening, skim the expanded reading.

THINK

How does Peter feel to be in the courtyard? What has happened since his bold declaration of devotion to Jesus no matter what, earlier in the chapter? What thoughts shoot through Peter's mind that lead him to leave the fireside for the gateway?

Now imagine that the rooster has crowed and reality is caving in on Peter. Sit beside him in his anguish. What is he experiencing? As he remembers Jesus' words, what does Jesus' face look like in his mind's eye? What are the tones of Jesus' voice?

PRAY/LIVE

Let your meditation on Peter's failure lead you to consider your own heart and life. Where have you blown it lately? Talk to Jesus about this. Bravely let yourself feel the depth of what you've done. You might speak a prayer of humility or thanksgiving, or a request for something you need. Notice what you expect Jesus to do or say in response.

Now read the passage again slowly. What is Jesus saying in response to you? Be open to how he may be reacting differently to you or to your failure than you expected. Write down what Jesus' response was and what experiencing that was like.

SPOKESMAN FOR JESUS

LUKE 3:16-20

[16]John answered them all, saying, "I baptize you with water, but he who is mightier than I is coming, the strap of whose sandals I am not worthy to untie. He will baptize you with the Holy Spirit and fire. [17]His winnowing fork is in his hand, to clear his threshing floor and to gather the wheat into his barn, but the chaff he will burn with unquenchable fire."

[18]So with many other exhortations he preached good news to the people. [19]But Herod the tetrarch, who had been reproved by him for Herodias, his brother's wife, and for all the evil things that Herod had done, [20]added this to them all, that he locked up John in prison.

READ

Read the passage aloud four times, each time reading it with a different volume.

THINK

These verses tell us about John the Baptist, a torchbearer for the coming of Jesus' ministry, calling people to repent.

Focus first on the words describing "he who is mightier than I." In your life, what would it mean to be a mere spokesman where the main character is Jesus? What might be some areas of your life where the Holy Spirit will burn the chaff, changing you?

Now think about John's responses in the first few verses of the passage, concerning generosity, justice, and honesty.

PRAY

What do you need to repent of in areas where you have failed to be generous, just, and honest in the past week? Invite the Holy Spirit to burn everything that is chaff.

Ask God to help you grow in generosity—for example, with your money, time, gifts, passions, energy, and so on.

Ask God to help you grow as an advocate for justice—for example, in your neighborhood, in your city, for the poor, for the unborn, for other people in the world, and so on.

Ask God to reveal areas of dishonesty or deception in your life. Implore him to give you the grace and courage to live a life of honesty and integrity.

LIVE

Live generously, justly, and honestly today, as a spokesman for Jesus.

DAY 224

GOD ENCOUNTERS

On this seventh day, review and reflect on all you have read this week. Take the time to revel in the ways you've encountered God in the past six days.

LOVE YOUR ENEMIES

LUKE 6:27-36

[27]"But I say to you who hear, Love your enemies, do good to those who hate you, [28]bless those who curse you, pray for those who abuse you. [29]To one who strikes you on the cheek, offer the other also, and from one who takes away your cloak do not withhold your tunic either. [30]Give to everyone who begs from you, and from one who takes away your goods do not demand them back. [31]And as you wish that others would do to you, do so to them.

[32]"If you love those who love you, what benefit is that to you? For even sinners love those who love them. [33]And if you do good to those who do good to you, what benefit is that to you? For even sinners do the same. [34]And if you lend to those from whom you expect to receive, what credit is that to you? Even sinners lend to sinners, to get back the same amount. [35]But love your enemies, and do good, and lend, expecting nothing in return, and your reward will be great, and you will be sons of the Most High, for he is kind to the ungrateful and the evil. [36]Be merciful, even as your Father is merciful."

READ
Read the passage aloud slowly.

THINK
Read the passage aloud a second time, but pretend you are Jesus. Get into it and read it like you mean it; say the words and phrases the way you think he would have. Perhaps gently? Perhaps warmly? Perhaps passionately?

Read the passage aloud one more time, but this time put yourself in the place of Jesus' listener; you're sitting in the front row as Jesus speaks and looks directly at you.

1. If Jesus spoke these words to you, what would they mean?
2. Which words would stand out to you?
3. What might Jesus be trying to get across to you?

PRAY
Thank our kind God that he loves his enemies. Thank God that he loves you when you act as if you barely know him. Take the words that stood out to you (see question 2) and paraphrase those back to God in prayer.

LIVE
Sit quietly and picture the kind of person you would be if you were to:

- love your enemies
- pray for those who abuse you
- turn the other cheek
- give generously to those who steal from you
- give without expecting in return

DO YOU SEE THIS WOMAN?

LUKE 7:37-47

37And behold, a woman of the city, who was a sinner, when she learned that he was reclining at table in the Pharisee's house, brought an alabaster flask of ointment, 38and standing behind him at his feet, weeping, she began to wet his feet with her tears and wiped them with the hair of her head and kissed his feet and anointed them with the ointment. 39Now when the Pharisee who had invited him saw this, he said to himself, "If this man were a prophet, he would have known who and what sort of woman this is who is touching him, for she is a sinner." 40And Jesus answering said to him, "Simon, I have something to say to you." And he answered, "Say it, Teacher."

41"A certain moneylender had two debtors. One owed five hundred denarii, and the other fifty. 42When they could not pay, he cancelled the debt of both. Now which of them will love him more?" 43Simon answered, "The one, I suppose, for whom he cancelled the larger debt." And he said to him, "You have judged rightly." 44Then turning toward the woman he said to Simon, "Do you see this woman? I entered your house; you gave me no water for my feet, but she has wet my feet with her tears and wiped them with her hair. 45You gave me no kiss, but from the time I came in she has not ceased to kiss my feet. 46You did not anoint my head with oil, but she has anointed my feet with ointment. 47Therefore I tell you, her sins, which are many, are forgiven — for she loved much. But he who is forgiven little, loves little."

READ

Read the passage slowly, noticing the major players and actions in the story. Picture the setting's sounds, smells, and sights.

THINK

Now choose one person in the story with whom you identify most — the Pharisee, the sinful woman, or an onlooker — and read the story again. Imaginatively enter the scene, experiencing everything from that person's perspective. Hear the conversations. Feel the silence in the room as Jesus' feet are tenderly washed. Now listen to Jesus' voice and watch his face as he speaks. What do you feel? What thoughts go through your head?

PRAY

Talk with Jesus about what this experience has stirred up in you.

LIVE

Oswald Chambers said, "If human love does not carry a man beyond himself, it is not love. If love is always discreet, always wise, always sensible and calculating, never carried beyond itself, it is not love at all. It may be affection, it may be warmth of feeling, but it has not the true nature of love in it."[15]

Think about the degree of restraint or abandon you show in your relationship with Jesus (and with others). Consider the conscious or unconscious decisions you are constantly making about the way you'll act in that relationship. When does emotional momentum stir you? What do you do when it does? Under what circumstances do you set limits or hold back? What expectations or fears underlie your decisions? Share these with Jesus. What is something you could do today that would have the true nature of love in it?

SITTING AT THE LORD'S FEET

LUKE 10:38-42

[38]Now as they went on their way, Jesus entered a village. And a woman named Martha welcomed him into her house. [39]And she had a sister called Mary, who sat at the Lord's feet and listened to his teaching. [40]But Martha was distracted with much serving. And she went up to him and said, "Lord, do you not care that my sister has left me to serve alone? Tell her then to help me." [41]But the Lord answered her, "Martha, Martha, you are anxious and troubled about many things, [42]but one thing is necessary. Mary has chosen the good portion, which will not be taken away from her."

READ

This passage might be very familiar to you. So before reading, pause and ask God to give you fresh eyes and an open heart to absorb it. Then read it carefully.

THINK

Prayerfully let your creativity loose as you engage with this text. First put yourself in the skin of Mary. On that day, what might you be doing? What's going on around you in the house? What are you thinking and feeling when Martha complains about you?

Now, put yourself in Martha's shoes. What are you preparing? What are your motivations? What are you feeling? What might you be thinking and feeling after Jesus says those words to you?

LIVE

The text says that Mary "sat at the Lord's feet." Now it's your turn. Take an empty chair and place it in the middle of the room. Sit or kneel in front of it, imagining Jesus seated there. Read the passage again. Stay in this posture, in the silence, and ponder who Jesus is.

PRAY

As you remain before the chair, whisper, "Jesus, who am I more like today: Mary or Martha?" Don't rush this experience. Even if an urge to get up comes, continue to be still and sit in silence. Anticipate that Jesus will communicate with you. Wait for him and allow him to speak words of promise, correction, or comfort into your life.

SEEK HIS KINGDOM

LUKE 12:25-34

[25]And which of you by being anxious can add a single hour to his span of life? [26]If then you are not able to do as small a thing as that, why are you anxious about the rest? [27]Consider the lilies, how they grow: they neither toil nor spin, yet I tell you, even Solomon in all his glory was not arrayed like one of these. [28]But if God so clothes the grass, which is alive in the field today, and tomorrow is thrown into the oven, how much more will he clothe you, O you of little faith! [29]And do not seek what you are to eat and what you are to drink, nor be worried. [30]For all the nations of the world seek after these things, and your Father knows that you need them. [31]Instead, seek his kingdom, and these things will be added to you.

[32]"Fear not, little flock, for it is your Father's good pleasure to give you the kingdom. [33]Sell your possessions, and give to the needy. Provide yourselves with moneybags that do not grow old, with a treasure in the heavens that does not fail, where no thief approaches and no moth destroys. [34]For where your treasure is, there will your heart be also.

READ

Read the passage aloud slowly. Pretend you and Jesus are sitting in Starbucks, and he's saying these words to you quietly.

THINK

Now pretend that you've come home, and you're going over in your mind what Jesus said to you. Read the passage again.

1. What words or phrases draw you the most?
2. What do you think Jesus is trying to say to you?
3. In order to do what Jesus said, what are you going to have to really trust for?

   ☐ that he'll make sure you're clothed and fed
   ☐ that by *giving* instead of *getting,* you'll still have everything you need
   ☐ that God's provision is really enough
   ☐ other:

4. How do you feel about this?

PRAY

Respond to God about truly trusting him for these practical, important matters. Be honest about what you are — and are not — ready to do.

LIVE

Sit quietly before God. Receive from him the idea that he is your treasure: "For where your treasure is, there will your heart be also."

LOST AND FOUND

LUKE 15:1-10

¹Now the tax collectors and sinners were all drawing near to hear him.
²And the Pharisees and the scribes grumbled, saying, "This man receives sinners and eats with them."

³So he told them this parable: ⁴"What man of you, having a hundred sheep, if he has lost one of them, does not leave the ninety-nine in the open country, and go after the one that is lost, until he finds it? ⁵And when he has found it, he lays it on his shoulders, rejoicing. ⁶And when he comes home, he calls together his friends and his neighbors, saying to them, 'Rejoice with me, for I have found my sheep that was lost.' ⁷Just so, I tell you, there will be more joy in heaven over one sinner who repents than over ninety-nine righteous persons who need no repentance.

⁸"Or what woman, having ten silver coins, if she loses one coin, does not light a lamp and sweep the house and seek diligently until she finds it? ⁹And when she has found it, she calls together her friends and neighbors, saying, 'Rejoice with me, for I have found the coin that I had lost.' ¹⁰Just so, I tell you, there is joy before the angels of God over one sinner who repents."

READ

Open your hands with your palms facing up. Sit for a moment in stillness and ask your heavenly Father to tell you important words that you need to hear today. Communicate that you are open to his guidance. Now read the passage.

THINK

In this passage two things — a sheep and a coin — are lost and then found. And both are celebrated upon their return.

As you think about the two stories of the lost items, which story hits you the most right now? Contemplate why that story jumps out at you today. Read it again, and put yourself in it.

When have you felt lost? Why did you feel that way?

In both stories people — a shepherd, a woman — proactively went after the lost item. How does it feel to know that God himself is proactively pursuing you for the simple yet profound fact that he loves you deeply?

Notice the element of celebration in these stories. What does this celebration make you feel? What should you begin to celebrate in your life or in the lives of others?

PRAY

Listen for God in these areas: What might he be communicating to you regarding your lostness? Regarding the fact that he desires to find you? Regarding how he celebrates your life?

LIVE

Recognize what God is doing in the world today — in the spectacular and in the mundane — and then celebrate it.

DAY 230
EXPANDED PASSAGE: LUKE 17

RETURNING TO SAY THANK YOU

LUKE 17:11-19

¹¹On the way to Jerusalem he was passing along between Samaria and Galilee. ¹²And as he entered a village, he was met by ten lepers, who stood at a distance ¹³and lifted up their voices, saying, "Jesus, Master, have mercy on us." ¹⁴When he saw them he said to them, "Go and show yourselves to the priests." And as they went they were cleansed. ¹⁵Then one of them, when he saw that he was healed, turned back, praising God with a loud voice; ¹⁶and he fell on his face at Jesus' feet, giving him thanks. Now he was a Samaritan. ¹⁷Then Jesus answered, "Were not ten cleansed? Where are the nine? ¹⁸Was no one found to return and give praise to God except this foreigner?" ¹⁹And he said to him, "Rise and go your way; your faith has made you well."

READ

Read the passage, focusing especially on the questions Jesus asks.

THINK

Not only are lepers deformed by their disease, but Old Testament law also excludes them from community with others. Ten men come to Jesus with this horrific skin disease. These men are physical and relational outsiders. When Jesus heals them, he also helps restore them to their communities.

When have you felt like an outsider and then experienced God's restoring you to community with others or with himself? Do you tend to be like the nine, who asked for God's help and didn't return, or are you like the one who returned to say thank you? Why?

Think about your last several requests to God in prayer. Have you turned around and come back, shouting your gratitude for how he has answered your requests and blessed you in the process? Why or why not? What needs to happen in your life for you to remember to return when God answers your prayers?

PRAY

Make this prayer time one of intentional thankfulness. Consider your recent requests to God (being specific). Return now and thank him for answering those requests, big and small.

LIVE

Every time you make a request, turn around and shout your gratitude.

DAY 231

GOD ENCOUNTERS

On this seventh day, review and reflect on all you have read this week. Take the time to revel in the ways you've encountered God in the past six days.

HEALING THE ENEMY

LUKE 22:47-53

⁴⁷While he was still speaking, there came a crowd, and the man called Judas, one of the twelve, was leading them. He drew near to Jesus to kiss him, ⁴⁸but Jesus said to him, "Judas, would you betray the Son of Man with a kiss?" ⁴⁹And when those who were around him saw what would follow, they said, "Lord, shall we strike with the sword?" ⁵⁰And one of them struck the servant of the high priest and cut off his right ear. ⁵¹But Jesus said, "No more of this!" And he touched his ear and healed him. ⁵²Then Jesus said to the chief priests and officers of the temple and elders, who had come out against him, "Have you come out as against a robber, with swords and clubs? ⁵³When I was with you day after day in the temple, you did not lay hands on me. But this is your hour, and the power of darkness."

READ

Read the passage aloud slowly. Keep in mind that this occurs in the Garden of Gethsemane. Jesus has just prayed, "Father, if you are willing, remove this cup from me. Nevertheless, not my will, but yours, be done." Then Jesus noted that his disciples were sleeping when he'd asked them to watch with him (see verses 42-46).

THINK

Read the passage again. This time place yourself in the scene as one of the disciples watching what is going on.

1. How do you feel when Judas arrives with soldiers?
2. How do you feel when one of you strikes the chief priest's servant?
3. How do you feel when Jesus heals this servant — one of his attackers?
4. How do you feel when Jesus points out how silly and dramatic his assailants are? (He has been accessible to them for days and is now *letting them* arrest him.)

Finally, put yourself in the place of the servant of the chief priest who is healed by Jesus. How do you feel? What do you want to say to Jesus?

PRAY

Consider Jesus' behavior in this scene. What baffles you? What is awakened within you? Fear? A sense of worship? If there is any way this scene might help you trust Jesus more, tell him.

LIVE

Sit quietly with your hand on one of your ears. See yourself as someone who is about to injure Jesus, but instead he heals you from your own injuries. Sit in that sense of being healed by God. Sit in that sense of finally being able to hear Jesus in your heart with your willing ears.

SEEKING THE LIVING AMONG THE DEAD

LUKE 24:1-12

¹But on the first day of the week, at early dawn, they went to the tomb, taking the spices they had prepared. ²And they found the stone rolled away from the tomb, ³but when they went in they did not find the body of the Lord Jesus. ⁴While they were perplexed about this, behold, two men stood by them in dazzling apparel. ⁵And as they were frightened and bowed their faces to the ground, the men said to them, "Why do you seek the living among the dead? ⁶He is not here, but has risen. Remember how he told you, while he was still in Galilee, ⁷that the Son of Man must be delivered into the hands of sinful men and be crucified and on the third day rise." ⁸And they remembered his words, ⁹and returning from the tomb they told all these things to the eleven and to all the rest. ¹⁰Now it was Mary Magdalene and Joanna and Mary the mother of James and the other women with them who told these things to the apostles, ¹¹but these words seemed to them an idle tale, and they did not believe them. ¹²But Peter rose and ran to the tomb; stooping and looking in, he saw the linen cloths by themselves; and he went home marveling at what had happened.

READ

Read the passage carefully, paying attention to the various characters and their responses to the events of the story.

THINK

Which disciple or follower of Jesus do you most identify with in this passage? What is it about that person that reminds you of yourself?

Read the passage again, this time putting yourself in that person's position. What are your thoughts and feelings as you hear that Jesus is alive again? What runs through your mind as you see others' responses? What do you wonder about? Where do you go when you hear the news? What questions do you have?

PRAY

Now picture the risen Jesus approaching you later that day, inviting you to spend time with him. How do you interact with him? What do you say? Talk to him about what all of this has been like for you.

LIVE

Reflect on your prayer time. You might again consider the person in the story you chose and why, or you could think about how your understanding of faithfulness and discipleship was deepened or changed. Write down anything that seems significant.

THE LIGHT OF MEN

JOHN 1:12-18

¹²But to all who did receive him, who believed in his name, he gave the right to become children of God, ¹³who were born, not of blood nor of the will of the flesh nor of the will of man, but of God.

¹⁴And the Word became flesh and dwelt among us, and we have seen his glory, glory as of the only Son from the Father, full of grace and truth. ¹⁵(John bore witness about him, and cried out, "This was he of whom I said, 'He who comes after me ranks before me, because he was before me.'") ¹⁶For from his fullness we have all received, grace upon grace. ¹⁷For the law was given through Moses; grace and truth came through Jesus Christ. ¹⁸No one has ever seen God; the only God, who is at the Father's side, he has made him known.

READ

Read the passage slowly and repeatedly. Don't rush through it. Take your time. Ruminate on the passage. Let it sink into the well of your soul.

THINK

What sticks out to you the most in these verses? Why is the Word coming to Earth such a big deal in the great scope of human history?

"The Word became flesh and dwelt among us." What might your life be like if God moved into the house or apartment or locker or dorm room next to yours?

How might the environment of your neighborhood be different if he dwelled among you as your next-door neighbor? How might your own life be different? Be specific.

LIVE

Get a candle (if you don't have one, buy or borrow one). At night, go into a dark room (turn off any lights and shut any curtains). Light the candle and stare at the flame. Consider Jesus, the Word, coming to Earth in flesh and blood, becoming the Light for the world.

PRAY

Stand in the dark room, still looking at the small flame. Allow these words to guide your prayers: "In him was life, and the life was the light of men. The light shines in the darkness, and the darkness has not overcome it" (John 1:4-5).

DAY 235

EXPANDED PASSAGE: JOHN 3:1-21

WHOEVER BELIEVES

JOHN 3:9-11,14-15,17-21

⁹Nicodemus said to him, "How can these things be?" ¹⁰Jesus answered him, "Are you the teacher of Israel and yet you do not understand these things? ¹¹Truly, truly, I say to you, we speak of what we know, and bear witness to what we have seen, but you do not receive our testimony. . . . ¹⁴"And as Moses lifted up the serpent in the wilderness, so must the Son of Man be lifted up, ¹⁵that whoever believes in him may have eternal life. . . .

¹⁷"For God did not send his Son into the world to condemn the world, but in order that the world might be saved through him. ¹⁸Whoever believes in him is not condemned, but whoever does not believe is condemned already, because he has not believed in the name of the only Son of God. ¹⁹And this is the judgment: the light has come into the world, and people loved the darkness rather than the light because their works were evil. ²⁰For everyone who does wicked things hates the light and does not come to the light, lest his works should be exposed. ²¹But whoever does what is true comes to the light, so that it may be clearly seen that his works have been carried out in God."

READ

Before you read the passage, understand that Jesus has just told Nicodemus (a scholar and teacher) that he must be "born of the Spirit" (verse 8). But Nicodemus is confused! Now read the passage silently.

THINK

Read the passage again, aloud this time, putting yourself in the place of Nicodemus standing on the rooftop in the moonlight, receiving Jesus' words.

1. Which words or phrases stand out to you? Consider these:

   ☐ "Whoever believes in him may have eternal life."
   ☐ "God did not send his Son into the world to condemn the world, but in order that the world might be saved through him."
   ☐ "Whoever believes in him is not condemned."
   ☐ "The light has come into the world."
   ☐ "Whoever does what is true comes to the light, so that it may be clearly seen that his works have been carried out in God."

2. Why?

PRAY

Talk to Jesus about any phrases that confused you. Talk to him about the phrases that captivated you.

LIVE

Sit quietly before God. Put yourself in the place of Nicodemus again — possibly lying in your bed each night, going over these words Jesus said to you. Which words will you drift off with tonight?

DO YOU WANT TO BE HEALED?

JOHN 5:1-9

¹After this there was a feast of the Jews, and Jesus went up to Jerusalem.

²Now there is in Jerusalem by the Sheep Gate a pool, in Aramaic called Bethesda, which has five roofed colonnades. ³In these lay a multitude of invalids — blind, lame, and paralyzed. ⁵One man was there who had been an invalid for thirty-eight years. ⁶When Jesus saw him lying there and knew that he had already been there a long time, he said to him, "Do you want to be healed?" ⁷The sick man answered him, "Sir, I have no one to put me into the pool when the water is stirred up, and while I am going another steps down before me." ⁸Jesus said to him, "Get up, take up your bed, and walk." ⁹And at once the man was healed, and he took up his bed and walked.

READ

Read this passage, being especially aware of how it depicts sickness, lack of wholeness, and the process of healing. These details might remind you of a truth you've considered before, or they might reveal something altogether new.

THINK

Read the verses again. What stands out to you? Why might the Holy Spirit be bringing this to your attention? Perhaps you deeply desire to experience wholeness of mind or spirit because you have been experiencing your woundedness lately. Or perhaps you find yourself questioning whether Jesus really can heal a physical sickness — either your own or someone else's.

PRAY

Ask Jesus what he has specifically for you that calls for healing. Talk to him about what you hear.

These possibilities might help get you started: Allowing Jesus to bring healing might require you to let go of something that hurts too much to release, and you don't think you're ready for it right now. Or you desire freedom and wholeness, but you feel stuck, imprisoned, fragmented. Or in this moment you find yourself ready for your healing: Be open to the possibility of Jesus bringing healing when you least expect it, of being healed at once. On the other hand, perhaps you feel ready and are frustrated that nothing seems to be happening.

LIVE

If your time with Jesus and God's Word today moved you the tiniest bit closer to wholeness, rejoice. If not, simply let things be. Continue talking to Jesus about your situation, being alert to what he has for you.

NO CONDEMNATION

JOHN 8:1-11

¹But Jesus went to the Mount of Olives. ²Early in the morning he came again to the temple. All the people came to him, and he sat down and taught them. ³The scribes and the Pharisees brought a woman who had been caught in adultery, and placing her in the midst ⁴they said to him, "Teacher, this woman has been caught in the act of adultery. ⁵Now in the Law Moses commanded us to stone such women. So what do you say?" ⁶This they said to test him, that they might have some charge to bring against him. Jesus bent down and wrote with his finger on the ground. ⁷And as they continued to ask him, he stood up and said to them, "Let him who is without sin among you be the first to throw a stone at her." ⁸And once more he bent down and wrote on the ground. ⁹But when they heard it, they went away one by one, beginning with the older ones, and Jesus was left alone with the woman standing before him. ¹⁰Jesus stood up and said to her, "Woman, where are they? Has no one condemned you?" ¹¹She said, "No one, Lord." And Jesus said, "Neither do I condemn you; go, and from now on sin no more."

READ

Write out today's passage. Say each word aloud as you go.

THINK

Imagine yourself in the crowd the day these events unfold. Picture the embarrassed and shamed expression on the woman's face. Hear the condescending voices of the religious leaders. Feel the Middle Eastern dirt blowing against you as Jesus bends down and writes something in it.

Now imagine yourself in the same situation as this woman. You're caught in a horrendous sin, exposed. Imagine you and Jesus having the same conversation:

"Has no one condemned you?"

"No one, Lord."

He looks you in the eyes. "Neither do I condemn you; go, and from now on sin no more."

What are you feeling? Thinking?

PRAY

Confess those acts of spiritual adultery you've engaged in recently. Close your eyes and imagine Jesus standing before you. Hear him telling you that he doesn't condemn you but that he wants you to stop sinning from now on.

LIVE

Ask the Holy Spirit to give you wisdom and guidance not to condone other people's (or your own) sin and at the same time not to condemn those people (or yourself) either. Ask the Spirit to bring to your mind people you can love while avoiding condemning and condoning.

DAY 238

GOD ENCOUNTERS

On this seventh day, review and reflect on all you have read this week. Take the time to revel in the ways you've encountered God in the past six days.

KNOWING THE GOOD SHEPHERD

JOHN 10:2-5,14-18

²But he who enters by the door is the shepherd of the sheep. ³To him the gatekeeper opens. The sheep hear his voice, and he calls his own sheep by name and leads them out. ⁴When he has brought out all his own, he goes before them, and the sheep follow him, for they know his voice. ⁵A stranger they will not follow, but they will flee from him, for they do not know the voice of strangers. . . .

¹⁴I am the good shepherd. I know my own and my own know me, ¹⁵just as the Father knows me and I know the Father; and I lay down my life for the sheep. ¹⁶And I have other sheep that are not of this fold. I must bring them also, and they will listen to my voice. So there will be one flock, one shepherd. ¹⁷For this reason the Father loves me, because I lay down my life that I may take it up again. ¹⁸No one takes it from me, but I lay it down of my own accord. I have authority to lay it down, and I have authority to take it up again. This charge I have received from my Father.

READ

Read these words of Jesus aloud slowly. Notice the two sets of closeness expressed: between Jesus and the Father, and between Jesus and the sheep.

THINK

Read these words of Jesus again aloud, as if he were explaining this to you personally. Notice that the word *know* occurs six times. Jesus knows his sheep; they know Jesus. The Father knows Jesus; Jesus knows the Father.

1. What do you make of the centrality of knowing one another?
2. Jesus, the Good Shepherd, does the following for the sheep. Which of these do you most need for Jesus to do for you today?

    ☐ call his own sheep by name
    ☐ lead them out
    ☐ know his own sheep
    ☐ put the sheep before himself, sacrificing himself, if necessary
    ☐ gather and bring other sheep

3. The sheep recognize Jesus' voice and respond by following him and knowing him. How do you need to respond to Jesus today?
4. How are you growing in your capacity to recognize his voice, perhaps through your experiences in this book?

PRAY

Talk to Jesus about what you need from him. Especially talk about your capacity to recognize his voice. Ask for help with this.

LIVE

Sit quietly before God and practice alert waiting. Receive the assurance that such practice will help you be more alert to Jesus' voice when you hear it.

HOLDING ON TO LIFE

JOHN 12:20-26

²⁰Now among those who went up to worship at the feast were some Greeks. ²¹So these came to Philip, who was from Bethsaida in Galilee, and asked him, "Sir, we wish to see Jesus." ²²Philip went and told Andrew; Andrew and Philip went and told Jesus. ²³And Jesus answered them, "The hour has come for the Son of Man to be glorified. ²⁴Truly, truly, I say to you, unless a grain of wheat falls into the earth and dies, it remains alone; but if it dies, it bears much fruit. ²⁵Whoever loves his life loses it, and whoever hates his life in this world will keep it for eternal life. ²⁶If anyone serves me, he must follow me; and where I am, there will my servant be also. If anyone serves me, the Father will honor him."

READ

If possible, read the expanded passage to see the full picture of what is happening here. Then read this excerpt three times meditatively.

THINK

Write in your own words what you think Jesus means when he talks about a grain of wheat dying and reproducing itself. Think about what you wrote.

Now wait for Jesus to show you an area of your life — a relationship, a decision to be made, and so on — in which you love your life and are not allowing him to bring growth or change. In what ways might your stance be destructive or suffocating?

Ponder Romans 12:2: "Be transformed by the renewal of your mind, that by testing you may discern what is the will of God." What would this area of your life look like if you were to "be transformed," and in so doing, let go?

PRAY

Sit down. Hold your hands in tight fists. Then relax them, open them, and turn your palms upward. Talk with Jesus about what a life of open hands would look like. Ask him to show you what it means that "where I am, there will my servant be also."

LIVE

Think again about your tightly held part of life. Try letting go just a little bit, with Jesus' help. Serve Jesus today. Follow him today.

THE HELPER

JOHN 14:15-17

¹⁵If you love me, you will keep my commandments. ¹⁶And I will ask the Father, and he will give you another Helper, to be with you forever, ¹⁷even the Spirit of truth, whom the world cannot receive, because it neither sees him nor knows him. You know him, for he dwells with you and will be in you.

READ

Because this passage is about the Holy Spirit, ask him to guide you in a prayerful reading of it. Make your reading a prayer in itself.

THINK

The Holy Spirit is the most neglected personhood of God. We often treat the Spirit like a tagalong part of the Trinity. Yet Jesus promises to leave his disciples (and us as his followers) with this important Helper. Is it hard for you to imagine that the Holy Spirit is offered to you as a helper? Why or why not?

What does it mean to have the Holy Spirit in you and guiding you throughout your day, as this passage says: "You know him, for he dwells with you and will be in you"? Is it comforting? Discomforting? Frustrating? Hard to comprehend? Awe-inspiring? How can you grow today in awareness that the Helper lives in you?

PRAY

Ask the Holy Spirit, your Helper, to remind you of his presence. Pray the words of this Scripture, asking him to "teach you all things" (verse 26) and remind you of all the things that Jesus told the disciples (and you).

LIVE

As you drive, walk, work, study, and interact with others today, call on your Helper for his guidance with the thoughts you think, the words you speak, and the decisions you make.

BECOME PERFECTLY ONE

JOHN 17:20-23,26

[20]I do not ask for these only, but also for those who will believe in me through their word, [21]that they may all be one, just as you, Father, are in me, and I in you, that they also may be in us, so that the world may believe that you have sent me. [22]The glory that you have given me I have given to them, that they may be one even as we are one, [23]I in them and you in me, that they may become perfectly one, so that the world may know that you sent me and loved them even as you loved me. . . .

[26]I made known to them your name, and I will continue to make it known, that the love with which you have loved me may be in them, and I in them.

READ

Read the passage aloud slowly, remembering that this is Jesus praying for you ("those who will believe in me").

THINK

Read it again slowly, but this time substitute your name (or your name and "all of them") when you read *them* or *they*.

If you need to, read the passage one more time before considering these questions.

1. What are you most excited about Jesus praying for you or saying about you?

   ☐ your witness for Jesus
   ☐ to be one heart and mind with other followers of Jesus
   ☐ to be one heart and mind with God and Jesus
   ☐ that Jesus has given you glory
   ☐ that Jesus is in you
   ☐ that you'll be mature in oneness
   ☐ that you'll give the world evidence that God sent Jesus
   ☐ that Jesus made the very being of God known to you
   ☐ that God's love for Jesus is in you

2. Why?

PRAY

Thank Jesus for praying for you. Talk to him about the prayer phrases you found most meaningful. Pray Jesus' prayer for his followers alive today in the world.

LIVE

Walk around today with the sense that Jesus is in you and that this was always his plan — to be in you.

BELIEVE WITHOUT SEEING

JOHN 20:19-29

¹⁹On the evening of that day, the first day of the week, the doors being locked where the disciples were for fear of the Jews, Jesus came and stood among them and said to them, "Peace be with you." ²⁰When he had said this, he showed them his hands and his side. Then the disciples were glad when they saw the Lord. ²¹Jesus said to them again, "Peace be with you. As the Father has sent me, even so I am sending you." ²²And when he had said this, he breathed on them and said to them, "Receive the Holy Spirit. ²³If you forgive the sins of any, they are forgiven them; if you withhold forgiveness from any, it is withheld."

²⁴Now Thomas, one of the Twelve, called the Twin, was not with them when Jesus came. ²⁵So the other disciples told him, "We have seen the Lord." But he said to them, "Unless I see in his hands the mark of the nails, and place my finger into the mark of the nails, and place my hand into his side, I will never believe."

²⁶Eight days later, his disciples were inside again, and Thomas was with them. Although the doors were locked, Jesus came and stood among them and said, "Peace be with you." ²⁷Then he said to Thomas, "Put your finger here, and see my hands; and put out your hand, and place it in my side. Do not disbelieve, but believe." ²⁸Thomas answered him, "My Lord and my God!" ²⁹Jesus said to him, "Have you believed because you have seen me? Blessed are those who have not seen and yet have believed."

READ

Read John's description of the first time Jesus appeared to his disciples after his death and resurrection. Pay special attention to Jesus' words to them.

THINK

What does Thomas's response to Jesus' resurrection make you feel? How do you react to Thomas's disbelief? What about Jesus' response to him?

PRAY

Read the passage once more. This time pretend you are one of the disciples. Maybe you will be a believing disciple; maybe you will be Thomas. Pick a role that corresponds with where you actually are in your relationship with Jesus right now. Now play out the story. As you hear Jesus speak to you, respond to him from your heart. Let him engage you in conversation.

LIVE

If you're a Thomas, wonder what it would be like to believe without seeing. If you're like the other disciples, remember to offer grace to others who need to see before believing. Thank God for the faith he has given you — either way.

GOD'S REDEMPTIVE PLAN

ACTS 1:1-11

[1]In the first book, O Theophilus, I have dealt with all that Jesus began to do and teach, [2]until the day when he was taken up, after he had given commands through the Holy Spirit to the apostles whom he had chosen. [3]He presented himself alive to them after his suffering by many proofs, appearing to them during forty days and speaking about the kingdom of God.

[4]And while staying with them he ordered them not to depart from Jerusalem, but to wait for the promise of the Father, which, he said, "you heard from me; [5]for John baptized with water, but you will be baptized with the Holy Spirit not many days from now."

[6]So when they had come together, they asked him, "Lord, will you at this time restore the kingdom to Israel?" [7]He said to them, "It is not for you to know times or seasons that the Father has fixed by his own authority. [8]But you will receive power when the Holy Spirit has come upon you, and you will be my witnesses in Jerusalem and in all Judea and Samaria, and to the end of the earth." [9]And when he had said these things, as they were looking on, he was lifted up, and a cloud took him out of their sight. [10]And while they were gazing into heaven as he went, behold, two men stood by them in white robes, [11]and said, "Men of Galilee, why do you stand looking into heaven? This Jesus, who was taken up from you into heaven, will come in the same way as you saw him go into heaven."

READ

Read the passage from the perspective of someone who has never read it before.

THINK

When are you tempted to be a spectator to the movements of God's redemptive plan rather than a participant involved in the action? Why? What are specific ways you can get off the bench and get up to bat for what God is up to in the world? What are some ways you can be a witness to others in your circle of influence?

You know that Jesus will come again in the future. What implications does that reality have on your life?

PRAY

Ask God to give you the courage to take the risk and get into the game, to participate in God's redemptive plan.

LIVE

Ask a close friend or family member to help pray, brainstorm, and discern the ways you can be a participant in God's redemptive plan for your life and the lives of those around you. Ask this person to keep you in check, reminding you that God wants his followers to act on what Jesus said and did.

DAY 245

GOD ENCOUNTERS

On this seventh day, review and reflect on all you have read this week. Take the time to revel in the ways you've encountered God in the past six days.

SPEAKING THE WORD WITH BOLDNESS

ACTS 4:24-31

24And when they heard it, they lifted their voices together to God and said, "Sovereign Lord, who made the heaven and the earth and the sea and everything in them, 25who through the mouth of our father David, your servant, said by the Holy Spirit,

"'Why did the Gentiles rage,
    and the peoples plot in vain?
26 The kings of the earth set themselves,
    and the rulers were gathered together,
    against the Lord and against his Anointed'—

27for truly in this city there were gathered together against your holy servant Jesus, whom you anointed, both Herod and Pontius Pilate, along with the Gentiles and the peoples of Israel, 28to do whatever your hand and your plan had predestined to take place. 29And now, Lord, look upon their threats and grant to your servants to continue to speak your word with all boldness, 30while you stretch out your hand to heal, and signs and wonders are performed through the name of your holy servant Jesus." 31And when they had prayed, the place in which they were gathered together was shaken, and they were all filled with the Holy Spirit and continued to speak the word of God with boldness.

READ

Read the passage aloud slowly, keeping in mind that Peter and John were just released from police custody for preaching about Jesus. Most of this passage is their prayer.

THINK

Read the passage aloud again. What touches you most? How do you explain the boldness of these men who have just suffered for Jesus?

Read the passage one more time, noting when a member of the Trinity is mentioned: God, Jesus (and his designation, Anointed), the Holy Spirit. Clearly, Peter and John, as well as these followers of Jesus, were living in the reality of the Trinity — active and living among them! What might it look like to live your life today immersed in the reality and power of the Trinity?

PRAY

Paraphrase the prayer of Peter, John, and Jesus' followers (verses 24-30) as it fits your life today, including what God has done in the past (verses 24-28), what is happening today (verse 29), and how you wish for God to work today (verse 30).

LIVE

Remind yourself throughout the day that a follower of Jesus is immersed in the Trinitarian reality — really!

JESUS, THE LORD

ACTS 7:51–8:1

[51]"You stiff-necked people, uncircumcised in heart and ears, you always resist the Holy Spirit. As your fathers did, so do you. [52]Which of the prophets did your fathers not persecute? And they killed those who announced beforehand the coming of the Righteous One, whom you have now betrayed and murdered, [53]you who received the law as delivered by angels and did not keep it."

[54]Now when they heard these things they were enraged, and they ground their teeth at him. [55]But he, full of the Holy Spirit, gazed into heaven and saw the glory of God, and Jesus standing at the right hand of God. [56]And he said, "Behold, I see the heavens opened, and the Son of Man standing at the right hand of God." [57]But they cried out with a loud voice and stopped their ears and rushed together at him. [58]Then they cast him out of the city and stoned him. And the witnesses laid down their garments at the feet of a young man named Saul. [59]And as they were stoning Stephen, he called out, "Lord Jesus, receive my spirit." [60]And falling to his knees he cried out with a loud voice, "Lord, do not hold this sin against them." And when he had said this, he fell asleep.

[1]And Saul approved of his execution.

And there arose on that day a great persecution against the church in Jerusalem, and they were all scattered throughout the regions of Judea and Samaria, except the apostles.

READ

Read the passage aloud once. Then read it again silently and slowly, paying careful attention to your response.

THINK

Stephen calls Jesus "Lord," and his actions agree. Have you ever read or heard stories of other martyrs like Stephen, people who died for Jesus' sake? What do these stories make you feel?

PRAY

Become aware of Jesus inviting you to share with him your thoughts and feelings. Perhaps stories of martyrdom make you angry, grieved, or afraid. Maybe you find yourself pulling away from such stories. You might have questions. Maybe you want only to sit silently with Jesus. As you open your heart's reaction to him, let that become your prayer.

LIVE

Read the passage again, this time prayerfully. Look for clues to help you discern Jesus' response to Stephen's martyrdom, as well as Jesus' response to you. Write down anything you want to remember or think about later.

THE MIRACULOUS RELEASE

ACTS 12:7-15

[7]And behold, an angel of the Lord stood next to him, and a light shone in the cell. He struck Peter on the side and woke him, saying, "Get up quickly." And the chains fell off his hands. [8]And the angel said to him, "Dress yourself and put on your sandals." And he did so. And he said to him, "Wrap your cloak around you and follow me." [9]And he went out and followed him. He did not know that what was being done by the angel was real, but thought he was seeing a vision. [10]When they had passed the first and the second guard, they came to the iron gate leading into the city. It opened for them of its own accord, and they went out and went along one street, and immediately the angel left him. [11]When Peter came to himself, he said, "Now I am sure that the Lord has sent his angel and rescued me from the hand of Herod and from all that the Jewish people were expecting."

[12]When he realized this, he went to the house of Mary, the mother of John whose other name was Mark, where many were gathered together and were praying. [13]And when he knocked at the door of the gateway, a servant girl named Rhoda came to answer. [14]Recognizing Peter's voice, in her joy she did not open the gate but ran in and reported that Peter was standing at the gate. [15]They said to her, "You are out of your mind." But she kept insisting that it was so, and they kept saying, "It is his angel!"

READ

Imagine you are in a roomful of your friends, and they have asked you to read them a story. With this scenario in mind, read the passage.

THINK

Good stories grab hold of us and won't let go. This story is no exception. Scripture sometimes "messes" with us in appropriate ways. How does this passage mess with you and your understanding of God?

The people praying for Peter's release from prison didn't believe it when he was standing at the door. They thought Rhoda was crazy or it must be someone else or an angel of Peter (but not Peter himself). Is it hard to believe that the Holy Spirit is powerful enough to perform such sensational acts? Why or why not? If this were to happen today, would you be skeptical or cynical? Why or why not?

How often do you pray for God to work and, when he does, react with shock or disbelief? What does this reveal about the faith behind your prayers?

PRAY

What can you pray that God will do — and *wholeheartedly believe* that he will answer? Pray for that with bold confidence and hope, knowing that God is powerful and is listening to your prayer.

LIVE

Be keenly aware today of how the Holy Spirit is working — in the sensational, in the mundane, or in both.

LIVE AS YOU WERE MEANT TO LIVE

ACTS 16:25-34

²⁵About midnight Paul and Silas were praying and singing hymns to God, and the prisoners were listening to them, ²⁶and suddenly there was a great earthquake, so that the foundations of the prison were shaken. And immediately all the doors were opened, and everyone's bonds were unfastened. ²⁷When the jailer woke and saw that the prison doors were open, he drew his sword and was about to kill himself, supposing that the prisoners had escaped. ²⁸But Paul cried with a loud voice, "Do not harm yourself, for we are all here." ²⁹And the jailer called for lights and rushed in, and trembling with fear he fell down before Paul and Silas. ³⁰Then he brought them out and said, "Sirs, what must I do to be saved?" ³¹And they said, "Believe in the Lord Jesus, and you will be saved, you and your household." ³²And they spoke the word of the Lord to him and to all who were in his house. ³³And he took them the same hour of the night and washed their wounds; and he was baptized at once, he and all his family. ³⁴Then he brought them up into his house and set food before them. And he rejoiced along with his entire household that he had believed in God.

READ

Read the passage aloud slowly, keeping in mind that just before this, Paul and Silas (after doing good) are stripped by a crowd, beaten black-and-blue by officials, and put in jail.

THINK

Read the passage again and be mindful that the Greek word for "salvation" has to do with deliverance for the future but also living a new kind of life in the here and now.

1. Why do you think the jailer is so dramatically affected by Paul's and Silas's behavior?
2. Why would the jailer have an idea of what it meant to "believe in the Lord Jesus"?
3. Picture these scenes:

   - the jailer making his prisoners feel at home with his family
   - the jailer dressing the wounds his coworkers had inflicted
   - Paul and Silas baptizing the family
   - the group eating a festive meal together, not knowing what would happen to Paul and Silas the next day

PRAY

Talk to God about what touches you most in this passage. What does that tell you about what you need from God? Ask God for that.

LIVE

Ponder the next twenty-four hours. In what area might you rejoice even though circumstances might not be happy? Who might you love who isn't expecting it? Watch for unexpected events and celebrate them.

PAINFUL CONSEQUENCES

ACTS 19:11-17

[11]And God was doing extraordinary miracles by the hands of Paul, [12]so that even handkerchiefs or aprons that had touched his skin were carried away to the sick, and their diseases left them and the evil spirits came out of them. [13]Then some of the itinerant Jewish exorcists undertook to invoke the name of the Lord Jesus over those who had evil spirits, saying, "I adjure you by the Jesus whom Paul proclaims." [14]Seven sons of a Jewish high priest named Sceva were doing this. [15]But the evil spirit answered them, "Jesus I know, and Paul I recognize, but who are you?" [16]And the man in whom was the evil spirit leaped on them, mastered all of them and overpowered them, so that they fled out of that house naked and wounded. [17]And this became known to all the residents of Ephesus, both Jews and Greeks. And fear fell upon them all, and the name of the Lord Jesus was extolled.

READ

Read the passage.

THINK

Often God allows us to experience unpleasant consequences of choices we make, sometimes so we realize how our choices affect our relationship with him and other people. For example, he might allow ugly parts of our character to be exposed, with embarrassing and painful results. Why do you think God uses consequences to draw people's attention to the thorny parts of their hearts? What do you think God wanted the sons of Sceva to learn about themselves through this experience?

PRAY

Recall a difficult experience that helped you see more of your weaknesses or faults. Ponder the state of your relationship with God before the experience. How did it change? Think about your relationships with others, both before and after the experience. What changed? In other words, in what ways did your newfound awareness impact how you relate to others?

LIVE

Mull over these words, written by Teresa of Avila in her *Interior Castle:* "We are fonder of consolations than we are of the cross. Test us, Lord — for You know the truth — so that we may know ourselves."[16] Can you identify with her confession? Can you identify with her request to be more fully exposed to God and to see herself more clearly? Sit and talk with Jesus about your reaction to testing from God, contrasting it with your reaction to feel-good experiences.

FAITH JOURNEY

ACTS 22:1-10

[1]"Brothers and fathers, hear the defense that I now make before you."

[2]And when they heard that he was addressing them in the Hebrew language, they became even more quiet. And he said:

[3]"I am a Jew, born in Tarsus in Cilicia, but brought up in this city, educated at the feet of Gamaliel according to the strict manner of the law of our fathers, being zealous for God as all of you are this day. [4]I persecuted this Way to the death, binding and delivering to prison both men and women, [5]as the high priest and the whole council of elders can bear me witness. From them I received letters to the brothers, and I journeyed toward Damascus to take those also who were there and bring them in bonds to Jerusalem to be punished.

[6]"As I was on my way and drew near to Damascus, about noon a great light from heaven suddenly shone around me. [7]And I fell to the ground and heard a voice saying to me, 'Saul, Saul, why are you persecuting me?' [8]And I answered, 'Who are you, Lord?' And he said to me, 'I am Jesus of Nazareth, whom you are persecuting.' [9]Now those who were with me saw the light but did not understand the voice of the one who was speaking to me. [10]And I said, 'What shall I do, Lord?' And the Lord said to me, 'Rise, and go into Damascus, and there you will be told all that is appointed for you to do.'"

READ

Read the passage from the perspective of Paul's mother. What might she be thinking as she hears these words?

THINK

Paul's faith began in an amazing way on the road to Damascus (see the beginning of Acts 9 for more details). He was bold to share his story and ultimately The Story, the one of God and man. This passage gives us a thorough yet succinct explanation of the person Paul was before he met Christ, how he met Christ, and the person he became after he met Christ.

Reflect on your story—how you came to faith and how your faith journey is continuing today. Who were you before Christ? What was meeting Christ like? In what ways is your life different now as a result of meeting him? Are other people different today because of your interaction with Jesus?

LIVE

Think about how you might describe your life-altering encounter with the Living God and your faith journey. Now write or type your story of faith in just two or three paragraphs. Finally, ask someone you know to help you hone it to include the most appropriate details.

PRAY

Pray that God will provide you an opportunity to present your story and The Story (of God and man) with another person in the next week. When you sense the open door plainly before you, take the risk and share the stories.

DAY 252

GOD ENCOUNTERS

On this seventh day, review and reflect on all you have read this week. Take the time to revel in the ways you've encountered God in the past six days.

WHY ARE YOU PERSECUTING ME?

ACTS 26:12-18

[12]In this connection I journeyed to Damascus with the authority and commission of the chief priests. [13]At midday, O king, I saw on the way a light from heaven, brighter than the sun, that shone around me and those who journeyed with me. [14]And when we had all fallen to the ground, I heard a voice saying to me in the Hebrew language, "Saul, Saul, why are you persecuting me? It is hard for you to kick against the goads." [15]And I said, "Who are you, Lord?" And the Lord said, "I am Jesus whom you are persecuting. [16]But rise and stand upon your feet, for I have appeared to you for this purpose, to appoint you as a servant and witness to the things in which you have seen me and to those in which I will appear to you, [17]delivering you from your people and from the Gentiles—to whom I am sending you [18]to open their eyes, so that they may turn from darkness to light and from the power of Satan to God, that they may receive forgiveness of sins and a place among those who are sanctified by faith in me."

READ

Read the passage aloud slowly. This is Paul speaking before King Agrippa, telling about his conversion.

THINK

Read the passage aloud again, this time noting all the personal pronouns in this very personal conversation: *I, me, you.*

Read it a third time, noting how the conversation focuses on the past and the future.

1. Why do you think Jesus doesn't just say, "I'm the Son of God. Your doctrine is wrong. Change it"?
2. How do you respond to Jesus' giving Saul a job to do even though he's been murdering Christians? What does this tell you about Jesus?
3. Consider what Paul might have prayed next; there he is, blind, with his underlings leading him to safety.

PRAY

Have a conversation with Jesus similar to Paul's.

First, Jesus asks you, "Why are you . . . ?" How do you respond?

Next, Jesus tells you exactly who he is — a glimpse of him you have missed: "I am Jesus, the One you're . . ."

Finally, Jesus says, "Stand upon your feet, for I have appeared to you for this purpose." What is the job? How do you respond?

Live today asking Jesus this question: *Is there anything about you I'm missing out on? That I don't understand or accept? Show me.*

PRIDE COMES BEFORE A FALL

ROMANS 2:17-24

[17]But if you call yourself a Jew and rely on the law and boast in God [18]and know his will and approve what is excellent, because you are instructed from the law; [19]and if you are sure that you yourself are a guide to the blind, a light to those who are in darkness, [20]an instructor of the foolish, a teacher of children, having in the law the embodiment of knowledge and truth — [21]you then who teach others, do you not teach yourself? While you preach against stealing, do you steal? [22]you who say that one must not commit adultery, do you commit adultery? You who abhor idols, do you rob temples? [23]You who boast in the law dishonor God by breaking the law. [24]For, as it is written, "The name of God is blasphemed among the Gentiles because of you."

READ

Whisper to yourself the words of this passage.

THINK

Paul, writing mostly to Gentiles (non-Jews) in the church in Rome, finds himself addressing Jews in this passage, and warns those who have become arrogant because of their ancestral heritage. He warns that their arrogance, laziness, and apathy do not sit well with God. It leads to all sorts of thoughts and behaviors that dishonor God, including saying one thing and actually doing another.

You may or may not have Jewish roots, but this passage is relevant to all of us. What areas of your own heart might be arrogant or apathetic because of your upbringing, your heritage, or what you have done (and not done) in the past?

What might your friends who are far from God think or feel about this? What can be done about it?

When was the last time you said or taught one thing yet acted quite differently? What emotions might God feel when he sees us thinking or acting contrary to his character?

PRAY

Sit for a few minutes in silence, asking God to help you know the feeling of true humility. Then call on him to forgive you where your life has not lived up to what you claim to believe. (Be specific.)

LIVE

Courageously invite others around you to help you remain humble. Give them permission to do what it takes to help your life match your words.

DAY 255
EXPANDED PASSAGE: ROMANS 4

TRUSTING WHEN IT'S HOPELESS

ROMANS 4:16-21

[16]That is why it depends on faith, in order that the promise may rest on grace and be guaranteed to all his offspring—not only to the adherent of the law but also to the one who shares the faith of Abraham, who is the father of us all, [17]as it is written, "I have made you the father of many nations"—in the presence of the God in whom he believed, who gives life to the dead and calls into existence the things that do not exist. [18]In hope he believed against hope, that he should become the father of many nations, as he had been told, "So shall your offspring be." [19]He did not weaken in faith when he considered his own body, which was as good as dead (since he was about a hundred years old), or when he considered the barrenness of Sarah's womb. [20]No distrust made him waver concerning the promise of God, but he grew strong in his faith as he gave glory to God, [21]fully convinced that God was able to do what he had promised.

READ

Read the passage aloud slowly.

THINK

Read the passage again, but silently.

1. What did God do for Abraham?
2. If you were Abraham, which of the following efforts would be most difficult for you?

   - ☐ daring to trust God to call into existence the things that do not exist
   - ☐ believing in spite of hopeless circumstances
   - ☐ living on the basis of what God says he will do
   - ☐ not weakening in faith
   - ☐ not wavering concerning the promise of God
   - ☐ fully convinced that God is able to do what he has promised
   - ☐ other:

Read the passage again. What words or phrases stand out to you?

PRAY

Thank God for Abraham, "our *faith* father." Ask God to help you trust him and his way. Ask God to help you simply embrace him and what he does.

LIVE

Sit quietly before God. Get used to the idea that you really can embrace him and what he does. Imagine one way your life might be different if you do this.

SLAVES OF RIGHTEOUSNESS

ROMANS 6:15-21

[15]What then? Are we to sin because we are not under law but under grace? By no means! [16]Do you not know that if you present yourselves to anyone as obedient slaves, you are slaves of the one whom you obey, either of sin, which leads to death, or of obedience, which leads to righteousness? [17]But thanks be to God, that you who were once slaves of sin have become obedient from the heart to the standard of teaching to which you were committed, [18]and, having been set free from sin, have become slaves of righteousness. [19]I am speaking in human terms, because of your natural limitations. For just as you once presented your members as slaves to impurity and to lawlessness leading to more lawlessness, so now present your members as slaves to righteousness leading to sanctification.

[20]For when you were slaves of sin, you were free in regard to righteousness. [21]But what fruit were you getting at that time from the things of which you are now ashamed? For the end of those things is death.

THINK

Search yourself for an area where you don't walk in freedom but continue to struggle with sin. When do you easily give in to temptation? Why? Are there times when you don't feel the pull so strongly? Why? What comfort, relief, or pleasure does the sin give you (no matter how short-lived or shallow)? What pain or discomfort does it bring? What do you fear you would lose if you gave up the sin?

READ

Read the passage with your specific sin in mind. Sift these verses through your life experience. How do they hold up? Do you find Paul's description of "sin because we are not under law but under grace"? What about his perspective on living in obedience, which leads to righteousness? Take time to identify what you do and don't agree with.

PRAY

Talk to God about the things you've uncovered. If you have unanswered questions or problems you can't reconcile, share them. If you're frustrated, express it to him. Maybe you will challenge him to show you freedom, as you agree to take on the challenge of giving his ways a shot.

LIVE

"Present your members as slaves to righteousness leading to sanctification." Rest in this today.

NOTHING CAN SEPARATE US FROM GOD'S LOVE

ROMANS 8:31-39

³¹What then shall we say to these things? If God is for us, who can be against us? ³²He who did not spare his own Son but gave him up for us all, how will he not also with him graciously give us all things? ³³Who shall bring any charge against God's elect? It is God who justifies. ³⁴Who is to condemn? Christ Jesus is the one who died — more than that, who was raised — who is at the right hand of God, who indeed is interceding for us. ³⁵Who shall separate us from the love of Christ? Shall tribulation, or distress, or persecution, or famine, or nakedness, or danger, or sword? ³⁶As it is written,

> "For your sake we are being killed all the day long;
>   we are regarded as sheep to be slaughtered."

³⁷No, in all these things we are more than conquerors through him who loved us. ³⁸For I am sure that neither death nor life, nor angels nor rulers, nor things present nor things to come, nor powers, ³⁹nor height nor depth, nor anything else in all creation, will be able to separate us from the love of God in Christ Jesus our Lord.

READ

Read the passage four times very slowly.

THINK

Logically understanding that God loves us is fairly easy. But grasping this truth to its fullest extent in our hearts and souls — in every corner of our everyday existence — requires more. We think we know God loves us, but we don't often ponder this profound truth, this important element of our identity as God's children.

Read the passage again. This time underline the phrases that speak directly to you and encourage your heart. With each underline, say aloud, "Thank you, God, for how much you love me."

"Do you think anyone is going to be able to drive a wedge between [you] and Christ's love for [you]? . . . No way!" When you read Paul's words, what flows through your mind and heart?

PRAY

Sit in silence with one thought in mind: *I am loved by God.* If your mind begins to wander, simply whisper, "Thank you for loving me, Jesus." Claim the promises of this passage as your own.

LIVE

Live confidently knowing that nothing "will be able to separate us from the love of God in Christ Jesus our Lord." He loves you that much!

THE WORD OF FAITH

ROMANS 10:8-13

⁸But what does it say? "The word is near you, in your mouth and in your heart" (that is, the word of faith that we proclaim); ⁹because, if you confess with your mouth that Jesus is Lord and believe in your heart that God raised him from the dead, you will be saved. ¹⁰For with the heart one believes and is justified, and with the mouth one confesses and is saved. ¹¹For the Scripture says, "Everyone who believes in him will not be put to shame." ¹²For there is no distinction between Jew and Greek; for the same Lord is Lord of all, bestowing his riches on all who call on him. ¹³For "everyone who calls on the name of the Lord will be saved."

READ

Read the passage aloud slowly.

THINK

Read the passage again silently.

1. Look at the rich phrases and see which one speaks to you most:

   ☐ "the word is near you, in your mouth and in your heart"
   ☐ "the word of faith that we proclaim"
   ☐ "believe in your heart that God raised him from the dead, you will be saved"
   ☐ "with the mouth one confesses"
   ☐ "Everyone who believes in him will not be put to shame."
   ☐ "Everyone who calls on the name of the Lord will be saved."

2. Why does this phrase touch you?
3. In what way would you like this phrase to become a stronger reality in your life?

PRAY

Thank God for his nearness, his willingness to be embraced, his willingness to hear us and set things right. Talk to God about your next step in trusting him heart and soul.

LIVE

Sit quietly before God, imagining what it feels like to live trusting him and embracing him — a life without shame.

DAY 259

GOD ENCOUNTERS

On this seventh day, review and reflect on all you have read this week. Take the time to revel in the ways you've encountered God in the past six days.

A LIVING SACRIFICE

ROMANS 12:1-3

¹I appeal to you therefore, brothers, by the mercies of God, to present your bodies as a living sacrifice, holy and acceptable to God, which is your spiritual worship. ²Do not be conformed to this world, but be transformed by the renewal of your mind, that by testing you may discern what is the will of God, what is good and acceptable and perfect.

³For by the grace given to me I say to everyone among you not to think of himself more highly than he ought to think, but to think with sober judgment, each according to the measure of faith that God has assigned.

READ

Read the passage twice, aloud.

THINK

Choose a theme that speaks to you — perhaps the idea of presenting your body as a living sacrifice or perhaps the idea of being transformed instead of conformed to this world. What does this passage say about that issue?

PRAY

Pick one phrase from the passage that pinpoints the theme that impacts you. Repeat that phrase to yourself slowly several times. Each time you say it, notice your internal response. What thoughts, memories, or feelings does it stir up?

Now bring these thoughts back to the passage, line by line, in a conversation with God: He speaks to you through the words in the passage, then you respond to what he said. (For example, if you feel you are being conformed to the world, you bring that feeling to each line of the passage and see how God replies.) When you're finished, repeat the phrase to yourself one last time, checking your heart's reaction. Is it different? Don't worry if this process leaves unanswered questions. Just be open to what God is showing you through your meditation.

LIVE

Consider the idea of presenting your body as a "living sacrifice." What would this look like as an act of "spiritual worship"? How would it affect your day-to-day activities? Think about these activities today.

GOVERNMENT AND GOD

ROMANS 13:1-7

[1]Let every person be subject to the governing authorities. For there is no authority except from God, and those that exist have been instituted by God. [2]Therefore whoever resists the authorities resists what God has appointed, and those who resist will incur judgment. [3]For rulers are not a terror to good conduct, but to bad. Would you have no fear of the one who is in authority? Then do what is good, and you will receive his approval, [4]for he is God's servant for your good. But if you do wrong, be afraid, for he does not bear the sword in vain. For he is the servant of God, an avenger who carries out God's wrath on the wrongdoer. [5]Therefore one must be in subjection, not only to avoid God's wrath but also for the sake of conscience. [6]For because of this you also pay taxes, for the authorities are ministers of God, attending to this very thing. [7]Pay to all what is owed to them: taxes to whom taxes are owed, revenue to whom revenue is owed, respect to whom respect is owed, honor to whom honor is owed.

THINK

There are all sorts of opinions out there regarding how our government should be run. And people have a hard time talking about church and government in the same paragraphs. *Separation of church and state,* we think.

But when was the last time you thanked God for people in office or prayed for their leadership? Have you ever thought about the truth that God is powerful and in control of the world in such a way that he is not surprised by who is in office, regardless of that person's political views?

In this passage, Paul commands, "Pay to all what is owed to them: taxes to whom taxes are owed, revenue to whom revenue is owed, respect to whom respect is owed, honor to whom honor is owed." What is your obligation as a citizen to this country and to the kingdom of God? In what specific ways can you respect your leaders?

READ

Read the passage.

PRAY

Find a list of names of your local officials (mayor, city council members, county officials), as well as your state and federal officials (governor, congressmen and women, senators, Supreme Court justices, vice president, and president). Pray for each one of them by name. Pray that God would use them to lead wisely and justly.

LIVE

Consider writing a short note or letter of encouragement to one or two of the government officials you prayed for, telling them you are thankful for what they do.

DEBATABLE MATTERS

ROMANS 14:6-10,13

⁶The one who observes the day, observes it in honor of the Lord. The one who eats, eats in honor of the Lord, since he gives thanks to God, while the one who abstains, abstains in honor of the Lord and gives thanks to God. ⁷For none of us lives to himself, and none of us dies to himself. ⁸For if we live, we live to the Lord, and if we die, we die to the Lord. So then, whether we live or whether we die, we are the Lord's. ⁹For to this end Christ died and lived again, that he might be Lord both of the dead and of the living.

¹⁰Why do you pass judgment on your brother? Or you, why do you despise your brother? For we will all stand before the judgment seat of God....

¹³Therefore let us not pass judgment on one another any longer, but rather decide never to put a stumbling block or hindrance in the way of a brother.

READ

Read the passage aloud slowly, keeping in mind that Paul has been addressing a controversy about what foods are right to eat.

THINK

Read the passage aloud again, imagining that Paul, your brother in Christ, is sitting next to you in a window seat, saying these things to you.

1. Why do people insist on their own way about debatable matters?
2. When you're critical, what words and tone do you usually use? When you're being condescending, what facial expression and arm gestures do you use?
3. What does this passage say about why moral superiority is so silly?

Read the passage aloud again. Which phrase speaks most deeply to you?

PRAY

Take the phrase that spoke to you and talk to God about it. Ask him to let that truth sink into your deepest self. Ask him to guide you in that truth.

LIVE

When Mother Teresa was asked how someone might pray for her, she asked that person to pray that she would not get in the way of what God wanted to do. Move through life with that consciousness, acting with God's love but not getting in the way of what God wants to do.

STRENGTH IS FOR SERVICE

ROMANS 15:1-6

[1]We who are strong have an obligation to bear with the failings of the weak, and not to please ourselves. [2]Let each of us please his neighbor for his good, to build him up. [3]For Christ did not please himself, but as it is written, "The reproaches of those who reproached you fell on me." [4]For whatever was written in former days was written for our instruction, that through endurance and through the encouragement of the Scriptures we might have hope. [5]May the God of endurance and encouragement grant you to live in such harmony with one another, in accord with Christ Jesus, [6]that together you may with one voice glorify the God and Father of our Lord Jesus Christ.

THINK

Paul specifies that we are to help others in areas where we are strong. What are some areas in which you have received training, direction, or guidance? What are some of your natural gifts and strengths?

READ

Read the passage with a heart of gratitude for those who, past and present, helped to build you up, even if you don't remember specific details.

PRAY

Ponder what this passage says about Jesus and how he dealt with people's troubles. Now think about his call to follow him (see Matthew 16:24). When you think about being like Jesus in this way, what questions, thoughts, and feelings come up? Share these with him.

LIVE

Contemplate the role that service to others plays in your daily life. There are a variety of forms this might take, for example, lending a listening ear or emotional support, doing manual labor or other chores for someone, or giving money, food, shelter, or clothing to a person in need. Has your service to others become another form of overwork? Or is it truly integrated into your life in a comfortable and valuable way? Have you been selfish in the use of your time? Should you be giving more of yourself to others than you currently do?[17]

CONSIDER YOUR CALLING

1 CORINTHIANS 1:26-31

[26]For consider your calling, brothers: not many of you were wise according to worldly standards, not many were powerful, not many were of noble birth. [27]But God chose what is foolish in the world to shame the wise; God chose what is weak in the world to shame the strong; [28]God chose what is low and despised in the world, even things that are not, to bring to nothing things that are, [29]so that no human being might boast in the presence of God. [30]And because of him you are in Christ Jesus, who became to us wisdom from God, righteousness and sanctification and redemption, [31]so that, as it is written, "Let the one who boasts, boast in the Lord."

READ
Ruminate over these verses. Take your time and read them slowly.

THINK
What sticks out to you in this passage concerning God and your relationship with him?

When have you tried to "boast in the presence of God," either overtly or subtly?

Consider the entire story of Scripture, starting with Genesis. Think about the types of people God fights for and the types he uses to impact human history: Abraham, Moses, Gideon, Saul (later Paul), Peter, and so on. Many of them started out inadequate or less-than-qualified for the job. How does this make you feel about God's desire to use you in his grand plan for the world?

PRAY
Write down your thoughts and prayers in these two areas:

1. "Consider your calling: . . . not many of you were wise." Think about what your life was like — specifically and generally — before meeting Christ. (If you don't remember because you let Christ in when you were really young, think about the person you were even five years ago.)
2. Reflect on the person you are today — the ways you are different due to God's involvement in your life.

Thank God for what he's done.

LIVE

Live confidently today, knowing that God wants to use you — yes, even you — for his ultimate purpose and plan. Live openly before him, realizing that you are an instrument in a world desperately in need of hope.

YOU ARE A TEMPLE

1 CORINTHIANS 3:11-17

¹¹For no one can lay a foundation other than that which is laid, which is Jesus Christ. ¹²Now if anyone builds on the foundation with gold, silver, precious stones, wood, hay, straw — ¹³each one's work will become manifest, for the Day will disclose it, because it will be revealed by fire, and the fire will test what sort of work each one has done. ¹⁴If the work that anyone has built on the foundation survives, he will receive a reward. ¹⁵If anyone's work is burned up, he will suffer loss, though he himself will be saved, but only as through fire.

¹⁶Do you not know that you are God's temple and that God's Spirit dwells in you? ¹⁷If anyone destroys God's temple, God will destroy him. For God's temple is holy, and you are that temple.

READ

Read the passage aloud slowly.

THINK

Read it aloud again, imagining Paul speaking to you as a good father would speak to you (see 1 Corinthians 4:14-17).

In the metaphor where each of us is a building, Jesus is the foundation. What might someone use for a foundation that will be "revealed by fire"? (In general, this would be anything other than Jesus, but be specific for yourself and others like you.)

The sort of building that you are is a temple. A temple is where people go to pray. Not only is God himself present in the temple (you), but both the Holy Spirit and Jesus also live inside you and intercede for you (see Romans 8:26-27,34). What might you do to keep your temple a sacred space?

Read the passage again silently. What does it make you want to be or do or entrust to God?

PRAY

Talk to God about your being a temple for him — even celebrate it! Then ask what you need to know and do to make the Trinity feel at home inside you.

LIVE

Move through life today, musing to yourself about truly being a temple in which the Trinity dwells. Do something to celebrate that.

DAY 266 _____

GOD ENCOUNTERS

On this seventh day, review and reflect on all you have read this week. Take the time to revel in the ways you've encountered God in the past six days.

SIN AND TOLERANCE

1 CORINTHIANS 5:1-6

¹It is actually reported that there is sexual immorality among you, and of a kind that is not tolerated even among pagans, for a man has his father's wife. ²And you are arrogant! Ought you not rather to mourn? Let him who has done this be removed from among you.

³For though absent in body, I am present in spirit; and as if present, I have already pronounced judgment on the one who did such a thing. ⁴When you are assembled in the name of the Lord Jesus and my spirit is present, with the power of our Lord Jesus, ⁵you are to deliver this man to Satan for the destruction of the flesh, so that his spirit may be saved in the day of the Lord.

⁶Your boasting is not good. Do you not know that a little leaven leavens the whole lump?

READ

Read the passage.

THINK

Have you ever observed the process of baking bread? By the work of a pinch of yeast, a small ball of dough doubles in size. Consider how this process is similar to what happens with sin and tolerance among Christians. In what way does arrogance and boasting make the problem worse?

PRAY

Think of a particular experience you've had with sin lately — either your own or that of someone you're close to. How did you respond? Did the sin break your heart? Did you confront it? Did you avoid or ignore it?

Picture Jesus sitting with you. Talk to him about what happened. Explore your heart with him and ask him to uncover why you responded the way you did.

LIVE

Consider this statement by Julian of Norwich: "[God] comes down to the lowest part of our need. For he never despises that which he himself has made."[18] Do you believe it's true about you? About others you know? Write down what this touches in you and anything you sense God is inviting you to do in response.

DAY 268
EXPANDED PASSAGE: 1 CORINTHIANS 8

RISKING SOMEONE'S ETERNAL RUIN

1 CORINTHIANS 8:7-9

[7]However, not all possess this knowledge. But some, through former association with idols, eat food as really offered to an idol, and their conscience, being weak, is defiled. [8]Food will not commend us to God. We are no worse off if we do not eat, and no better off if we do. [9]But take care that this right of yours does not somehow become a stumbling block to the weak.

READ

This passage was part of an actual letter. Pretend you have just pulled this letter from your mailbox. Read the words as though they are handwritten by a friend.

THINK

Paul gives instruction here to the church in Corinth regarding meat sacrificed to idols. Translated to our current culture, this instruction would be similar to Christians who believe that people should never drink alcohol versus Christians who believe that people have the freedom to drink alcohol, depending on their maturity in their Christian walk.

Think of a situation when you could have been more sensitive to other believers who may have a different understanding than you. How can you grow to be more sensitive to others without becoming soft on the truth? What sacrifices in your own life need to be made to ensure you aren't "a stumbling block to the weak"?

Where is the limit on our freedom in Christ?

PRAY

Ask God to search your heart in the area of sensitive interaction with other believers. Consider not only *what* you say or do but also *how* you say or do it. Ask the Holy Spirit to give you wisdom and compassion for healthy, God-honoring relationships with other believers.

Finally, ask God to show you if there is anyone you need to request forgiveness from due to an interaction that involved differing views on these types of issues.

LIVE

If applicable, boldly but humbly seek out those individuals and ask their forgiveness for your lack of sensitivity. Consider also talking with friends or family members in the near future about what freedom in Christ expressed appropriately might look like.

DRINKING FROM THE SPIRITUAL ROCK

1 CORINTHIANS 10:1-10

[1]For I do not want you to be unaware, brothers, that our fathers were all under the cloud, and all passed through the sea, [2]and all were baptized into Moses in the cloud and in the sea, [3]and all ate the same spiritual food, [4]and all drank the same spiritual drink. For they drank from the spiritual Rock that followed them, and the Rock was Christ. [5]Nevertheless, with most of them God was not pleased, for they were overthrown in the wilderness.

[6]Now these things took place as examples for us, that we might not desire evil as they did. [7]Do not be idolaters as some of them were; as it is written, "The people sat down to eat and drink and rose up to play." [8]We must not indulge in sexual immorality as some of them did, and twenty-three thousand fell in a single day. [9]We must not put Christ to the test, as some of them did and were destroyed by serpents, [10]nor grumble, as some of them did and were destroyed by the Destroyer.

READ

Read the passage aloud slowly, realizing that Paul is referring to how the Israelites exited Egypt, crossed the Red Sea, and journeyed to the Promised Land.

THINK

Read the passage again.

1. What miracles did the Israelites experience? (Note: Some people read verse 4 to mean that the same rock followed them or appeared at each of their resting places — and "the Rock was Christ." So Christ journeyed with them.)
2. "Nevertheless, with most of them God was not pleased, for they were overthrown in the wilderness." Try to understand and explain how they could have developed this attitude.
3. Which of these ways that the Israelites wanted their own way captivates you most?

   ☐ becoming idolaters
   ☐ being sexually immoral
   ☐ putting Christ to the test
   ☐ grumbling

PRAY

Read the passage one more time. Thank God that he draws you to experience his wonder and grace every day. Ask him to keep you away from temptation and to teach you how to deal with it.

LIVE

Be alert and expectant today, noticing God's wonder and grace, and thanking him for it. See yourself as learning from the Israelites' mistakes.

MY BODY, BROKEN FOR YOU

1 CORINTHIANS 11:23-29

[23]For I received from the Lord what I also delivered to you, that the Lord Jesus on the night when he was betrayed took bread, [24]and when he had given thanks, he broke it, and said, "This is my body which is for you. Do this in remembrance of me." [25]In the same way also he took the cup, after supper, saying, "This cup is the new covenant in my blood. Do this, as often as you drink it, in remembrance of me." [26]For as often as you eat this bread and drink the cup, you proclaim the Lord's death until he comes.

[27]Whoever, therefore, eats the bread or drinks the cup of the Lord in an unworthy manner will be guilty concerning the body and blood of the Lord. [28]Let a person examine himself, then, and so eat of the bread and drink of the cup. [29]For anyone who eats and drinks without discerning the body eats and drinks judgment on himself.

THINK

Briefly think back on the last time you took Communion. What was it like for you? Did it feel routine or special? In what ways? Who was there with you? Did the presence of that person(s) change the experience for you in any way? How did you prepare yourself?

READ

Read the passage, being especially aware of how you usually approach Communion.

PRAY

Be aware of the Holy Spirit's presence with you now. Meditate on what stands out to you in Paul's description of the communion experience. What is your reaction to his words? Do you resonate with his serious tone? Do you feel challenged by anything in particular? Invite the Holy Spirit to examine your heart and to filter out any junk he finds there — and make you clean.

LIVE

Take time to examine your heart now, as at Communion. What do you need to clear up with God? With another person? Meditate on this Anglican prayer from *The Book of Common Prayer*: "We do not presume to come to this thy Table, O merciful Lord, trusting in our own righteousness, but in thy manifold and great mercies. We are not worthy so much as to gather up the crumbs under thy Table. But thou art the same Lord whose property is always to have mercy. Grant us therefore, gracious Lord, so to eat the flesh of thy dear Son Jesus Christ, and to drink his blood, that we may evermore dwell in him, and he in us. *Amen.*"[19]

Find out the next time your church plans to offer Communion, and set aside time on your calendar to revisit this prayer of examination before you participate.

NOTHING WITHOUT LOVE

1 CORINTHIANS 13:3-7

[3]If I give away all I have, and if I deliver up my body to be burned, but have not love, I gain nothing.

[4]Love is patient and kind; love does not envy or boast; it is not arrogant [5]or rude. It does not insist on its own way; it is not irritable or resentful; [6]it does not rejoice at wrongdoing, but rejoices with the truth. [7]Love bears all things, believes all things, hopes all things, endures all things.

READ

Ask God to give you fresh insight into these familiar words, allowing you to learn things that you haven't before. Now read the passage.

THINK

Whether we know Scripture well or not, most of us have heard this passage read during a wedding ceremony. Its words are encouraging and uplifting, and we might hope the couple won't forget them (and us either). But as you know, reading the words is much easier than living by them.

Ponder this sentence: "If I deliver up my body to be burned, but have not love, I gain nothing." What specifically does this mean in your own life?

Consider the list that defines love. Read line by line, asking yourself these two questions: In what ways am I living this out well? In what ways do I need to improve?

PRAY

Pick the one that needs more improvement, and communicate it to God. Ask him to remodel your life in such a way that you quickly see changes in this area. Ask for the ability to recognize when you're not exemplifying the godly love described in this passage.

LIVE

Someplace where you will see it often today—in your cell phone, on your hand, or at the top of a notebook—write the one way you want to improve. When you see it, ask yourself how you might express that attribute to those around you.

BE STEADFAST

1 CORINTHIANS 15:51-58

[51]Behold! I tell you a mystery. We shall not all sleep, but we shall all be changed, [52]in a moment, in the twinkling of an eye, at the last trumpet. For the trumpet will sound, and the dead will be raised imperishable, and we shall be changed. [53]For this perishable body must put on the imperishable, and this mortal body must put on immortality. [54]When the perishable puts on the imperishable, and the mortal puts on immortality, then shall come to pass the saying that is written:

"Death is swallowed up in victory."
[55] "O death, where is your victory?
    O death, where is your sting?"

[56]The sting of death is sin, and the power of sin is the law. [57]But thanks be to God, who gives us the victory through our Lord Jesus Christ.

[58]Therefore, my beloved brothers, be steadfast, immovable, always abounding in the work of the Lord, knowing that in the Lord your labor is not in vain.

READ

Read this passage a few times, slowly and meditatively.

THINK

What phrase or idea in this passage stands out to you? Perhaps you are drawn toward the "last trumpet" or being free from the fear of death, or maybe you are more drawn to the concept of not holding back in your work. Allow this idea to unfold in your mind. What does it mean for your life today?

PRAY

Talk to the Master about how this makes you feel. If you have questions for him, don't hold on to them: Let Jesus hear them and then let them go. Trust that your questions will be answered at the right time.

Once you have shared your concerns with Jesus, sit with him in silence, being open to whatever he might say in response.

LIVE

Consider Paul's instruction to the Christians in Corinth to be "always abounding in the work of the Lord." Ponder: What is the "work" you have been made for? Consider your interests, abilities, skills, passions. When do you feel most alive? (The work you've been made for may or may not correspond to your current vocation.)

What holds you back from pursuing this work with your whole heart—however that might look at this stage in your life? Consider the legitimate reasons, as well as the reasons that might be illegitimate but are still preventing you from moving ahead. Talk to God about this. Ask him to show you what he would have you do, even if that's the simple step of waiting on him to slowly reveal your work over time.

DAY 273

GOD ENCOUNTERS

On this seventh day, review and reflect on all you have read this week. Take the time to revel in the ways you've encountered God in the past six days.

YES!

2 CORINTHIANS 1:17-22

[17]Was I vacillating when I wanted to do this? Do I make my plans according to the flesh, ready to say "Yes, yes" and "No, no" at the same time? [18]As surely as God is faithful, our word to you has not been Yes and No. [19]For the Son of God, Jesus Christ, whom we proclaimed among you, Silvanus and Timothy and I, was not Yes and No, but in him it is always Yes. [20]For all the promises of God find their Yes in him. That is why it is through him that we utter our Amen to God for his glory. [21]And it is God who establishes us with you in Christ, and has anointed us, [22]and who has also put his seal on us and given us his Spirit in our hearts as a guarantee.

READ

Read the passage slowly, at least three times.

THINK

In these verses, Paul writes to the church in the city of Corinth about the promises of God through the fulfillment of Jesus. Read the passage again and circle the word *yes* each time it appears in the text.

So often we hear the word *no,* but this passage says, "For all the promises of God find their Yes in him." What does it mean to hear *yes* from God?

What will your life look like (specifically) if you "utter [your] Amen to God for his glory"?

PRAY

Allow God to affirm you as you simply sit with him.

Invite him to bring his promises of "yes" to your mind and heart. What specific promises has he given to you? Embrace those promises and ask him to place these stamps of "yes" on your heart so you can carry them with you.

LIVE

Write down one or two specific "yeses" God has given you. Carry that note around with you. Consider sharing these promises with a friend, roommate, family member, classmate, or coworker today.

EXPANDED PASSAGE: EXODUS 34:29-35; 2 CORINTHIANS 3:7-18

LIFTING THE VEIL

2 CORINTHIANS 3:12-18

[12]Since we have such a hope, we are very bold, [13]not like Moses, who would put a veil over his face so that the Israelites might not gaze at the outcome of what was being brought to an end. [14]But their minds were hardened. For to this day, when they read the old covenant, that same veil remains unlifted, because only through Christ is it taken away. [15]Yes, to this day whenever Moses is read a veil lies over their hearts. [16]But when one turns to the Lord, the veil is removed. [17]Now the Lord is the Spirit, and where the Spirit of the Lord is, there is freedom. [18]And we all, with unveiled face, beholding the glory of the Lord, are being transformed into the same image from one degree of glory to another. For this comes from the Lord who is the Spirit.

READ

Read the passage aloud slowly.

THINK

Again, slowly read verses 12-15 with a mood of despair. Then read verses 16-18 with a mood of joy, mystery, and surprise.

1. What words or phrases stand out to you? Why?
2. If you didn't choose words or phrases from verses 16-18, do that now. Read them again and note the frequency of these words: *veil, face, Spirit, freedom, glory, image.*

PRAY

Paraphrase verses 16-18 back to God, something like: Whenever I turn my face to you, O God, you remove the veil and there we are — face-to-face! I will suddenly recognize you as a living, personal presence, not [fill in, perhaps: a remote, unknown figure]. And when you are personally present, a living Spirit, that old, constricting legalism is recognized as obsolete. I'm free of it! All of us are! Nothing between me and you, my face shining with your glory. And so I am transformed much like the Messiah. My life gradually becomes brighter and more beautiful as you enter my life and I become like you.

LIVE

Sit quietly before God, basking in one of these phrases:

- You are living Spirit.
- The veil is removed.
- I am being transformed into your image.

JARS OF CLAY

2 CORINTHIANS 4:5-13

⁵For what we proclaim is not ourselves, but Jesus Christ as Lord, with ourselves as your servants for Jesus' sake. ⁶For God, who said, "Let light shine out of darkness," has shone in our hearts to give the light of the knowledge of the glory of God in the face of Jesus Christ.

⁷But we have this treasure in jars of clay, to show that the surpassing power belongs to God and not to us. ⁸We are afflicted in every way, but not crushed; perplexed, but not driven to despair; ⁹persecuted, but not forsaken; struck down, but not destroyed; ¹⁰always carrying in the body the death of Jesus, so that the life of Jesus may also be manifested in our bodies. ¹¹For we who live are always being given over to death for Jesus' sake, so that the life of Jesus also may be manifested in our mortal flesh. ¹²So death is at work in us, but life in you.

¹³Since we have the same spirit of faith according to what has been written, "I believed, and so I spoke," we also believe, and so we also speak.

READ

Read the passage aloud once. Read it a second time, and if a word catches your attention, stop and toss it around in your mind. Listen briefly for what your heart is saying in reply. Then keep reading.

THINK

In the silence that follows your reading, meditate on what you heard. How do you relate to the troubled, terrorized, and battered lifestyle Paul and other Christians in the first century led? If you can't relate, what other people around you might be run-down and struggling?

PRAY

Tell God what you've been thinking about. What is your response to the trouble and pain in or around you? If it's your own pain, share with God what you wish you could do in response. If it's the pain of another, notice your impulse to help, fix, or ignore. Be open to God's response to you. Let your sharing lead you into a silent prayer of thankfulness, humility, or request.

LIVE

In her book *Going on Retreat*, Margaret Silf describes what she calls a "retreat on the streets": Small groups of people meet to pray, then they go off into the city with only a few dollars to spend on food that day, taking opportunities to talk with the homeless, unemployed, disturbed, or addicted. At the end of the day, the group gathers to share thoughts and feelings, and to pray.[20]

While this kind of retreat may not be appropriate for you at this time, think about how you could intentionally seek to engage with the needs and feelings of disadvantaged people around you. What would your ordinary life look like if you let the light within you shine amid the darkness?

A NEW CREATION

2 CORINTHIANS 5:14-21

[14]For the love of Christ controls us, because we have concluded this: that one has died for all, therefore all have died; [15]and he died for all, that those who live might no longer live for themselves but for him who for their sake died and was raised.

[16]From now on, therefore, we regard no one according to the flesh. Even though we once regarded Christ according to the flesh, we regard him thus no longer. [17]Therefore, if anyone is in Christ, he is a new creation. The old has passed away; behold, the new has come. [18]All this is from God, who through Christ reconciled us to himself and gave us the ministry of reconciliation; [19]that is, in Christ God was reconciling the world to himself, not counting their trespasses against them, and entrusting to us the message of reconciliation. [20]Therefore, we are ambassadors for Christ, God making his appeal through us. We implore you on behalf of Christ, be reconciled to God. [21]For our sake he made him to be sin who knew no sin, so that in him we might become the righteousness of God.

READ
Read the passage.

THINK
What implications does this passage have for your life right now?

Meditate on these words: "If anyone is in Christ, he is a new creation. The old has passed away; behold, the new has come." (You might consider their radical inclusiveness.)

"Be reconciled to God." How can you become reconciled to God? What would that entail? Do you feel deserving of his reconciliation? Why or why not?

PRAY
Thank God that he makes you a new creation and gives you a fresh start every single morning. Let your thankfulness spill over; tell God that you are grateful to have new life in him.

Ask God to help you become a better friend to him and to help you understand what a friend he is to you!

LIVE
"We are ambassadors for Christ, God making his appeal through us." Who can you tell today about what God is doing in the world?

A HEART WIDE OPEN

2 CORINTHIANS 6:1-13

[1]Working together with him, then, we appeal to you not to receive the grace of God in vain. [2]For he says,

> "In a favorable time I listened to you,
>   and in a day of salvation I have helped you."

Behold, now is the favorable time; behold, now is the day of salvation. [3]We put no obstacle in anyone's way, so that no fault may be found with our ministry, [4]but as servants of God we commend ourselves in every way: by great endurance, in afflictions, hardships, calamities, [5]beatings, imprisonments, riots, labors, sleepless nights, hunger; [6]by purity, knowledge, patience, kindness, the Holy Spirit, genuine love; [7]by truthful speech, and the power of God; with the weapons of righteousness for the right hand and for the left; [8]through honor and dishonor, through slander and praise. We are treated as impostors, and yet are true; [9]as unknown, and yet well known; as dying, and behold, we live; as punished, and yet not killed; [10]as sorrowful, yet always rejoicing; as poor, yet making many rich; as having nothing, yet possessing everything.

[11]We have spoken freely to you, Corinthians; our heart is wide open. [12]You are not restricted by us, but you are restricted in your own affections. [13]In return (I speak as to children) widen your hearts also.

READ

Read the passage aloud slowly.

THINK

Read the passage again, noting any words that stand out to you.

1. What does this passage have to say to someone who thinks life is boring?
2. What does it say to someone who thinks living for God is boring?
3. With what sort of heart did Paul and his friends do their work for God?

Read the passage one more time — very slowly.

4. What words or phrases are most meaningful to you?
5. How do they connect with your life right now?

PRAY

Talk to God about the opportunity to live with your heart wide open. Ask him to show you how to work hard with a heart of patience, kindness, and genuine love, and with a life of power and joy.

LIVE

Sit in the word *live*. Picture yourself fully alive, partnering with God in what he is doing (or wants to do) in you, and in the people and circumstances around you.

GRIEF THAT LEADS TO REPENTANCE

2 CORINTHIANS 7:8-13

[8]For even if I made you grieve with my letter, I do not regret it — though I did regret it, for I see that that letter grieved you, though only for a while. [9]As it is, I rejoice, not because you were grieved, but because you were grieved into repenting. For you felt a godly grief, so that you suffered no loss through us.

[10]For godly grief produces a repentance that leads to salvation without regret, whereas worldly grief produces death. [11]For see what earnestness this godly grief has produced in you, but also what eagerness to clear yourselves, what indignation, what fear, what longing, what zeal, what punishment! At every point you have proved yourselves innocent in the matter. [12]So although I wrote to you, it was not for the sake of the one who did the wrong, nor for the sake of the one who suffered the wrong, but in order that your earnestness for us might be revealed to you in the sight of God. [13]Therefore we are comforted.

And besides our own comfort, we rejoiced still more at the joy of Titus, because his spirit has been refreshed by you all.

LIVE

Since we are spirits in bodies, tangible objects or physical activities can help us enter into prayer. If it's daytime, close the curtains or go into a room without windows. Light a candle and spend a few minutes watching the flame before you read and pray today. Let your awareness of the flame quiet your tendency to be aware only of yourself.

READ

Read the passage twice. According to Paul, what are God's reasons for using grief to bring us to repentance? How does Paul describe a life that's been turned around and brought back closer to God?

THINK

Now set the text aside and take a few moments to sit with your eyes closed and recall recent experiences you've had with sin. Did you repent? If so, how did God lead you to that? Did you resist? What turned you around? If you didn't repent, do you notice ways that God was reaching out to you that you refused? What were the thoughts that held you back?

PRAY

Go back to the passage again. Prayerfully reread Paul's perspective on repentance. How does his outlook interact with your current situation? Is there a message you sense God is speaking to you?

DAY 280

GOD ENCOUNTERS

On this seventh day, review and reflect on all you have read this week. Take the time to revel in the ways you've encountered God in the past six days.

GENEROUS OFFERINGS

2 CORINTHIANS 9:8-15

[8]And God is able to make all grace abound to you, so that having all sufficiency in all things at all times, you may abound in every good work. [9]As it is written,

> "He has distributed freely, he has given to the poor;
>   his righteousness endures forever."

[10]He who supplies seed to the sower and bread for food will supply and multiply your seed for sowing and increase the harvest of your righteousness. [11]You will be enriched in every way to be generous in every way, which through us will produce thanksgiving to God. [12]For the ministry of this service is not only supplying the needs of the saints but is also overflowing in many thanksgivings to God. [13]By their approval of this service, they will glorify God because of your submission that comes from your confession of the gospel of Christ, and the generosity of your contribution for them and for all others, [14]while they long for you and pray for you, because of the surpassing grace of God upon you. [15]Thanks be to God for his inexpressible gift!

READ

Read the passage, imagining that Paul is speaking these words specifically to you.

THINK

Paul talks here about generosity as an important element of God's character. Taking care of the poor is close to the heart of God. Jesus spoke — and lived — generously, just like his Father.

Do you think followers of God are known as being generous people? Why or why not?

In what ways can you grow in your generosity with your time? Your love? Your money? Your abilities? Your possessions? Your life?

PRAY

Walk around inside and outside your home. Look at your possessions: clothes, electronic equipment, books, furniture, paintings on the walls, maybe even the car in your driveway, and so on. What does all this stuff make you think? (Even if most of it belongs to others, like your parents, what's running through your head and heart?) Use Paul's words as the foundation for your communication with God, praying as you are walking around.

Talk with God about your desire to be more generous with the objects you possess. Ask him to bring to mind the people you could be more generous with today and in what way. Ask God to make you more like him — a person of generosity.

LIVE

Go and live with generosity at the forefront of your mind.

GOD'S HIDDEN SERVANTS

2 CORINTHIANS 11:21,23-30

[21]To my shame, I must say, we were too weak for that!

But whatever anyone else dares to boast of—I am speaking as a fool—I also dare to boast of that.... [23]Are they servants of Christ? I am a better one—I am talking like a madman—with far greater labors, far more imprisonments, with countless beatings, and often near death. [24]Five times I received at the hands of the Jews the forty lashes less one. [25]Three times I was beaten with rods. Once I was stoned. Three times I was shipwrecked; a night and a day I was adrift at sea; [26]on frequent journeys, in danger from rivers, danger from robbers, danger from my own people, danger from Gentiles, danger in the city, danger in the wilderness, danger at sea, danger from false brothers; [27]in toil and hardship, through many a sleepless night, in hunger and thirst, often without food, in cold and exposure. [28]And, apart from other things, there is the daily pressure on me of my anxiety for all the churches. [29]Who is weak, and I am not weak? Who is made to fall, and I am not indignant?

[30]If I must boast, I will boast of the things that show my weakness.

READ

Read the passage aloud slowly, keeping in mind that the Corinthians were partial to slick preachers.

THINK

Which sort of teachers (of the Bible, of spiritual things) do you gravitate toward: the animated, joking, smooth servants of God or the hidden, suffering, unrecognized servants of God?

Paul was the second type. In those days, they didn't know him as we do — the great apostle Paul who wrote nearly half the New Testament. He may not have been all that popular a fellow.

Read the passage again silently. If you were to admire the apostle Paul, what in this passage describes what you would admire him for?

Keep in mind that Paul was also a person of joy. His joy was not in being well-known and appreciated. Instead he was one who encouraged his reader to "rejoice in the Lord always; again I will say, rejoice" (Philippians 4:4). When do you need Paul's sort of joy in your life?

PRAY

Ask God to give you discernment (not judgment) about his servants and which ones are best to follow. Ask God to give you great satisfaction in serving him regardless of how successful that service may look.

LIVE

Watch today for an opportunity to feel the desperation for another who is at the end of his or her rope, or to have an angry fire in your gut when someone is duped into sin. Make an effort to weep for those who weep and rejoice with those who rejoice.

RELATIONSHIPS ARE MESSY

2 CORINTHIANS 12:16-21

[16]But granting that I myself did not burden you, I was crafty, you say, and got the better of you by deceit. [17]Did I take advantage of you through any of those whom I sent to you? [18]I urged Titus to go, and sent the brother with him. Did Titus take advantage of you? Did we not act in the same spirit? Did we not take the same steps?

[19]Have you been thinking all along that we have been defending ourselves to you? It is in the sight of God that we have been speaking in Christ, and all for your upbuilding, beloved. [20]For I fear that perhaps when I come I may find you not as I wish, and that you may find me not as you wish — that perhaps there may be quarreling, jealousy, anger, hostility, slander, gossip, conceit, and disorder. [21]I fear that when I come again my God may humble me before you, and I may have to mourn over many of those who sinned earlier and have not repented of the impurity, sexual immorality, and sensuality that they have practiced.

READ

Read the passage aloud slowly.

THINK

Enter the scenes that Paul is describing. Envision the individual members of the Corinthian church he's writing to. Replay Paul's history with them—how he first came to the cosmopolitan city preaching the message of Christ for the first time. Many believed and repented, and many formed new churches. Since then, those churches have helped support him financially, and he's acted as a spiritual mentor and father to them. Imagine what goes on in his mind as he anticipates visiting them again; think about what his last visit was like.

PRAY

Now read the passage again aloud. Notice the messiness of human relationships—misunderstandings, conflicts, and tensions. In the silence that follows your reading, consider your own relationships. Pick one in which you've felt the most recent tension or problems. Open up to God, asking him to show you what he wants you to know about it.

LIVE

Write down in a journal what God uncovered for you about your problematic relationship. Ask him to make clear anything he is asking you to notice or do about it, then sit quietly and attentively as you wait for his response. Don't assume that you should necessarily do anything; instead be open to how God leads you.

IN NEED OF CORRECTION

GALATIANS 1:6-12

[6]I am astonished that you are so quickly deserting him who called you in the grace of Christ and are turning to a different gospel — [7]not that there is another one, but there are some who trouble you and want to distort the gospel of Christ. [8]But even if we or an angel from heaven should preach to you a gospel contrary to the one we preached to you, let him be accursed. [9]As we have said before, so now I say again: If anyone is preaching to you a gospel contrary to the one you received, let him be accursed.

[10]For am I now seeking the approval of man, or of God? Or am I trying to please man? If I were still trying to please man, I would not be a servant of Christ.

[11]For I would have you know, brothers, that the gospel that was preached by me is not man's gospel. [12]For I did not receive it from any man, nor was I taught it, but I received it through a revelation of Jesus Christ.

READ

Read the passage aloud. Reflect by writing your thoughts down in a journal or typing them into your computer.

THINK

This feels like a scathing lecture from Paul—and it certainly is. He is disgusted because the church in Galatia has turned from the true gospel to other slick teachers and optimistic (but empty) ways of thinking.

Consider carefully: What are the essentials of the gospel—the good news of Jesus Christ? What does it most certainly include? What does it most certainly not include?

Have you ever been tempted to turn from the message of the gospel or to add to, delete, or alter portions of it to make it conveniently fit your life? Have you ever heard others add to, delete, or alter the message of the gospel? What might be done about that? What are the consequences of doing such a thing?

What might Paul say to you if he were here today?

PRAY

Prayerfully reflect on the importance of the gospel message. Ask God to give you a mind that discerns and carefully weighs the truth of the gospel and that knows how the gospel should be applied to your life.

LIVE

Spend a few minutes searching for and reading at least three key passages in your Bible that speak specifically to the meaning of the gospel.

JUSTIFIED BY FAITH

GALATIANS 2:16,19-21

[16]Yet we know that a person is not justified by works of the law but through faith in Jesus Christ, so we also have believed in Christ Jesus, in order to be justified by faith in Christ and not by works of the law, because by works of the law no one will be justified. . . .

[19]For through the law I died to the law, so that I might live to God. [20]I have been crucified with Christ. It is no longer I who live, but Christ who lives in me. And the life I now live in the flesh I live by faith in the Son of God, who loved me and gave himself for me. [21]I do not nullify the grace of God, for if righteousness were through the law, then Christ died for no purpose.

READ

Read the passage aloud slowly.

THINK

Read it again silently.

1. What did Paul find that was better than trying to obey the law?
2. Which of the following astonishing statements by Paul do you find most intriguing? (The first three are truer the more the last two come to pass.)

   ☐ "A person is not justified by works of the law."
   ☐ "I died to the law, so I might live to God."
   ☐ "The life I now live in the flesh I live by faith in the Son of God."
   ☐ "Christ lives in me."
   ☐ "The life I now live in the flesh I live by faith in the Son of God."

Read the passage one more time—very slowly—letting it sink into the innermost parts of you.

PRAY

Talk to God about Paul's amazing statements. Which of them do you want help in making true of yourself? To what degree do you really believe that "Christ lives in [you]"? If you need help believing this, tell God.

LIVE

Take something with you through your day to remind yourself that the life you now live is not yours, but is Christ's life in you. The item could be a cross, a piece of paper with this statement written on it, a stone on which you have written *LIFE*, or whatever will help remind you.

GROWTH: A RESULT OF HOW HARD YOU TRY?

GALATIANS 3:2-6

²Let me ask you only this: Did you receive the Spirit by works of the law or by hearing with faith? ³Are you so foolish? Having begun by the Spirit, are you now being perfected by the flesh? ⁴Did you suffer so many things in vain — if indeed it was in vain? ⁵Does he who supplies the Spirit to you and works miracles among you do so by works of the law, or by hearing with faith — ⁶just as Abraham "believed God, and it was counted to him as righteousness"?

READ

As you read this passage, try not to identify yourself too firmly with the author's anger, but stay open to any similarities you recognize between yourself and his listeners.

THINK/PRAY

Ponder one question that particularly challenges you. For example, "Does he who supplies the Spirit to you and works miracles among you do so by works of the law, or by hearing with faith?" Or ask yourself what "foolish" efforts you're making toward a transformational work that he's begun in you. Share your heart's response openly with the Father. Bring him your questions and concerns, and ask for his help in opening up to his model of growth.

LIVE

Take several minutes to try stepping outside your usual foolishness. Taste what it could be like to see growth as a process of "hearing with faith." Rest in the presence of his Holy Spirit. Don't worry about how you'll grow spiritually; don't try to make a plan for how you'll change yourself. Use this time to practice simply being, finding out what it is to be yourself in the presence of Love.

DAY 287

GOD ENCOUNTERS

On this seventh day, review and reflect on all you have read this week. Take the time to revel in the ways you've encountered God in the past six days.

HEIRS THROUGH GOD

GALATIANS 4:1-7

[1]I mean that the heir, as long as he is a child, is no different from a slave, though he is the owner of everything, [2]but he is under guardians and managers until the date set by his father. [3]In the same way we also, when we were children, were enslaved to the elementary principles of the world. [4]But when the fullness of time had come, God sent forth his Son, born of woman, born under the law, [5]to redeem those who were under the law, so that we might receive adoption as sons. [6]And because you are sons, God has sent the Spirit of his Son into our hearts, crying, "Abba! Father!" [7]So you are no longer a slave, but a son, and if a son, then an heir through God.

READ

Read the passage at least five times. Take your time. Slow down and reflect on what you read.

THINK

Paul is a master craftsman of metaphors. And so we find him here in the middle of another word picture, contrasting the difference between the rights and privileges of a slave and those of an heir. We were once slaves, but as believers we are now called sons and daughters — heirs — and God desires for us to live in freedom, not slavery: "God sent forth his Son . . . to redeem those who were under the law, so that we might receive adoption as sons."

What does it mean for you to experience your rightful heritage in Christ? What does it mean to have freedom in your relationship with him? How do you temper that freedom so as not to abuse God's grace?

In what ways does being an heir rather than a slave change your interaction with your Father? Be specific.

PRAY

Imagine yourself in the lap of your Father, remembering that you have the privilege of calling him "Abba! Father!" With the mind-set of a child, pray like a child. Begin your prayer with "Papa." Pray freely and without fear, knowing that this childlike and intimate language is not only permissible but desirable. Tell him your fears. Tell him your joys. Tell him your dreams.

LIVE

Pray frequently, creatively, and confidently, knowing that you have great freedom to approach your heavenly Papa, who is always accessible to you.

FRUITFUL LOVE

GALATIANS 5:16-17,19-23

[16]But I say, walk by the Spirit, and you will not gratify the desires of the flesh. [17]For the desires of the flesh are against the Spirit, and the desires of the Spirit are against the flesh, for these are opposed to each other, to keep you from doing the things you want to do. . . .

[19]Now the works of the flesh are evident: sexual immorality, impurity, sensuality, [20]idolatry, sorcery, enmity, strife, jealousy, fits of anger, rivalries, dissensions, divisions, [21]envy, drunkenness, orgies, and things like these. I warn you, as I warned you before, that those who do such things will not inherit the kingdom of God. [22]But the fruit of the Spirit is love, joy, peace, patience, kindness, goodness, faithfulness, [23]gentleness, self-control; against such things there is no law.

READ

Read the passage aloud slowly. Read verses 16-17 and 19-21 again slowly. What words or phrases stand out to you? Why do you think they stand out? Read verses 22-23 again slowly. What words or phrases stand out to you? Why do you think they stand out?

THINK

These two ways of life — the flesh and the Spirit — negate each other. To live the first way shuts out the second. To live the second way shuts out the first. The first is empowered by the idea that we must get what we want when we want it. The second is empowered by a faithful, fruitful love for God.

PRAY

Talk to God about the ideas that stood out to you in verses 22-23. Tell God why these are attractive to you. Tell God how they reflect his deep character.

LIVE

Hold one of the following words in front of you today: *love, joy, peace, patience, kindness, goodness, faithfulness, gentleness, self-control.* Let that word permeate what you do.

FREE FROM PLEASING OTHERS

GALATIANS 6:11-16

[11]See with what large letters I am writing to you with my own hand. [12]It is those who want to make a good showing in the flesh who would force you to be circumcised, and only in order that they may not be persecuted for the cross of Christ. [13]For even those who are circumcised do not themselves keep the law, but they desire to have you circumcised that they may boast in your flesh. [14]But far be it from me to boast except in the cross of our Lord Jesus Christ, by which the world has been crucified to me, and I to the world. [15]For neither circumcision counts for anything, nor uncircumcision, but a new creation. [16]And as for all who walk by this rule, peace and mercy be upon them, and upon the Israel of God.

READ

Carefully read the passage.

THINK

This passage is rebuking first-century Christians for believing that cere-monial Jewish acts like circumcision could alleviate all guilt before God. Consider how you relate to this message. Who are you interested in impressing? How much energy do you expend figuring out ways to be more accepted by others? Is your security rooted in others, or is it rooted in your total acceptance by God?

Do you ever imagine God taking sides — either with you against the world or with everyone else against you? How would your life look if you lived to please only him?

PRAY

Let your thoughts lead you into conversation with God. Interact with him on what you're thinking about, remembering that he loves and accepts you. You might write things down as they come to mind, but don't let your writing shrink your awareness so you forget God's presence. Confide in him why you do what you do, even if you know your reasons are selfish or foolish.

LIVE

Return to the question of how your life would look if you lived only to please him — to boast about nothing "except in the cross of our Lord Jesus Christ." What one thing, even if tiny and internal, could you do to start living this way? Maybe you begin by asking God to help you get beyond pleasing others."

WHO WE ARE

EPHESIANS 1:11-19

[11]In him we have obtained an inheritance, having been predestined according to the purpose of him who works all things according to the counsel of his will, [12]so that we who were the first to hope in Christ might be to the praise of his glory. [13]In him you also, when you heard the word of truth, the gospel of your salvation, and believed in him, were sealed with the promised Holy Spirit, [14]who is the guarantee of our inheritance until we acquire possession of it, to the praise of his glory.

[15]For this reason, because I have heard of your faith in the Lord Jesus and your love toward all the saints, [16]I do not cease to give thanks for you, remembering you in my prayers, [17]that the God of our Lord Jesus Christ, the Father of glory, may give you the Spirit of wisdom and of revelation in the knowledge of him, [18]having the eyes of your hearts enlightened, that you may know what is the hope to which he has called you, what are the riches of his glorious inheritance in the saints, [19]and what is the immeasurable greatness of his power toward us who believe, according to the working of his great might.

THINK

Consider your identity. Who are you—*really*? In what do you find your true identity and sense of worth? In other words, what makes you, you? Are the sources of your self-worth healthy or unhealthy? Jot down a few notes about how you see your identity.

READ

Read the passage silently, but mouth the words of the verses as you read. What does this passage say about your identity? What is Christ's role in shaping your identity? Refer to your notes. How does this picture of your identity compare to those initial thoughts?

PRAY

Paul includes several elements in his prayers for the church at Ephesus. It is full of thanksgiving, petitions for wisdom and revelation in the Father, enlightened hearts, hope, knowledge of the inheritance, and the greatness of his power.

Make Paul's prayer in verses 15-19 your own. For example, *I ask you—the God of my Lord, Jesus Christ, the God of glory—to give me wisdom and the revelation of knowing you personally.* And so on.

Next, ask God to bring to mind an individual who needs prayer. Come before God and pray these verses for that person's current situation and overall life. Pray for his or her identity. Make your prayer specific by replacing the applicable words in today's passage with the individual's name.

Are there others for whom you could pray this prayer? Spend time interceding for them as well.

LIVE

If the Spirit nudges you to do so, tell the person that you prayed specifically for him or her. Read that person the prayer from Scripture.

ALIVE WITH CHRIST

EPHESIANS 2:1-6

¹And you were dead in the trespasses and sins ²in which you once walked, following the course of this world, following the prince of the power of the air, the spirit that is now at work in the sons of disobedience — ³among whom we all once lived in the passions of our flesh, carrying out the desires of the body and the mind, and were by nature children of wrath, like the rest of mankind. ⁴But God, being rich in mercy, because of the great love with which he loved us, ⁵even when we were dead in our trespasses, made us alive together with Christ — by grace you have been saved — ⁶and raised us up with him and seated us with him in the heavenly places in Christ Jesus.

READ

Read the passage aloud slowly.

THINK

Read the passage again, noting the "sins in which you once walked" as described in the first part of the paragraph and all that God has done in the second part.

1. How do you relate to the former life of sin described in verses 1-3?
2. How difficult or easy is it for you to believe that the old life is not in sync with the life Christ offers us?
3. Repeat in your own words what God has done in verses 4-6. What does this tell you about what God is really like?
4. How difficult or easy is it for you to believe that God is like that?

PRAY

Ask God to help you more easily believe in the goodness of life with him (verses 1-3) and in the goodness of God's own self (verses 4-6). Respond to God about what it's like to be surrounded by such goodness.

LIVE

Be aware of having an interactive life with this God who is unendingly compassionate and who makes us really alive all day long.

CHRIST'S EXTRAVAGANT LOVE

EPHESIANS 3:10-21

¹⁰So that through the church the manifold wisdom of God might now be made known to the rulers and authorities in the heavenly places. ¹¹This was according to the eternal purpose that he has realized in Christ Jesus our Lord, ¹²in whom we have boldness and access with confidence through our faith in him. ¹³So I ask you not to lose heart over what I am suffering for you, which is your glory.

¹⁴For this reason I bow my knees before the Father, ¹⁵from whom every family in heaven and on earth is named, ¹⁶that according to the riches of his glory he may grant you to be strengthened with power through his Spirit in your inner being, ¹⁷so that Christ may dwell in your hearts through faith — that you, being rooted and grounded in love, ¹⁸may have strength to comprehend with all the saints what is the breadth and length and height and depth, ¹⁹and to know the love of Christ that surpasses knowledge, that you may be filled with all the fullness of God.

²⁰Now to him who is able to do far more abundantly than all that we ask or think, according to the power at work within us ²¹to him be glory in the church and in Christ Jesus throughout all generations, forever and ever.

READ

As you read this passage, look for a word or theme that refreshes you. Maybe this will be Paul's specific description of God's strength and power, or the picture of having "boldness and access with confidence through our faith in him."

THINK/PRAY

Think about the portion of the passage you chose. Why do you think it touches you today? Are you feeling tired? Trapped? Discouraged?

Now sit in silence, picturing yourself opening the door to Christ and letting him come inside to be with you in your troubles. Talk to him about what is bringing you down.

Look back at the passage, and read — a few times, slowly — the part that spoke to you. What message does Christ want you to hear today? Savor this message and let it speak to your need.

LIVE

Pick a word from the passage that symbolizes what uplifted you. Write it down or doodle a picture that represents its meaning to you. Now put it where you will often see it and reflect on it. Maybe you'll use a sticky note and put it on your steering wheel, your bathroom mirror, or your microwave door. When you see it throughout the day, pause to recall Christ's message to you.

DAY 294

GOD ENCOUNTERS

On this seventh day, review and reflect on all you have read this week. Take the time to revel in the ways you've encountered God in the past six days.

UNITY OF THE SPIRIT

EPHESIANS 4:1-6

[1]I therefore, a prisoner for the Lord, urge you to walk in a manner worthy of the calling to which you have been called, [2]with all humility and gentleness, with patience, bearing with one another in love, [3]eager to maintain the unity of the Spirit in the bond of peace. [4]There is one body and one Spirit—just as you were called to the one hope that belongs to your call—[5]one Lord, one faith, one baptism, [6]one God and Father of all, who is over all and through all and in all.

READ

Read this passage with another believer, if possible.

THINK

Think about "walk[ing] in a manner worthy of the calling to which you have been called." Ponder Paul's words: "eager to maintain the unity of the Spirit in the bond of peace." What does "unity of the Spirit" look like? Do you know other followers of Christ who are walking in unity with you?

"There is one body and one Spirit . . . one Lord, one faith, one baptism." Does this describe your relationships? Your church community? The body of Christ around the world? What can be done to strengthen this oneness with other believers?

With another believer (or several), brainstorm ways — little and big — to help create greater oneness in Christ.

PRAY

When you drive on or walk beside roads today, use that as a trigger to pray for unity among other believers — in your personal circles, in your town, and around the world.

LIVE

Do what you can to live in unity with others.

BE FILLED WITH THE SPIRIT

EPHESIANS 5:15-20

[15]Look carefully then how you walk, not as unwise but as wise, [16]making the best use of the time, because the days are evil. [17]Therefore do not be foolish, but understand what the will of the Lord is. [18]And do not get drunk with wine, for that is debauchery, but be filled with the Spirit, [19]addressing one another in psalms and hymns and spiritual songs, singing and making melody to the Lord with your heart, [20]giving thanks always and for everything to God the Father in the name of our Lord Jesus Christ.

READ

Read the passage aloud slowly.

THINK

Read the passage again, picturing yourself in the crowd of people listening to this letter read aloud (as was done in those days). The writer, Paul, spent two years with your group and knows you well.

1. What does "be foolish" mean to you?
2. How would you go about being "filled with the Spirit"? What would that look like for you?

Read the passage again and notice what words or phrases stand out to you. Why do you think they speak to you that way?

PRAY

Speak back to God the words that spoke to you. Tell God what they mean to you and what you would like to do about them. Talk to God about how well he knows you, that he would speak to you so personally.

LIVE

Each time you drink a liquid today, pause and picture yourself being filled with the liquid Spirit of God. Enjoy that.

RELATIONSHIPS FOR LIVING WELL

EPHESIANS 6:1-9

¹Children, obey your parents in the Lord, for this is right. ²"Honor your father and mother" (this is the first commandment with a promise), ³"that it may go well with you and that you may live long in the land." ⁴Fathers, do not provoke your children to anger, but bring them up in the discipline and instruction of the Lord.

⁵Bondservants, obey your earthly masters with fear and trembling, with a sincere heart, as you would Christ, ⁶not by the way of eye-service, as people-pleasers, but as bondservants of Christ, doing the will of God from the heart, ⁷rendering service with a good will as to the Lord and not to man, ⁸knowing that whatever good anyone does, this he will receive back from the Lord, whether he is a bondservant or is free. ⁹Masters, do the same to them, and stop your threatening, knowing that he who is both their Master and yours is in heaven, and that there is no partiality with him.

READ

Read the passage, letting it call to mind the relevant relationships in your life.

THINK

Mull over what this passage is saying about whole and healthy relationships — children to parents, fathers to children, and employees to employers. What is your reaction to the description given of each relationship? Perhaps you feel longing or maybe sadness or annoyance? Explore your reaction.

PRAY

Pick one relationship this passage brought to mind and take a few minutes to observe what kind of child, parent, employee, or student you are. How does your fulfillment of this role compare to the standard Paul sets? Ponder the models in your life for that role. How were you parented? How do your role models relate to their employers? Talk to Jesus about this, and share with him any disappointment, gratitude, or frustration you feel about your own role and your role models.

LIVE

What is Jesus' invitation to you in the relationship you selected? Perhaps it is just to continue growing in your awareness of what kind of person you are in relationships. Or perhaps you sense Jesus leading you toward a specific action. Make a note of what you hear so you can refer to it.

THE POSTURE OF GRATEFULNESS

PHILIPPIANS 1:3-6

[3]I thank my God in all my remembrance of you, [4]always in every prayer of mine for you all making my prayer with joy, [5]because of your partnership in the gospel from the first day until now. [6]And I am sure of this, that he who began a good work in you will bring it to completion at the day of Jesus Christ.

READ

Read the passage. After doing so, write out the entire passage. Then read it again.

THINK

The subject of thankfulness in prayer will come up many times in this devotional, but there's no way to offer too much gratitude when we communicate with God. Of course it seems to be in our nature to approach God only when times are tough, when we feel like venting, or when we have a need. God listens to all our prayers, but it's hard to pray heartfelt, God-honoring prayers with an ungrateful and complaining spirit. We should *always* be grateful for *something* in prayer.

Paul models a thankful heart for us here as he reflects on the church in Philippi. On a scale of one to ten — one being "frequently ungrateful" and ten being "always thankful" — what number would you give your prayers? What number would your friends give your prayers? What would it take for your prayers to move toward ten?

LIVE/PRAY

Find a small photo of an old friend or family member. Place it in a location where you will see it often. Every time you look at the photo, pause and thank God for who that person is, what that person means to you, and who God is forming that person to become. Be reminded that God, who started this great work in him or her, will "bring it to completion at the day of Jesus Christ."

HE HUMBLED HIMSELF

PHILIPPIANS 2:2-11

[2]Complete my joy by being of the same mind, having the same love, being in full accord and of one mind. [3]Do nothing from selfish ambition or conceit, but in humility count others more significant than yourselves. [4]Let each of you look not only to his own interests, but also to the interests of others. [5]Have this mind among yourselves, which is yours in Christ Jesus, [6]who, though he was in the form of God, did not count equality with God a thing to be grasped, [7]but emptied himself, by taking the form of a servant, being born in the likeness of men. [8]And being found in human form, he humbled himself by becoming obedient to the point of death, even death on a cross. [9]Therefore God has highly exalted him and bestowed on him the name that is above every name, [10]so that at the name of Jesus every knee should bow, in heaven and on earth and under the earth, [11]and every tongue confess that Jesus Christ is Lord, to the glory of God the Father.

READ

Read the passage aloud slowly, noticing the recurring words, such as *interests, humilty, humbled, obedient.*

THINK

1. Read verses 5-8 again and consider what amazes you about Jesus, perhaps that he:

   - "did not count equality with God a thing to be grasped"
   - "humbled himself"
   - "made himself nothing"
   - "took the form of a servant"
   - "was obedient to the point of death, even death on a cross"

2. Read verses 9-11 again and consider what amazes you about God, perhaps that:

   - he "exalted him and bestowed on him the name that is above every name"
   - "every knee should bow . . . to the glory of God"

3. Now read verses 2-4 again and consider what God is calling you to be or do.

4. In what way does your admiration for Jesus' and God's radical behavior (verses 5-11) inspire you to the behavior described in verses 2-4?

PRAY

Tell Jesus what you admire about his willingness to come to earth and his way of being while here. Tell God what you admire about his humility. Ask them to help you do whatever came to you in question 3.

LIVE

Look for opportunities today to help someone get ahead. If and when you do, sense Jesus' companionship in your efforts.

THINK THIS WAY

PHILIPPIANS 3:15-21

[15]Let those of us who are mature think this way, and if in anything you think otherwise, God will reveal that also to you. [16]Only let us hold true to what we have attained.

[17]Brothers, join in imitating me, and keep your eyes on those who walk according to the example you have in us. [18]For many, of whom I have often told you and now tell you even with tears, walk as enemies of the cross of Christ. [19]Their end is destruction, their god is their belly, and they glory in their shame, with minds set on earthly things. [20]But our citizenship is in heaven, and from it we await a Savior, the Lord Jesus Christ, [21]who will transform our lowly body to be like his glorious body, by the power that enables him even to subject all things to himself.

READ

Read the passage two times slowly.

THINK

Read again what Paul says about how the mature should "hold true to what we have attained." Write down honestly what you feel and think about it, without judging your own reaction.

Now read again what Paul says about those who are "enemies of the cross of Christ" rather than knowing Jesus. What thoughts, memories, or feelings do you have as you read this? Jot them down.

Finally, read again, paying special attention to what Christians have to look forward to. What does this make you feel? Note the promise that evokes the greatest response in you.

LIVE

Think about a circumstance in your life that frustrates you with its monotony or pointlessness. Once again become aware of the goal in this passage: a simple and trusting openness to God and total commitment to what he has for you.

Now consider the following statement by Oswald Chambers: "The spiritual saint never believes circumstances to be haphazard, or thinks of his life as secular and sacred; he sees everything he is dumped down in as the means of securing the knowledge of Jesus Christ."[21] Do you believe that the God who intends to "transform our lowly body to be like his glorious body" is the same God who has allowed your circumstance? Why or why not?

PRAY

Ask Jesus to help you become totally committed to "hold[ing] true to what we have attained." Ask him to help you recognize and avoid taking other paths, choosing other goals. Thank him that "our citizenship is in heaven."

DAY 301

GOD ENCOUNTERS

On this seventh day, review and reflect on all you have read this week. Take the time to revel in the ways you've encountered God in the past six days.

SHAPING WORRIES INTO PRAYERS

PHILIPPIANS 4:6-9

[6]Do not be anxious about anything, but in everything by prayer and supplication with thanksgiving let your requests be made known to God. [7]And the peace of God, which surpasses all understanding, will guard your hearts and your minds in Christ Jesus.

[8]Finally, brothers, whatever is true, whatever is honorable, whatever is just, whatever is pure, whatever is lovely, whatever is commendable, if there is any excellence, if there is anything worthy of praise, think about these things. [9]What you have learned and received and heard and seen in me — practice these things, and the God of peace will be with you.

READ

Read the passage, including the expanded passage, if possible.

THINK

How do you handle something that worries you? Do you ignore the problem so you can put off thinking about it for as long as possible? Do you feel depressed and pessimistic about it, pretty sure of negative results, no matter what? Do you spend a lot of energy identifying a solution and working toward it? Whatever your answer, pinpoint your primary way of reacting. See if you know why you handle worry the way you do.

Now consider one worry you have today and how you've been dealing (or not dealing) with it.

PRAY

Sit in silence for a few minutes with your eyes closed. Breathe deeply and let your mind quiet down. Become aware of God's presence.

Express to God your concern. Even though he knows the situation, tell him all about it, every detail. In what way has your anxiety affected other areas of your life, such as relationships, work, or school? What's the worst-case scenario you're afraid might happen? Whether rational or irrational, share with God what you fear.

LIVE

Recall the Person you've experienced God to be in the past weeks and months. Reflect on previous notes you've made about experiencing God through his Word and prayer. From that, focus on three of his attributes. How do these elements of his character relate to your situation? What do they indicate about his presence with you right now? Picture this God in your mind. Remember today that this is the God who has heard your concern, the God whose peace will be with you.

HE IS SUPREME

COLOSSIANS 1:15-23

[15]He is the image of the invisible God, the firstborn of all creation. [16]For by him all things were created, in heaven and on earth, visible and invisible, whether thrones or dominions or rulers or authorities — all things were created through him and for him. [17]And he is before all things, and in him all things hold together. [18]And he is the head of the body, the church. He is the beginning, the firstborn from the dead, that in everything he might be preeminent. [19]For in him all the fullness of God was pleased to dwell, [20]and through him to reconcile to himself all things, whether on earth or in heaven, making peace by the blood of his cross.

[21]And you, who once were alienated and hostile in mind, doing evil deeds, [22]he has now reconciled in his body of flesh by his death, in order to present you holy and blameless and above reproach before him, [23]if indeed you continue in the faith, stable and steadfast, not shifting from the hope of the gospel that you heard, which has been proclaimed in all creation under heaven, and of which I, Paul, became a minister.

READ

Wherever you are, stand up and read the passage aloud. Stand prayerfully in a posture that communicates to God respect and receptivity to his Word.

THINK

This passage speaks of the supremacy and power of God manifested through Jesus Christ. What specific attribute or characteristic of Jesus sticks out to you most in this passage? Why do you think it does?

"He is the image of the invisible God, the firstborn of all creation." What are specific, practical ways in which you can see the "invisible God" in Jesus?

What does the following mean? "He is the beginning, the firstborn from the dead, that in everything he might be preeminent." What implications does this have in your life today? Wonder about the supremacy of Christ.

PRAY

Reflect on the attribute of Christ that struck you (for example, maybe it was that "in him all things hold together"). In what ways would the world be different if Christ did not possess that attribute? In what ways would your life be different? How and why?

LIVE

Live your day knowing that you serve — and are loved by — the God who holds the entire world together!

THE BOND OF PERFECT HARMONY

COLOSSIANS 3:3-5,12-17

[3]For you have died, and your life is hidden with Christ in God. [4]When Christ who is your life appears, then you also will appear with him in glory.

[5]Put to death therefore what is earthly in you: sexual immorality, impurity, passion, evil desire, and covetousness, which is idolatry. . . .

[12]Put on then, as God's chosen ones, holy and beloved, compassionate hearts, kindness, humility, meekness, and patience, [13]bearing with one another and, if one has a complaint against another, forgiving each other; as the Lord has forgiven you, so you also must forgive. [14]And above all these put on love, which binds everything together in perfect harmony. [15]And let the peace of Christ rule in your hearts, to which indeed you were called in one body. And be thankful. [16]Let the word of Christ dwell in you richly, teaching and admonishing one another in all wisdom, singing psalms and hymns and spiritual songs, with thankfulness in your hearts to God. [17]And whatever you do, in word or deed, do everything in the name of the Lord Jesus, giving thanks to God the Father through him.

READ

Read the passage aloud slowly.

THINK

Read the passage again and consider these segments included in the process of stepping into the new life.

1. A new life is possible (verses 3-4).
2. We get rid of the old life (verse 5).
3. We put on the new life (verses 12-14).
4. We consider background thoughts and behavior needed to put on new life (verses 15-17).

Which segment of this process speaks to you most right now? Reread the verses that correspond to that segment. Now, what word or phrase in that segment speaks to you? Why do you think that is? How does that idea relate to the other segments? How does it relate to love, "which binds everything together"?

PRAY

Pray back to God the segment that speaks to you, personalizing it. For example, based on verse 15, *Please let the peace of Christ rule in my heart—show me that true peace of Christ!*

LIVE

Sit quietly in the idea that your old life really is dead. All the good, loving attitudes and behaviors of Jesus are open to you. Allow yourself to be invited to step into that today.

VIRTUE CHECKLIST

COLOSSIANS 4:2-6

[2]Continue steadfastly in prayer, being watchful in it with thanksgiving. [3]At the same time, pray also for us, that God may open to us a door for the word, to declare the mystery of Christ, on account of which I am in prison — [4]that I may make it clear, which is how I ought to speak.

[5]Walk in wisdom toward outsiders, making the best use of the time. [6]Let your speech always be gracious, seasoned with salt, so that you may know how you ought to answer each person.

READ

Read this passage several times, each time narrowing your focus to the part that challenges you the most.

THINK

What did you focus on? Was it a virtuous action that is not part of your lifestyle? Or perhaps it was something you already do, but you noticed something different about the way or reason why Paul says to do it. What is your emotional response when you think of changing this area of your life? Do you feel eager? Overwhelmed? Threatened or protective? Unsure?

PRAY

Talk with Jesus about the item on Paul's list of virtues that challenged you most and about how you responded to it. Sit in silence to wait for what Jesus might have to say to you.

LIVE

As you read the following statement made by Saint Bernard of Clairvaux, also consider what Paul tells Christians to do in today's passage: "If then you are wise, you will show yourself rather as a reservoir than as a canal. For a canal spreads abroad water as it receives it, but a reservoir waits until it is filled before overflowing, and thus communicates, without loss to itself, its superabundant water. In the Church at the present day, we have many canals, few reservoirs."[22]

Are you more like a canal, a reservoir, or something else altogether? Would others who know you agree? Talk with Jesus about this and be open to what he is showing you about yourself. In what way is he inviting you to live differently?

ONLY GOD APPROVAL

1 THESSALONIANS 2:3-8

[3]For our appeal does not spring from error or impurity or any attempt to deceive, [4]but just as we have been approved by God to be entrusted with the gospel, so we speak, not to please man, but to please God who tests our hearts. [5]For we never came with words of flattery, as you know, nor with a pretext for greed—God is witness. [6]Nor did we seek glory from people, whether from you or from others, though we could have made demands as apostles of Christ. [7]But we were gentle among you, like a nursing mother taking care of her own children. [8]So, being affectionately desirous of you, we were ready to share with you not only the gospel of God but also our own selves, because you had become very dear to us.

READ

Read the passage, noting the word *approved*.

THINK

It's tempting to promote ourselves, to see ourselves more highly than we ought. If we examine ourselves honestly, we will have to admit that we are often trying to win the approval of the crowd.

Think back over the past week. What decisions did you make solely to look good in the eyes of others? What would it take for you to go through today without making decisions based on trying to make yourself look good? What would it take for you to live today for only God's approval?

PRAY

Confess those recent circumstances when you were tempted to seek approval from other people. Ask God to help you be free from "words of flattery" or "pretext of greed." Ask him to help you focus your desire for acceptance and approval entirely on him.

LIVE

Before every decision, before every comment, ask yourself, *What is my motive? Is it to get approval from the crowd or to get approval from God?* Let these questions make you aware today of how — and why — you make decisions.

SOMEONE ELSE'S FAITH AND LOVE

1 THESSALONIANS 3:6-13

⁶But now that Timothy has come to us from you, and has brought us the good news of your faith and love and reported that you always remember us kindly and long to see us, as we long to see you — ⁷for this reason, brothers, in all our distress and affliction we have been comforted about you through your faith. ⁸For now we live, if you are standing fast in the Lord. ⁹For what thanksgiving can we return to God for you, for all the joy that we feel for your sake before our God, ¹⁰as we pray most earnestly night and day that we may see you face to face and supply what is lacking in your faith?

¹¹Now may our God and Father himself, and our Lord Jesus, direct our way to you, ¹²and may the Lord make you increase and abound in love for one another and for all, as we do for you, ¹³so that he may establish your hearts blameless in holiness before our God and Father, at the coming of our Lord Jesus with all his saints.

READ

Read the passage aloud slowly.

THINK

Ask God to bring to mind those you know who live their lives before God routinely showing "faith and love" (a really alive faith) and giving others joy. You may not know these people well or see them often (they may be missionaries from your church, friends of friends, or speakers you've listened to), but the way they live reassures you that this kind of life is possible. Read the passage again in light of these people.

PRAY

First, thank God for these people, that:

- their faith and love comfort you
- they think well of you and you want to see them
- their faith is so alive it keeps you more alive
- you experience joy because of them

Second, pray for these people who, although they may seem so mature, still need your prayers. Pray that:

- if their faith falters, someone (maybe you) can help supply what is lacking
- God the Father and the Lord Jesus will direct your way to them
- Jesus will make them "increase and abound in love for . . . all"
- they may be "blameless in holiness before our God"
- they may be blameless at the coming of our Lord Jesus

LIVE

Rejoice restfully that people who love God and live his Word really do exist in this world.

DAY 308

GOD ENCOUNTERS

On this seventh day, review and reflect on all you have read this week. Take the time to revel in the ways you've encountered God in the past six days.

HOPE OF SALVATION

1 THESSALONIANS 5:1-10

[1]Now concerning the times and the seasons, brothers, you have no need to have anything written to you. [2]For you yourselves are fully aware that the day of the Lord will come like a thief in the night. [3]While people are saying, "There is peace and security," then sudden destruction will come upon them as labor pains come upon a pregnant woman, and they will not escape. [4]But you are not in darkness, brothers, for that day to surprise you like a thief. [5]For you are all children of light, children of the day. We are not of the night or of the darkness. [6]So then let us not sleep, as others do, but let us keep awake and be sober. [7]For those who sleep, sleep at night, and those who get drunk, are drunk at night. [8]But since we belong to the day, let us be sober, having put on the breastplate of faith and love, and for a helmet the hope of salvation. [9]For God has not destined us for wrath, but to obtain salvation through our Lord Jesus Christ, [10]who died for us so that whether we are awake or asleep we might live with him.

READ

Read the passage twice.

THINK

When you think about the end of the world and Jesus' return to Earth, what do you feel? Nervous? Excited? Halfhearted interest? In everyday life, how often do you think, feel, act, or plan as though you really believe that Jesus will come back someday soon?

PRAY

Prayerfully think about Paul's statement: "But you are not in darkness . . . for that day to surprise you." What does it stir up in you? Do you feel confident or uncertain about where you stand with Jesus? Talk to him about your reaction to this phrase.

LIVE

Ruth Haley Barton voices the questions "Is God really good? If I trust myself to him, isn't there a good chance that I will wind up where I least want to be or that God will withhold what I want the most? Isn't God a little bit like Lucy in the Peanuts comic strip, who pulls the football away just as Charlie Brown gives himself completely to the kick, causing him to fall flat on his face?"[23]

Take a moment to absorb these questions and reconsider Paul's statement that "God has not destined us for wrath, but to obtain salvation." How do your deep-down-inside expectations of God correspond with Paul's perspective? With the perspective Barton describes? Share with God your honest beliefs about him and your expectations of how he'll treat you.

Suspend for a few minutes whatever disbelief you have, and imagine you truly believe God is trustworthy. How might you live differently?

309

WE GIVE THANKS

2 THESSALONIANS 1:3-4

³We ought always to give thanks to God for you, brothers, as is right, because your faith is growing abundantly, and the love of every one of you for one another is increasing. ⁴Therefore we ourselves boast about you in the churches of God for your steadfastness and faith in all your persecutions and in the afflictions that you are enduring.

READ

Read this passage very slowly and cautiously. Imagine yourself as a surgeon carefully cutting and dissecting it. Give focused attention to each word.

THINK/PRAY

What or whom are you grateful for today? Why? Pause and give thanks to God for these now.

Who is growing in their faith, maturing into God's likeness, and loving others well? Thank God for them now, including names and details.

Who needs to grow more in their faith, needs to mature further into God's likeness, and could love others more appropriately and generously? Thank God for them and pray for them now, including names and details.

Which followers of Christ have fallen on hard times but are determined and are persevering? Thank God for them and pray for them now, including names and details. Pray also for the persecuted church — those Christ-followers around the globe who are being arrested and tortured and murdered simply because of what they believe. Thank God for their incredible passion and commitment to Jesus. Finally, ask God to give you the same courage, commitment, and love for Christ.

LIVE

Carry all these individuals in your thoughts today. Ask God to bring them to mind during the coming week. As you remember them thank God for them and pray for them.

LIFE IN THE SPIRIT

2 THESSALONIANS 2:13-17

[13]But we ought always to give thanks to God for you, brothers beloved by the Lord, because God chose you as the firstfruits to be saved, through sanctification by the Spirit and belief in the truth. [14]To this he called you through our gospel, so that you may obtain the glory of our Lord Jesus Christ. [15]So then, brothers, stand firm and hold to the traditions that you were taught by us, either by our spoken word or by our letter.

[16]Now may our Lord Jesus Christ himself, and God our Father, who loved us and gave us eternal comfort and good hope through grace, [17]comfort your hearts and establish them in every good work and word.

READ

Read the passage aloud slowly. Then recall the small, inconsequential things that have occupied your thoughts in the last few moments, hours, or days.

THINK

Read the passage again, noting how Paul viewed an average life as so spectacular because he was immersed in the Trinitarian reality (God, Jesus, and Holy Spirit in verses 13-14).

1. Which of these truths about God's unseen reality most captivate you?

   □ You are "beloved by the Lord."
   □ You were chosen as the firstfruits to be saved.
   □ You're sanctified by the Spirit.
   □ You "obtain the glory of our Lord Jesus Christ."
   □ God reaches out to you in love.
   □ God gives us "eternal comfort and good hope through grace."
   □ God can "comfort your hearts."
   □ God can establish every good work.
   □ God can establish every word.

2. Think about today's events — even mundane ones. Which of the truths mentioned in question 1 do you need to link with each event?

PRAY

Pray about each event, that you will live in this unseen reality, that you'll see how these truths are present. For example, pray about a conversation or a homework assignment or a work project, that you'll participate in it knowing you are loved and receiving God's gifts of unending help and confidence.

LIVE

Pick one of these truths about life in the Spirit and sense its reality. If you have trouble doing this, ask God to help you.

IF YOU DON'T WORK, YOU DON'T EAT

2 THESSALONIANS 3:6-15

⁶Now we command you, brothers, in the name of our Lord Jesus Christ, that you keep away from any brother who is walking in idleness and not in accord with the tradition that you received from us. ⁷For you yourselves know how you ought to imitate us, because we were not idle when we were with you, ⁸nor did we eat anyone's bread without paying for it, but with toil and labor we worked night and day, that we might not be a burden to any of you. ⁹It was not because we do not have that right, but to give you in ourselves an example to imitate. ¹⁰For even when we were with you, we would give you this command: If anyone is not willing to work, let him not eat. ¹¹For we hear that some among you walk in idleness, not busy at work, but busybodies. ¹²Now such persons we command and encourage in the Lord Jesus Christ to do their work quietly and to earn their own living.

¹³As for you, brothers, do not grow weary in doing good. ¹⁴If anyone does not obey what we say in this letter, take note of that person, and have nothing to do with him, that he may be ashamed. ¹⁵Do not regard him as an enemy, but warn him as a brother.

READ

Read the passage carefully.

THINK

Why do you think Paul is making such a big deal out of Christians who won't work? Why is he encouraging those in Thessalonica to make a big deal out of it? In what ways do you think laziness and freeloading impact relationships?

PRAY

Read the passage again, this time listening for a word or phrase that stands out to you, such as "doing good," "idle," or "do not regard him as an enemy, but warn him as a brother." Chew on this for a few minutes. Share with God what pops up in you as you consider it.

Now read again the part of the passage that contains the word or phrase. Why do you think this word is standing out to you today? Does it trigger a fear? Does it challenge you? What part of your life does it touch?

LIVE

Read the whole passage one last time. This time, listen for the action or attitude God is inviting you to take on this week. Maybe he's asking you to lovingly sit down with a friend and speak plainly about her freeloading. Maybe he wants you to start looking for a job or to stop borrowing or using stuff that isn't yours. Make a note of how you can take steps in the direction God is indicating. If you are especially aware of God's presence with you when you take these steps, what might the impact be?

LOVE FROM A PURE HEART

1 TIMOTHY 1:3-7

[3]As I urged you when I was going to Macedonia, remain at Ephesus so that you may charge certain persons not to teach any different doctrine, [4]nor to devote themselves to myths and endless genealogies, which promote speculations rather than the stewardship from God that is by faith. [5]The aim of our charge is love that issues from a pure heart and a good conscience and a sincere faith. [6]Certain persons, by swerving from these, have wandered away into vain discussion, [7]desiring to be teachers of the law, without understanding either what they are saying or the things about which they make confident assertions.

THINK

Paul as mentor has sent carefully written instructions to his disciple Timothy. This is the first volume of his guidance for Timothy, urging him as a young leader to mature in Christ. Among the complexities of life, Paul boils the message down to one simple concept: love. Not just love, but "love that issues from a pure heart and a good conscience and a sincere faith."

READ

With this background in mind, meditate on the passage.

PRAY

While remaining open to God, consider what love looks like when it's "from a pure heart and a good conscience and a sincere faith." Then ask God the following questions, pausing between each one to listen to the Holy Spirit's response:

God, what about my love is not from a pure heart? Ask God to help remove the contamination of selfishness in your life.

Father, what about my love is not from a good conscience? Ask for courage to be authentic and truthful with God, others, and yourself.

Lord, what about my life and love is not from a sincere faith? Ask God to give you the willingness and to help you be more open to his purposes, even if doing so feels uncertain and scary.

LIVE

Go live and love selflessly, authentically, and openly.

PEACEFUL AND QUIET LIFE

1 TIMOTHY 2:1-2,8-9

[1]First of all, then, I urge that supplications, prayers, intercessions, and thanksgivings be made for all people, [2]for kings and all who are in high positions, that we may lead a peaceful and quiet life, godly and dignified in every way. . . .

[8]I desire then that in every place the men should pray, lifting holy hands without anger or quarreling; [9]likewise also that women should adorn themselves in respectable apparel, with modesty and self-control, not with braided hair and gold or pearls or costly attire.

READ

Read the passage aloud slowly.

THINK

Read the passage again, noting what is said about prayer:

- how to pray: "supplications, prayers, intercessions, and thanksgivings" and "raising holy hands"
- government-related prayer: peaceful and quiet life, godly and dignified
- tone of prayer: "without anger or quarreling" and women praying in humility
- pray for: "all people" and "kings and all who are in high positions"
- outcome of prayer: the gospel will spread, women will adorn themselves with good works (verse 10)

Read the passage one more time. What do you think God is telling you about how you need to pray?

PRAY

Lift holy hands as you ask God to lead you in praying that governments will rule well so "we may lead a peaceful and quiet life, godly and dignified in every way."

LIVE

Sit quietly with your hands raised, outstretched, eager for the gospel to permeate the nations of our planet.

DAY 315

GOD ENCOUNTERS

On this seventh day, review and reflect on all you have read this week. Take the time to revel in the ways you've encountered God in the past six days.

PRECONDITIONS OF LEADERSHIP

1 TIMOTHY 3:1-13

[1]The saying is trustworthy: If anyone aspires to the office of overseer, he desires a noble task. [2]Therefore an overseer must be above reproach, the husband of one wife, sober-minded, self-controlled, respectable, hospitable, able to teach, [3]not a drunkard, not violent but gentle, not quarrelsome, not a lover of money. [4]He must manage his own household well, with all dignity keeping his children submissive, [5]for if someone does not know how to manage his own household, how will he care for God's church? [6]He must not be a recent convert, or he may become puffed up with conceit and fall into the condemnation of the devil. [7]Moreover, he must be well thought of by outsiders, so that he may not fall into disgrace, into a snare of the devil.

[8]Deacons likewise must be dignified, not double-tongue, not addicted to much wine, not greedy for dishonest gain. [9]They must hold the mystery of the faith with a clear conscience. [10]And let them also be tested first; then let them serve as deacons if they prove themselves blameless. [11]Their wives likewise must be dignified, not slanderers, but sober-minded, faithful in all things. [12]Let deacons each be the husband of one wife, managing their children and their own households well. [13]For those who serve well as deacons gain a good standing for themselves and also great confidence in the faith that is in Christ Jesus.

READ

Read this passage a few times slowly and carefully.

THINK

As you absorb the moral expectations presented in this passage, what is your reaction? Perhaps you desire to change, or perhaps you feel irritated. Maybe you feel shame or guilt. Maybe relief. Does reading this make you want to be a leader? If not, why not? Share your reaction with God.

PRAY

Take several minutes to read the text again slowly, letting each instruction direct you toward a new area of your heart to examine with the Holy Spirit. (Don't feel that you must work your way through the entire passage: The goal is to uncover content for prayer, not get through the entire list.) In which areas does your life look different from the model Paul is describing? For example, you've been more pushy than gentle with someone, or you've been more unreliable than dependable. Tell God about what you find.

LIVE

Ask God to show you what it would look like to embrace transformation in an area you've examined today, realizing that starting with baby steps might be just right for you. Take courage that "our personalities are transformed — not lost — in the furnace of God's love."[24] God's transformation will not obliterate your personality; instead, the process will make you more into the one-of-a-kind person God intended you to be.

TEACH WITH YOUR LIFE

1 TIMOTHY 4:10-16

¹⁰For to this end we toil and strive, because we have our hope set on the living God, who is the Savior of all people, especially of those who believe.

¹¹Command and teach these things. ¹²Let no one despise you for your youth, but set the believers an example in speech, in conduct, in love, in faith, in purity. ¹³Until I come, devote yourself to the public reading of Scripture, to exhortation, to teaching. ¹⁴Do not neglect the gift you have, which was given you by prophecy when the council of elders laid their hands on you. ¹⁵Practice these things, immerse yourself in them, so that all may see your progress. ¹⁶Keep a close watch on yourself and on the teaching. Persist in this, for by so doing you will save both yourself and your hearers.

READ

Read the passage, focusing on the words *teach* and *practice*.

THINK

In these verses, Paul, as almost a father figure, passes on wise words to young Timothy — and to us — about modeling our faith.

How can we be a part of that, no matter how old we are?

On a scale of one to ten — one being spiritual flabbiness and ten being spiritually fit — how would you rate your spiritual fitness? Why did you give yourself that rating?

How well are you "set[ting] the believers an example" in these five areas: "in speech, in conduct, in love, in faith, in purity"? Very well? In which areas? Not so well? In which areas? How can you make your life a better teacher in all of these?

PRAY

See if you can open your life to God like you would open a book. Consider the areas (such as school, family, work, and other activities), and write them down if that helps. Acknowledge to God your openness, then invite him to do his work in your life — whatever that might be — encouraging you, challenging you, and shaping your words, your demeanor, your love, your faith, and your integrity.

LIVE

Write these five words on an index card: *speech, conduct, love, faith, purity*. Ask God to help you be an example with your life in these specific areas throughout your day.

DEVOTED TO GOOD WORKS

1 TIMOTHY 5:1-4,7-10

¹Do not rebuke an older man but encourage him as you would a father, younger men as brothers, ²older women as mothers, younger women as sisters, in all purity.

³Honor widows who are truly widows. ⁴But if a widow has children or grandchildren, let them first learn to show godliness to their own household and to make some return to their parents, for this is pleasing in the sight of God.... ⁷Command these things as well, so that they may be without reproach. ⁸But if anyone does not provide for his relatives, and especially for members of his household, he has denied the faith and is worse than an unbeliever.

⁹Let a widow be enrolled if she is not less than sixty years of age, having been the wife of one husband, ¹⁰and having a reputation for good works: if she has brought up children, has shown hospitality, has washed the feet of the saints, has cared for the afflicted, and has devoted herself to every good work.

READ

Read the passage aloud slowly.

THINK

Before reading the passage again, consider the following cultural ideas. Which ones have you unconsciously accepted?

- ☐ Older people and younger people don't mix much.
- ☐ Older people are retired, so they don't do "special ministry." (You don't know many people who have brought up children, shown hospitality, washed the feet of the saints, cared for the afflicted, and devoted themselves to every good work.
- ☐ Older people are tired and don't want to do much at church anymore.
- ☐ Older people aren't generally the people you go to for advice.
- ☐ Older people have Social Security benefits and don't need anyone's help.
- ☐ Older people are people you feel sorry for, not reverently honor.

Read the passage again. Envision the sort of older person Paul was talking about. What older person do you know who is like the one Paul describes? In what small ways might you honor this person? Try to wrap your mind around the idea that you can *look forward* to being such an older person.

PRAY

Thank God for older people in your life who resemble Paul's description. Pray for those who need more of what Paul describes. Pray for yourself that you'll be this sort of older person.

LIVE

Sit quietly. Pretend your joints don't work as well as they used to. Ponder what it would be like to still be eager to get up every day to be with Jesus and partner with him in what he's doing in the world.

GODLINESS WITH CONTENTMENT

1 TIMOTHY 6:6-12

⁶But godliness with contentment is great gain, ⁷for we brought nothing into the world, and we cannot take anything out of the world. ⁸But if we have food and clothing, with these we will be content. ⁹But those who desire to be rich fall into temptation, into a snare, into many senseless and harmful desires that plunge people into ruin and destruction. ¹⁰For the love of money is a root of all kinds of evils. It is through this craving that some have wandered away from the faith and pierced themselves with many pangs.

¹¹But as for you, O man of God, flee these things. Pursue righteousness, godliness, faith, love, steadfastness, gentleness. ¹²Fight the good fight of the faith. Take hold of the eternal life to which you were called and about which you made the good confession in the presence of many witnesses.

READ

Read the passage twice.

THINK

Mull over Paul's advice to Timothy. Do you agree with his statements and assumptions about material wealth? About the value of being yourself before God? Why or why not? Explore your thoughts and share them with God.

PRAY

Consider your belongings, including favorite things and stuff you don't usually think about. In what ways might some of these items get in the way of you being yourself, plain and simple, before God? In what way does your attachment to these possessions alter your view of who you are? (Don't be too quick to answer here.)

LIVE

Read the passage again, considering more carefully Paul's description of righteousness. Do you notice an especially strong desire for any of these qualities? Listen for what God may be saying to you through the text and through your desire. Is he inviting you to do anything — even something small — in response to this time today?

PURSUE RIGHTEOUSNESS

2 TIMOTHY 2:22-26

[22]So flee youthful passions and pursue righteousness, faith, love, and peace, along with those who call on the Lord from a pure heart. [23]Have nothing to do with foolish, ignorant controversies; you know that they breed quarrels. [24]And the Lord's servant must not be quarrelsome but kind to everyone, able to teach, patiently enduring evil, [25]correcting his opponents with gentleness. God may perhaps grant them repentance leading to a knowledge of the truth, [26]and they may come to their senses and escape from the snare of the devil, after being captured by him to do his will.

READ

Slowly read these verses. Let their message saturate your heart and mind.

THINK

In Paul's second leadership letter to Timothy, he writes words of encouragement and challenge that we, too, need to take to heart in the coming week. Paul is talking about some aspects of a mature faith.

Imagine he is sitting beside you, speaking these words to you directly. How do you feel when you hear them? What part of the passage resonates most with you? Why? Maybe "youthful passions" seems a little patronizing. Perhaps righteousness seems impossible or defeating. Maybe with some people you've lost hope that "God may perhaps grant them repentance leading to a knowledge of the truth."

PRAY

Sit in a comfortable position, being silent and as still as you can. Ask God *why* he has given you this particular piece of instruction through Paul (the one that resonated most with you). Listen for the gentle whisper of God's voice in the midst of the silence. Maybe he will show you a spot of childishness or one of righteousness. Maybe he will offer you hope.

LIVE

As you continue to sit in silence, explore what God might want you to do with this piece of instruction. How are you to live it out today? This week? This month?

GOD-BREATHED AND PROFITABLE

2 TIMOTHY 3:1-5,15-17

¹But understand this, that in the last days there will come times of difficulty. ²For people will be lovers of self, lovers of money, proud, arrogant, abusive, disobedient to their parents, ungrateful, unholy, ³heartless, unappeasable, slanderous, without self-control, brutal, not loving good, ⁴treacherous, reckless, swollen with conceit, lovers of pleasure rather than lovers of God, ⁵having the appearance of godliness, but denying its power. Avoid such people. . . .

¹⁵From childhood you have been acquainted with the sacred writings, which are able to make you wise for salvation through faith in Christ Jesus. ¹⁶All Scripture is breathed out by God and profitable for teaching, for reproof, for correction, and for training in righteousness, ¹⁷that the man of God may be competent, equipped for every good work.

READ

Read the passage aloud slowly.

THINK

Before dismissing the first paragraph as a description of people other than yourself, consider that Western culture, in general (and our individual selves, in particular), tends to be lovers of self, proud, ungrateful, and lovers of pleasure.

Read the passage again. This time notice the enormous change from the first paragraph to the second.

1. How does the way Scripture moves us (verse 16) help us to be different from the general culture?
2. Scripture is God-breathed — words breathed to you from our relational God, not a bunch of rules. Picture God speaking to you, teaching His Word "for reproof, for correction, and for training in righteousness."

Can you picture God doing these things in ways exactly right for you? In gentle yet firm ways? To rescue you before you blow it?

PRAY

Ask God to help you be open to his teaching, reproof, correction, and training in righteousness. Ask him to show you specific details, if any, that you need to know at this moment.

LIVE

Imagine what living an interactive life with God would be like, one in which all day long you experience him gently showing you how to live in righteousness. Why would this be the best way to live?

DAY 322

GOD ENCOUNTERS

On this seventh day, review and reflect on all you have read this week. Take the time to revel in the ways you've encountered God in the past six days.

THE RIGHTEOUS JUDGE

2 TIMOTHY 4:1-8

[1]I charge you in the presence of God and of Christ Jesus, who is to judge the living and the dead, and by his appearing and his kingdom: [2]preach the word; be ready in season and out of season; reprove, rebuke, and exhort, with complete patience and teaching. [3]For the time is coming when people will not endure sound teaching, but having itching ears they will accumulate for themselves teachers to suit their own passions, [4]and will turn away from listening to the truth and wander off into myths. [5]As for you, always be sober-minded, endure suffering, do the work of an evangelist, fulfill your ministry.

[6]For I am already being poured out as a drink offering, and the time of my departure has come. [7]I have fought the good fight, I have finished the race, I have kept the faith. [8]Henceforth there is laid up for me the crown of righteousness, which the Lord, the righteous judge, will award to me on that Day, and not only to me but also to all who have loved his appearing.

READ

Read Paul's instructions to his apprentice Timothy, trying to identify the primary theme.

THINK

What common thread runs through all of Paul's statements and instructions here? Perhaps it's the tone of what he's saying (such as urgent or tender), or maybe it's that every statement somehow relates to a particular object or event (such as Christ's judgment of everyone, or people-pleasing versus God-pleasing). Write down the theme you see.

PRAY

Read the passage again with the theme in mind. Notice how each part of the passage unpacks the meaning even more. What especially stands out to you? Perhaps it's the reason that repentance and evangelism are so important or the anticipation of standing before God as he looks at your life. Think about what you discover, and be transparent with God about it.

LIVE

Now read the passage once more, this time listening for what you sense God, through the text, is saying to you personally. Maybe he's drawing your attention to your need to please people, or maybe you're relieved to understand more clearly that repentance isn't about being perfect but about living in accordance with reality. What will you do with what God is showing you? Sit in silence for a few minutes. Jot down your new intention.

APOSTLE OF CHRIST

TITUS 1:1-4

¹Paul, a servant of God and an apostle of Jesus Christ, for the sake of the faith of God's elect and their knowledge of the truth, which accords with godliness, ²in hope of eternal life, which God, who never lies, promised before the ages began ³and at the proper time manifested in his word through the preaching with which I have been entrusted by the command of God our Savior;

⁴To Titus, my true child in a common faith:

Grace and peace from God the Father and Christ Jesus our Savior.

READ

Read the opening words of greeting from Paul to Titus in these verses.

THINK

Paul describes himself as "an apostle of Jesus Christ, for the sake of the faith of God's elect and their knowledge of the truth." Are you a servant of God and an apostle of Christ? Do those terms accurately describe your life? Why or why not? How can your life be lived in such a way that you are living for the sake of God's elect and their knowledge of the truth? How can your life be "for the sake of the faith" among others by word and action? Take time to consider these questions, being specific.

Paul gives the purpose of his life to Titus by saying he lives "in hope of eternal life, which God, who never lies, promised before the ages began." In what way does God raise hopes? Has he raised your hopes?

PRAY

Ask Christ to help you be his agent. Invite him to reveal to you how you might best respond to his Word.

LIVE

Respond to what you hear from God, remembering that you go forth into this day as an agent of Christ.

OUR BLESSED HOPE

TITUS 2:11-14

[11]For the grace of God has appeared, bringing salvation for all people, [12]training us to renounce ungodliness and worldly passions, and to live self-controlled, upright, and godly lives in the present age, [13]waiting for our blessed hope, the appearing of the glory of our great God and Savior Jesus Christ, [14]who gave himself for us to redeem us from all lawlessness and to purify for himself a people for his own possession who are zealous for good works.

READ
Read the passage aloud slowly.

THINK
Read the passage aloud again, this time picturing the words being spoken by someone you look up to and admire. Which of these rich words or phrases stand out to you? Why do you need these words and ideas at this moment in your life?

Read it one more time, picturing yourself saying the words to someone you wish to encourage.

PRAY
Ask God to guide you in one or all of these movements of growth:

☐ renouncing "ungodliness and worldly passions"
☐ living a "self-controlled, upright, and godly" life
☐ "waiting for our blessed hope"
☐ being "zealous for good works"
☐ other:

LIVE
Consider God, who is "zealous for good works." Inhale that goodness. See how much God wishes to bring you along. Try on the belief that this new life starts right now.

WASHED INSIDE AND OUT

TITUS 3:1-11

[1]Remind them to be submissive to rulers and authorities, to be obedient, to be ready for every good work, [2]to speak evil of no one, to avoid quarreling, to be gentle, and to show perfect courtesy toward all people. [3]For we ourselves were once foolish, disobedient, led astray, slaves to various passions and pleasures, passing our days in malice and envy, hated by others and hating one another. [4]But when the goodness and loving kindness of God our Savior appeared, [5]he saved us, not because of works done by us in righteousness, but according to his own mercy, by the washing of regeneration and renewal of the Holy Spirit, [6]whom he poured out on us richly through Jesus Christ our Savior, [7]so that being justified by his grace we might become heirs according to the hope of eternal life. [8]The saying is trustworthy, and I want you to insist on these things, so that those who have believed in God may be careful to devote themselves to good works. These things are excellent and profitable for people. [9]But avoid foolish controversies, genealogies, dissensions, and quarrels about the law, for they are unprofitable and worthless. [10]As for a person who stirs up division, after warning him once and then twice, have nothing more to do with him, [11]knowing that such a person is warped and sinful; he is self-condemned.

READ

Read the passage.

PRAY

What parts of this passage do you react to more than others? Maybe an argument you've had comes to mind, or maybe you have trouble adopting the attitude toward authority described here. Perhaps you wish you could be given a "good bath" and made new. Try to summarize your primary thought. Express it to God.

THINK

Although being purified ("washing of regeneration and renewal of the Holy Spirit") is good for us and brings wonderfully satisfying results, the process often involves humbling, which isn't easy. Richard Foster said, "Humility means to live as close to the truth as possible: the truth about ourselves, the truth about others, the truth about the world in which we live."[25]

Think about Foster's statement, considering yourself, others, and the world around you. What elements of God's truth in this passage did you have trouble receiving? Maybe you're too hard on yourself and won't believe God's acceptance of you. Maybe you're afraid that if you admit the limitations of someone you look up to, it will unravel everything good you believe about that person. Or maybe you realize you don't want to get close to the real needs and problems of the world. Be open with God about the grime that keeps you from being clean and living closer to the truth.

LIVE

Now, keeping in mind how near or far you live from the truth about yourself, others, and the world, picture God as he's described in this passage: stepping in and washing you inside and out, removing the grime that separates you from the truth. What do you think or feel about that? Whatever surfaces, share it openly with him.

A BELOVED BROTHER

PHILEMON 8-20

[8]Accordingly, though I am bold enough in Christ to command you to do what is required, [9]yet for love's sake I prefer to appeal to you—I, Paul, an old man and now a prisoner also for Christ Jesus—[10]I appeal to you for my child, Onesimus, whose father I became in my imprisonment. [11](Formerly he was useless to you, but now he is indeed useful to you and to me.) [12]I am sending him back to you, sending my very heart. [13]I would have been glad to keep him with me, in order that he might serve me on your behalf during my imprisonment for the gospel, [14]but I preferred to do nothing without your consent in order that your goodness might not be by compulsion but of your own accord. [15]For this perhaps is why he was parted from you for a while, that you might have him back forever, [16]no longer as a bondservant but more than a bondservant, as a beloved brother—especially to me, but how much more to you, both in the flesh and in the Lord.

[17]So if you consider me your partner, receive him as you would receive me. [18]If he has wronged you at all, or owes you anything, charge that to my account. [19]I, Paul, write this with my own hand: I will repay it—to say nothing of your owing me even your own self. [20]Yes, brother, I want some benefit from you in the Lord. Refresh my heart in Christ.

READ

Read the passage and, if possible, the entire book of Philemon. (Don't worry — it's only twenty-five verses long!)

THINK

Here Paul writes a letter to Philemon concerning a slave named Onesimus. Paul has grown to see this man as a friend and — more specifically and importantly — as a brother in Christ. So Paul encourages Philemon to accept Onesimus in the same way.

Paul is saying that the greatest label we can have for one another is "true Christian brother" or true Christian sister.

What Christians do you have a hard time accepting as brothers or sisters in Christ? Why is it hard to think of other believers this way? Explore your heart: Is it their backgrounds, ethnicities, behaviors, cultural differences, theological differences, or something else? What would need to change in you for you to accept these people, seeing them as Christian brothers and sisters?

PRAY

Talk to God about this. Tell him about your struggle to accept others. Thank him that he accepts you, and thank him that he sees you and other believers as no less than his very own children. Ask God to help you see others with the same eyes.

LIVE

As you encounter people who are different from you, be reminded that God sees them with the label "my children" — and that means you too.

DAY 328

EXPANDED PASSAGE: HEBREWS 1

HE UPHOLDS THE UNIVERSE

HEBREWS 1:3

³He is the radiance of the glory of God and the exact imprint of his nature, and he upholds the universe by the word of his power. After making purification for sins, he sat down at the right hand of the Majesty on high.

READ

Read this verse over and over again. Let it resonate in your heart. Become familiar with the words. Memorize it before moving to the next section.

THINK

Though the authorship of Hebrews is uncertain, we can be certain of the message of the book: God's plan to redeem history came in the form of his Son, Jesus.

Spend time meditating on the passage. First, consider the purpose of a mirror: to display in perfect clarity a faithful representation of an object or person. How incredible to realize that Jesus' role was to be the exact imprint of God to the world! Second, consider the monumental act of holding the universe together. How amazing to know that Jesus does this, that he is vital to the vast scope of human history!

In what ways does the significance of Jesus in the world impact your view of him?

PRAY

Stand in front of a mirror and consider Jesus, who mirrors God. While looking at your reflection, ask God for the courage and guidance to help you mirror Jesus to the world, reflecting him as you go about every day.

LIVE

Consider how you might reflect Jesus today—and do it.

DAY 329

GOD ENCOUNTERS

On this seventh day, review and reflect on all you have read this week. Take the time to revel in the ways you've encountered God in the past six days.

RICHES OF GLORY

HEBREWS 2:6-10

⁶It has been testified somewhere,

> "What is man, that you are mindful of him,
>> or the son of man, that you care for him?
> ⁷ You made him for a little while lower than the angels;
>> you have crowned him with glory and honor,
> ⁸ putting everything in subjection under his feet."

Now in putting everything in subjection to him, he left nothing outside his control. At present, we do not yet see everything in subjection to him. ⁹But we see him who for a little while was made lower than the angels, namely Jesus, crowned with glory and honor because of the suffering of death, so that by the grace of God he might taste death for everyone.

¹⁰For it was fitting that he, for whom and by whom all things exist, in bringing many sons to glory, should make the founder of their salvation perfect through suffering.

READ

Read the passage aloud slowly.

THINK

Read the passage again, noting the diverse themes of death and suffering versus angels and glory. What words or phrases fascinate you most? Pause a moment and ask God to help you understand them and continue to be absorbed by them. Why do you think those words or phrases fascinate you? What is going on in your life right now — feelings, circumstances, decisions — that they might correspond to?

PRAY

Ask that you will be continually fascinated by God's glory, God's well-deserved honor and brightness.

LIVE

Sit in the quiet and reflect on how you would feel if God were degrading, dishonoring, and not at all beautiful. Why is it better to live and breathe on an earth created by such a magnificent God?

SHARPER THAN A TWO-EDGED SWORD

HEBREWS 4:12-13

[12]For the word of God is living and active, sharper than any two-edged sword, piercing to the division of soul and of spirit, of joints and of marrow, and discerning the thoughts and intentions of the heart. [13]And no creature is hidden from his sight, but all are naked and exposed to the eyes of him to whom we must give account.

READ

Read these two verses. Then read verse 13 first (beginning with "And no creature") and verse 12 next. Finally, read the verses in their proper order again.

THINK

Most of us believe that God's Word is important. In fact, you probably wouldn't be reading these words right now if you didn't believe God's Word is significant. But if you're like many people, reading it sometimes feels like a chore—less than enjoyable.

Most Jewish children in the first century would memorize the first five books of the Bible (the Pentateuch) before their thirteenth birthdays.[26] They were taught to believe that the words were a love letter to them from God himself.

Think now about how important Scripture is to *you*. What if you were unable to read or hear anything from the Bible for twelve months? Would you miss it? Why or why not? What do you think "no creature is hidden from his sight" means? In what ways have you experienced God's Word to be precise and powerful, "sharper than any two-edged sword"?

PRAY

Start praying by thanking God for the gift of his Word. Ask him to give you more passion and desire for it. Give God permission to let his Word leave you "exposed to the eyes of him to whom we must give account" in the days and weeks ahead.

LIVE

Memorize these verses, and pray them regularly as a way of asking God to make Scripture increasingly important in your life.

ANCHOR OF THE SOUL

HEBREWS 6:13-19

[13]For when God made a promise to Abraham, since he had no one greater by whom to swear, he swore by himself, [14]saying, "Surely I will bless you and multiply you." [15]And thus Abraham, having patiently waited, obtained the promise. [16]For people swear by something greater than themselves, and in all their disputes an oath is final for confirmation. [17]So when God desired to show more convincingly to the heirs of the promise the unchangeable character of his purpose, he guaranteed it with an oath, [18]so that by two unchangeable things, in which it is impossible for God to lie, we who have fled for refuge might have strong encouragement to hold fast to the hope set before us. [19]We have this as a sure and steadfast anchor of the soul, a hope that enters into the inner place behind the curtain.

READ

Read the passage aloud slowly.

THINK

Read the passage aloud again, noting the emphasis on promises and hope. Consider what part hope has played in your life. Its opposites are despair, suspicion, doubt, and cynicism. What does this passage tell you about hope?

Read the passage aloud one more time. What words or phrases stand out to you? Why are those words or phrases important for you today?

PRAY

Pick out phrases that you'd like to pray and converse with God about, such as:

- ☐ "guaranteed it with an oath"
- ☐ "it is impossible for God to lie"
- ☐ "hold fast to the hope"
- ☐ "sure and steadfast anchor of the soul"

LIVE

Walk through this day trying on an attitude of greater hope — expectancy, anticipation, trust. This is what everyday life in the kingdom of God looks like.

A NEW COVENANT

HEBREWS 8:1-2,6-12

¹Now the point in what we are saying is this: we have such a high priest, one who is seated at the right hand of the throne of the Majesty in heaven, ²a minister in the holy places, in the true tent that the Lord set up, not man. . . . ⁶But as it is, Christ has obtained a ministry that is as much more excellent than the old as the covenant he mediates is better, since it is enacted on better promises. ⁷For if that first covenant had been faultless, there would have been no occasion to look for a second.

⁸For he finds fault with them when he says:

Behold, the days are coming, declares the Lord,
    when I will establish a new covenant with the house of Israel
    and with the house of Judah,
⁹   not like the covenant that I made with their fathers
        on the day when I took them by the hand to bring them out of the
            land of Egypt.
    For they did not continue in my covenant,
        and so I showed no concern for them, declares the Lord.
¹⁰   For this is the covenant that I will make with the house of Israel
        after those days, declares the Lord:
    I will put my laws into their minds,
        and write them on their hearts,
    and I will be their God,
        and they shall be my people.
¹¹   And they shall not teach, each one his neighbor
        and each one his brother, saying, 'Know the Lord,'
    for they shall all know me,
        from the least of them to the greatest.
¹²   For I will be merciful toward their iniquities,
        and I will remember their sins no more."

READ

Read the passage from the perspective of someone living in Old Testament times, hearing the promise of a "new covenant" that has no form yet. What would life be like without Jesus? Sit and take in this picture of life. Let yourself imagine what it would be like to sin in that context and to relate to God.

THINK

Read the passage again, this time from your present-day perspective, noting contrasts with the Old Testament perspective. What does it mean to you to hear God say that the new covenant is "not like the covenant that I made with their fathers," which expects you to perfectly obey Old Testament laws? How does this reality make you see Jesus differently? What's it like to have such an approachable high priest who will be merciful and "will remember [your] sins no more"?

PRAY/LIVE

Talk with Jesus about what stands out to you from this time of meditation. Perhaps a new desire to be obedient arises in contrast to previous discouragement over trying to change. Maybe you want to thank Jesus for being near you, or maybe you feel like singing a song of praise to him. Maybe you just want to sit in quiet gratitude because God threw out the old covenant and established a new covenant, writing his laws on your heart.

THINGS NOT SEEN

HEBREWS 11:1-3,39-40

[1]Now faith is the assurance of things hoped for, the conviction of things not seen. [2]For by it the people of old received their commendation. [3]By faith we understand that the universe was created by the word of God, so that what is seen was not made out of things that are visible. . . .

[39]And all these, though commended through their faith, did not receive what was promised, [40]since God had provided something better for us, that apart from us they should not be made perfect.

READ

If possible, read all of Hebrews 11, but focus on verses 1-3 and 39-40.

THINK

This familiar passage of Scripture is often called the Faith Hall of Fame. It lists people of the Bible who exhibited the faith — sometimes at extreme personal cost — that made God famous. Talking about faith is much easier than living it out every day, but we can turn to these people's lives for inspiration.

You've heard, and possibly even uttered, the saying "Seeing is believing." The writer of Hebrews begins with a definition of faith that he connects to eyesight. Faith, he writes, is "the conviction of things not seen. . . . so that what is seen was not made out of things that are visible."

What do you have a hard time believing because you can't prove it by seeing or touching it yourself? Would faith be easier if you could physically see the object of your faith? (Would faith still be faith if you could see the object, or would faith cease to be faith and become fact?)

PRAY

Thank God for godly people who inspire you to the kind of faith described in this chapter of the Bible.

LIVE

Sometime today, choose one of the people mentioned in the Faith Hall of Fame and read his or her story in Scripture. (Use a concordance to find the story, if you need to.)

DISCIPLINED

HEBREWS 12:7-11

[7]It is for discipline that you have to endure. God is treating you as sons. For what son is there whom his father does not discipline? [8]If you are left without discipline, in which all have participated, then you are illegitimate children and not sons. [9]Besides this, we have had earthly fathers who disciplined us and we respected them. Shall we not much more be subject to the Father of spirits and live? [10]For they disciplined us for a short time as it seemed best to them, but he disciplines us for our good, that we may share his holiness. [11]For the moment all discipline seems painful rather than pleasant, but later it yields the peaceful fruit of righteousness to those who have been trained by it.

READ

Read the passage aloud slowly.

THINK

Read the passage again.

How might God use endurance to "discipline" you? Don't jump on the first thing that comes to mind. Sit quietly for a while and see what God brings to you.

How might you cooperate better in this discipline? Once again, the first thing that comes to mind might not be God, but an old tape from the past. So take time to listen.

PRAY

Tell God what sort of disciplined person you'd like to be. What would you look like? Express confidence that this picture would be a much better life for you.

LIVE

Try to crawl into the persona of the disciplined person you'd like to become. How would your burdens in life be lighter?

DAY 336

GOD ENCOUNTERS

On this seventh day, review and reflect on all you have read this week. Take the time to revel in the ways you've encountered God in the past six days.

BE CONTENT WITH WHAT YOU HAVE

HEBREWS 13:5-9

⁵Keep your life free from love of money, and be content with what you have, for he has said, "I will never leave you nor forsake you." ⁶So we can confidently say,

> "The Lord is my helper;
> I will not fear;
> what can man do to me?"

⁷Remember your leaders, those who spoke to you the word of God. Consider the outcome of their way of life, and imitate their faith. ⁸Jesus Christ is the same yesterday and today and forever. ⁹Do not be led away by diverse and strange teachings, for it is good for the heart to be strengthened by grace, not by foods, which have not benefited those devoted to them.

READ
Read the passage aloud.

THINK
Spend time pondering the connection the writer is making between obsession with material possessions and the belief that God might leave us or let us down. What do you make of this? How are the two ideas related to each other?

PRAY
Take several minutes to explore your life in light of this instruction. How do you relate to material things? Do you often wish you had more? Do you feel that nothing can harm you because of what you have? What fears do you have about God letting you down? What would it be like to "be content with what you have"? Talk with him about this subject. Attentively listen for his input.

LIVE
Continue praying by personalizing the verses, pausing frequently to notice your internal reaction to what you're saying. For example, *God, help me avoid being obsessed with getting more material things. I want to be content with what I have, since you assured me . . .*

When you're finished, look through the passage one more time, honestly confessing the contrary reactions, if any, you experienced when praying. With each, become aware of the possibility that your contrary feeling or belief could change. (Don't try to force that change; just be aware of the possibility.) For example, you could repeat to your soul that "the Lord is my helper," or you could ask God to increase your belief that he'll "never leave you nor forsake you."

BE DOERS OF THE WORD

JAMES 1:19-27

[19]Know this, my beloved brothers: let every person be quick to hear, slow to speak, slow to anger; [20]for the anger of man does not produce the righteousness of God. [21]Therefore put away all filthiness and rampant wickedness and receive with meekness the implanted word, which is able to save your souls.

[22]But be doers of the word, and not hearers only, deceiving yourselves. [23]For if anyone is a hearer of the word and not a doer, he is like a man who looks intently at his natural face in a mirror. [24]For he looks at himself and goes away and at once forgets what he was like. [25]But the one who looks into the perfect law, the law of liberty, and perseveres, being no hearer who forgets but a doer who acts, he will be blessed in his doing.

[26]If anyone thinks he is religious and does not bridle his tongue but deceives his heart, this person's religion is worthless. [27]Religion that is pure and undefiled before God, the Father, is this: to visit orphans and widows in their affliction, and to keep oneself unstained from the world.

READ

Meditate on this passage. Underline words or phrases that stick out to you. Circle repeated words.

THINK

Consider what roles specific body parts have in your spiritual formation. James says here that our lives as followers of Jesus can be shaped by how we choose to use (or refrain from using) our ears and our tongue.

How have your ears and tongue been beneficial or damaging to your interactions with others recently? Be specific. When have you said one thing and done the other? Think about what James says about that.

PRAY

Start your time of communication with God by putting your hands on your ears and saying aloud, "God, I desire to listen to what you want me to hear."

Remain in the silence. (You can lower your hands.)

Now put your hands over your mouth and say aloud, "God, I desire to use my tongue to speak words that are helpful and to refrain from speaking words that are hurtful."

Remain in the silence.

Confess those times when you have not listened and when you have spoken unnecessary and harmful words.

Remain in the silence.

LIVE

In conversations today, be mindful of the percentage of time you are speaking compared to the time you are listening to others. Then ask yourself whether the percentage is healthy.

SHOW NO PARTIALITY

JAMES 2:1-9

[1]My brothers, show no partiality as you hold the faith in our Lord Jesus Christ, the Lord of glory. [2]For if a man wearing a gold ring and fine clothing comes into your assembly, and a poor man in shabby clothing also comes in, [3]and if you pay attention to the one who wears the fine clothing and say, "You sit here in a good place," while you say to the poor man, "You stand over there," or, "Sit down at my feet," [4]have you not then made distinctions among yourselves and become judges with evil thoughts? [5]Listen, my beloved brothers, has not God chosen those who are poor in the world to be rich in faith and heirs of the kingdom, which he has promised to those who love him? [6]But you have dishonored the poor man. Are not the rich the ones who oppress you, and the ones who drag you into court? [7]Are they not the ones who blaspheme the honorable name by which you were called?

[8]If you really fulfill the royal law according to the Scripture, "You shall love your neighbor as yourself," you are doing well. [9]But if you show partiality, you are committing sin and are convicted by the law as transgressors.

READ

Read the passage aloud slowly. Who are the people who are shown partiality in your life? (They don't have to be wealthy, but just people you want to impress or want to think highly of you.)

THINK

Read the passage again, noticing these words: *partiality, dishonored, distinctions, judges.* James is urging us to love people and use things (as opposed to loving things and using people).

1. Whom do you "use" to entertain you? To help you? To make you feel better?
2. What does it look like to love others as you love yourself? To give others the same amount of time, energy, and attention you give yourself?

Set aside these thoughts and read the passage one more time. What comes to you from this passage? What might God be saying to you today?

PRAY

Pray for those in your life you are tempted to use. Ask God to show you how to care for them the way you already care for yourself.

LIVE

Sit quietly, picturing Jesus greeting people he encountered with great love (he never used anyone). What feeling did each person have in his presence? Feel that. You are in his presence now.

WISE LIVING

JAMES 3:13-18

[13]Who is wise and understanding among you? By his good conduct let him show his works in the meekness of wisdom. [14]But if you have bitter jealousy and selfish ambition in your hearts, do not boast and be false to the truth. [15]This is not the wisdom that comes down from above, but is earthly, unspiritual, demonic. [16]For where jealousy and selfish ambition exist, there will be disorder and every vile practice. [17]But the wisdom from above is first pure, then peaceable, gentle, open to reason, full of mercy and good fruits, impartial and sincere. [18]And a harvest of righteousness is sown in peace by those who make peace.

READ

Stand up and read the passage. Then read it a second time.

THINK

Defining something accurately involves stating what it is and what it is not. James does just that, telling us what wisdom is and is not. Review the passage again. Make two columns on a piece of paper, and in your own words write in one column what James says wisdom is not. Then in the other column write what James says wisdom is.

How do these characteristics of wisdom (and the lack thereof) line up with your actions recently? If James followed you around and observed your life for a week, what comments might he make about the presence — or absence — of wisdom? James says that wisdom is hard work. In what ways do you see it as hard work?

PRAY

Tell God your desire to become wise, to be "open to reason, full of mercy and good fruits." Ask him to help you.

LIVE

Ask a friend or family member you trust to give you honest feedback for the next few weeks about wisdom in your life. Give them permission to affirm wise areas of your life and wise decisions you make, as well as to point out unwise areas of your life and unwise decisions you make.

RESIST . . . DRAW NEAR

JAMES 4:7-10

[7]Submit yourselves therefore to God. Resist the devil, and he will flee from you. [8]Draw near to God, and he will draw near to you. Cleanse your hands, you sinners, and purify your hearts, you double-minded. [9]Be wretched and mourn and weep. Let your laughter be turned to mourning and your joy to gloom. [10]Humble yourselves before the Lord, and he will exalt you.

READ

This is a short passage of contrasts. Read the entire thing aloud. Read it again, this time reading every other sentence aloud. Read it again, this time reading the other sentences aloud. Then read it again in its entirety.

THINK

Someone has said that we usually think of Satan in one of two ways: We either give him too much credit for his work in the world or we don't give him any credit at all. Neither view is right. James tells us that we are to "resist the devil, and he will flee from you." So this means the Devil is active, but it also means that resisting him by Jesus' power in us is enough to scare him away.

In what ways have you seen Satan work destructively in your life, in the lives of others around you, and in the world? What do you think your practical response should be to the Devil's work?

James also tells us to "draw near to God, and he will draw near to you." Think about the times you need to draw near to him and experience his presence.

PRAY

Are you tempted to sin? Say no to Satan and be assured that he will leave you alone.

Are you in need of God's comfort and promises in your life? Whisper that you need him and be assured that he is at your side.

Rest in God's promises in Scripture.

LIVE

Remember the power that God has in your life and over the Devil. Live confidently that in Christ we always win, which means we don't have to be afraid. Utilize the tools of resisting and drawing near in your walk with Jesus.

THE PRAYER OF FAITH

JAMES 5:13-18

[13]Is anyone among you suffering? Let him pray. Is anyone cheerful? Let him sing praise. [14]Is anyone among you sick? Let him call for the elders of the church, and let them pray over him, anointing him with oil in the name of the Lord. [15]And the prayer of faith will save the one who is sick, and the Lord will raise him up. And if he has committed sins, he will be forgiven. [16]Therefore, confess your sins to one another and pray for one another, that you may be healed. The prayer of a righteous person has great power as it is working. [17]Elijah was a man with a nature like ours, and he prayed fervently that it might not rain, and for three years and six months it did not rain on the earth. [18]Then he prayed again, and heaven gave rain, and the earth bore its fruit.

READ

Read the passage aloud slowly.

THINK

Read the passage aloud again. What is God inviting you to do or be in this passage? How does this invitation resonate with what's going on in your life right now? Where are you hurting or sick or in need of forgiveness? Where do you need to sing?

PRAY

Offer a "prayer of faith" — one that trusts God. Confess your sins to God, and ask him if there is someone you could confess to so "you may be healed." If there is, ask God for the courage to speak to the person about it.

LIVE

Try to live in the reality that you are freshly confessed — whole and healed inside and out. What does that look like in your life today?

DAY 343

GOD ENCOUNTERS

On this seventh day, review and reflect on all you have read this week. Take the time to revel in the ways you've encountered God in the past six days.

BE HOLY IN ALL YOUR CONDUCT

1 PETER 1:13-22

[13]Therefore, preparing your minds for action, and being sober-minded, set your hope fully on the grace that will be brought to you at the revelation of Jesus Christ. [14]As obedient children, do not be conformed to the passions of your former ignorance, [15]but as he who called you is holy, you also be holy in all your conduct, [16]since it is written, "You shall be holy, for I am holy." [17]And if you call on him as Father who judges impartially according to each one's deeds, conduct yourselves with fear throughout the time of your exile, [18]knowing that you were ransomed from the futile ways inherited from your forefathers, not with perishable things such as silver or gold, [19]but with the precious blood of Christ, like that of a lamb without blemish or spot. [20]He was foreknown before the foundation of the world but was made manifest in the last times for the sake of you [21]who through him are believers in God, who raised him from the dead and gave him glory, so that your faith and hope are in God.

[22]Having purified your souls by your obedience to the truth for a sincere brotherly love, love one another earnestly from a pure heart.

READ

Read this passage, and the expanded passage, if possible.

THINK

Peter, the young apostle who denied Jesus during the last hours of Jesus' life, is now a grown man and mature Christ-follower. Here he writes words of encouragement and wisdom to other followers of Jesus.

Peter talks about being holy, meaning different, separate, set apart. He encourages followers to live differently from how the world lives — to "conduct yourselves with fear." What would it mean for your life's journey to travel through it with that holiness and fear of God?

What does "be holy in all your conduct" mean, practically? It sounds good, but what would it mean to really live that way?

Peter instructs, "Love one another earnestly from a pure heart." What would loving others this way require of you?

PRAY

Let these phrases guide your prayer life right now:

- "You shall be holy, for I am holy."
- "Conduct yourselves with fear."
- "Be holy in all your conduct."
- "Love one another earnestly form a pure heart."

LIVE

Ask God for a way to live separately, differently, and uniquely from the way the world lives.

FOLLOW IN HIS STEPS

1 PETER 2:11-17,21

[11]Beloved, I urge you as sojourners and exiles to abstain from the passions of the flesh, which wage war against your soul. [12]Keep your conduct among the Gentiles honorable, so that when they speak against you as evildoers, they may see your good deeds and glorify God on the day of visitation.

[13]Be subject for the Lord's sake to every human institution, whether it be to the emperor as supreme, [14]or to governors as sent by him to punish those who do evil and to praise those who do good. [15]For this is the will of God, that by doing good you should put to silence the ignorance of foolish people. [16]Live as people who are free, not using your freedom as a cover-up for evil, but living as servants of God. [17]Honor everyone. Love the brotherhood. Fear God. Honor the emperor. . . .

[21]For to this you have been called, because Christ also suffered for you, leaving you an example, so that you might follow in his steps.

READ

Read the passage aloud slowly.

THINK

Read the passage again aloud, noting that "to this you have been called . . . that you might follow in his steps."

1. What, if anything, surprises you in this description of the life Christ lived as an example?
2. What, if anything, in this description fits with what you've been doing lately?
3. What, if anything, in this description challenges you?
4. Consider the day you have in front of you. How might the ideas of respect, celebration, and living Christ's life fit into it?

PRAY

Thank God for the example Christ left for us. Ask God to draw you more deeply into that ongoing, vibrant life of Christ. Add anything else that came to you during today's meditation.

LIVE

Rest and delight in living Christ's example today. Consider that you won't be bored; rather, it will be an adventure.

DAY 346
EXPANDED PASSAGE: 1 PETER 3

HONOR CHRIST AS HOLY

1 PETER 3:13-18

¹³Now who is there to harm you if you are zealous for what is good? ¹⁴But even if you should suffer for righteousness' sake, you will be blessed. Have no fear of them, nor be troubled, ¹⁵but in your hearts honor Christ the Lord as holy, always being prepared to make a defense to anyone who asks you for a reason for the hope that is in you; yet do it with gentleness and respect, ¹⁶having a good conscience, so that, when you are slandered, those who revile your good behavior in Christ may be put to shame. ¹⁷For it is better to suffer for doing good, if that should be God's will, than for doing evil.

¹⁸For Christ also suffered once for sins, the righteous for the unrighteous, that he might bring us to God, being put to death in the flesh but made alive in the spirit.

READ

Read this passage a few times, slowly and meditatively.

THINK

Mull over Peter's exhortation to honor Christ as holy in every kind of circumstance. Do you agree with the link he makes between honoring Christ and doing good to others? When you're relating to others, what kinds of things do you give your attention to, if not to honoring Christ? Do you have other goals, like giving the person a good impression of you or making useful connections? In what ways does this approach to relationships leave you satisfied or dissatisfied?

PRAY

Share with Jesus what has surfaced for you, remembering that he, "the righteous One," already knows the unrighteousness in you, and suffered for you anyway: He loves you.

Sit with him in silence. Even if you don't sense him saying anything, that's okay. Just stay there, open to him. If you are led to genuine adoration of him, go ahead and take time to tell him what you think of him. If not, just receive his acceptance of you.

LIVE

Douglas Steere, a leading Quaker of the twentieth century, once said, "In the school of adoration the soul learns why the approach to every other goal has left it restless."[27] Think back to how you relate to others and notice any dissatisfaction or restlessness in that. What would it look like for you to give Peter's idea a shot and in your heart honor Christ the Lord? Try it.

NO LONGER FOR HUMAN PASSIONS

1 PETER 4:1-2,14,19

¹Since therefore Christ suffered in the flesh, arm yourselves with the same way of thinking, for whoever has suffered in the flesh has ceased from sin, ²so as to live for the rest of the time in the flesh no longer for human passions but for the will of God. . . .

¹⁴If you are insulted for the name of Christ, you are blessed, because the Spirit of glory and of God rests upon you. . . . ¹⁹Therefore let those who suffer according to God's will entrust their souls to a faithful Creator while doing good.

READ

Read the passage aloud slowly.

THINK

Read verses 1-2 again slowly. How does any suffering (which may be more like disappointment or frustration) you're going through relate to living "no longer for human passions," for example, wanting your own way but not getting it? In what ways does your "wanter" (the part of you that decides what you want) need to be invited to change?

Read verses 14 and 19 again slowly. Are you being discounted or badly treated because you're living a selfless, Christlike life? If so, in what ways? If not, how might that happen to you at some point?

PRAY

Ask the Holy Spirit to fill you and help you change the deep desires inside you. If you're being mistreated because of Christ, ask the Holy Spirit to help you absorb the truth that the Spirit and his glory is what brought you to the notice of others.

LIVE

Picture yourself as one who "the Spirit of glory and of God rests upon." Consider that such a suffering life is intimately linked with God and provides the companionship of the Spirit.

SUPPLEMENT YOUR FAITH

2 PETER 1:3-9

³His divine power has granted to us all things that pertain to life and godliness, through the knowledge of him who called us to his own glory and excellence, ⁴by which he has granted to us his precious and very great promises, so that through them you may become partakers of the divine nature, having escaped from the corruption that is in the world because of sinful desire. ⁵For this very reason, make every effort to supplement your faith with virtue, and virtue with knowledge, ⁶and knowledge with self-control, and self-control with steadfastness, and steadfastness with godliness, ⁷and godliness with brotherly affection, and brotherly affection with love. ⁸For if these qualities are yours and are increasing, they keep you from being ineffective or unfruitful in the knowledge of our Lord Jesus Christ. ⁹For whoever lacks these qualities is so nearsighted that he is blind, having forgotten that he was cleansed from his former sins.

READ

Go into a room by yourself and close the door behind you, then read the passage aloud.

THINK

God's power has provided everything we need that pertains to life and godliness. And Peter reminds us that "he has granted to us his precious and very great promises." And that is why we should supplement our faith with the following:

- virtue
- knowledge
- self-control
- steadfastness
- godliness
- brotherly affection
- love

Take your time to ponder each character trait. Then think about those you are doing well in. Think about those you need to grow in.

PRAY

Admit your need for God's guidance and help in your growth in him. Ask him to help you grow in those areas where you recognize you need the most improvement.

LIVE

On a small sheet of paper, write down the character traits you desire to develop. Review often what you wrote.

Ask the Holy Spirit for encouragement — to illuminate and reveal areas of your life that show these character traits when they become evident.

DESTRUCTIVE HERESIES

2 PETER 2:1-3

[1]But false prophets also arose among the people, just as there will be false teachers among you, who will secretly bring in destructive heresies, even denying the Master who bought them, bringing upon themselves swift destruction. [2]And many will follow their sensuality, and because of them the way of truth will be blasphemed. [3]And in their greed they will exploit you with false words. Their condemnation from long ago is not idle, and their destruction is not asleep.

READ
Read the passage aloud slowly.

THINK
Read the passage again slowly, noticing how "destructive heresies" originate. Keep in mind that the people who cause destruction rarely realize they're doing it. They may have good intentions (or *think* they have them) because they believe they're right about something.

1. Where have you witnessed destructive heresies within the body of Christ lately?
2. How might you grieve over having witnessed people:
   - bringing false teaching
   - denying Christ
   - blaspheming the truth
   - exploiting people with false words

3. In what ways do such destructive heresies lie (see verse 1) to the world about who God is and what God is like?
4. What might God be leading you to pray? What sort of person might God be leading you to *be*?

PRAY
Thank God for doing what he promises in this passage: "Their condemnation from long ago is not idle." Ask God to show you how you are not to stand by, but to be one who prays for the injured as well as the "false prophets" — for both to grasp truth and love and to find healing.

LIVE
Grieve with God over people's willingness to teach heresies within the church.

DAY 350

GOD ENCOUNTERS
On this seventh day, review and reflect on all you have read this week. Take the time to revel in the ways you've encountered God in the past six days.

IF ANYONE DOES SIN

1 JOHN 1:6–2:2

[6]If we say we have fellowship with him while we walk in darkness, we lie and do not practice the truth. [7]But if we walk in the light, as he is in the light, we have fellowship with one another, and the blood of Jesus his Son cleanses us from all sin. [8]If we say we have no sin, we deceive ourselves, and the truth is not in us. [9]If we confess our sins, he is faithful and just to forgive us our sins and to cleanse us from all unrighteousness. [10]If we say we have not sinned, we make him a liar, and his word is not in us.

[1]My little children, I am writing these things to you so that you may not sin. But if anyone does sin, we have an advocate with the Father, Jesus Christ the righteous. [2]He is the propitiation for our sins, and not for ours only but also for the sins of the whole world.

READ

Read the passage.

THINK

Truth. Grace. The two sides of a fence we often fall off of when responding to sin. In going to one extreme, we might rebuke sin but leave the sinner feeling condemned or rejected. In going to the other extreme, we might communicate acceptance to the sinner but minimize the sin, leaving the sinner in its bondage. John's perspective is different.

Look at the two halves of the problem presented in this passage: our attitude toward sin and our expectations of how God views sin. Notice what John points out about the role the Father and Jesus each play in the situation and the choice we have in how we view ourselves. Take a few moments to let John's statements about these things sink into you.

PRAY

What is your attitude toward the sins with which you struggle? What deeper desire lies beneath the draw that particular sin has on you? Does your guilt hold you back from Jesus? Talk to him about this.

Now sit silently, listening for Jesus' response to you. What is his desire for you?

LIVE

Consider a situation that holds temptation for you. Ask Jesus to remind you of his presence as advocate the next time you're faced with that temptation.

LOVE IN DEED AND IN TRUTH

1 JOHN 3:16-24

[16]By this we know love, that he laid down his life for us, and we ought to lay down our lives for the brothers. [17]But if anyone has the world's goods and sees his brother in need, yet closes his heart against him, how does God's love abide in him? [18]Little children, let us not love in word or talk but in deed and in truth.

[19]By this we shall know that we are of the truth and reassure our heart before him; [20]for whenever our heart condemns us, God is greater than our heart, and he knows everything. [21]Beloved, if our heart does not condemn us, we have confidence before God; [22]and whatever we ask we receive from him, because we keep his commandments and do what pleases him. [23]And this is his commandment, that we believe in the name of his Son Jesus Christ and love one another, just as he has commanded us. [24]Whoever keeps his commandments abides in God, and God in him. And by this we know that he abides in us, by the Spirit whom he has given us.

READ

Read the passage slowly and carefully until you understand the crux of John's argument: "Whenever our heart condemns us, God is greater than our heart."

PRAY

What role does condemnation play in your life? Maybe there's that voice in your head constantly telling you what you *should* have done. Maybe you can instantly think of six aspects of yourself that you'd change if you could. Maybe receiving compliments or affirmation from others is hard for you. Explore this with God, and talk with him about what you find. Be open to what he might want to show you about yourself.

THINK

Why do you think John so firmly ties together loving other people and freedom from condemnation? Ponder this connection. In what ways are the two related?

Become aware of how much you do and do not believe John's argument. Be honest with yourself and with God, remembering that it's okay to admit that, while you think something sounds true, you aren't sure you believe it.

LIVE

Pay special attention today to how much you criticize yourself or minimize praise given by others. Notice what runs through your head when you look in the mirror or if you beat yourself up over mistakes at work. Jot these things down if you need help remembering. Then, sometime later in the day, talk to God for a few minutes about what you are noticing. Recall what John says about loving others and condemnation, and ponder it some more.

352

GOD'S INDWELLING LOVE

1 JOHN 4:7,11-13,16-18

7Beloved, let us love one another, for love is from God, and whoever loves has been born of God and knows God. . . . 11Beloved, if God so loved us, we also ought to love one another. 12No one has ever seen God; if we love one another, God abides in us and his love is perfected in us.

13By this we know that we abide in him and he in us, because he has given us of his Spirit. . . . 16So we have come to know and to believe the love that God has for us. God is love, and whoever abides in love abides in God, and God abides in him. 17By this is love perfected with us, so that we may have confidence for the day of judgment, because as he is so also are we in this world. 18There is no fear in love, but perfect love casts out fear. For fear has to do with punishment, and whoever fears has not been perfected in love.

READ
Read the passage aloud slowly.

THINK
Read the passage again slowly, pausing after the word *love* each time you read it aloud. While the command to love one another can be difficult, consider also these things that empower people to love one another:

- Love is from God.
- We experience a relationship with God.
- We receive love from God, so we're turning that love around to others.
- God abides in us.
- God's love is perfected in us.
- God gives us his Spirit.
- God abides in us and we abide in God.
- There is no fear in love.

1. Which of the above ideas is the easiest for you to grasp? Why?
2. Which one is the most difficult for you to grasp? Why?

Draw a little stick figure of yourself as the recipient of what is being given (love or relationship or God's own Spirit).

3. How does it feel to receive like this?

PRAY
Thank God for pouring into you such things (your answers to 1 and 2, the entire list, or other phrases in the passage). Express your desire to be saturated with God's love so it overflows in you and pours out to others. (Or express the desire to have that desire.)

LIVE
Contemplate yourself as an absorber and container of God's love, as one who is taking up permanent residence in a life of love.

PROOF THAT WE LOVE GOD

1 JOHN 5:1-3

¹Everyone who believes that Jesus is the Christ has been born of God, and everyone who loves the Father loves whoever has been born of him. ²By this we know that we love the children of God, when we love God and obey his commandments. ³For this is the love of God, that we keep his commandments. And his commandments are not burdensome.

READ

Read the passage three times slowly.

THINK

What do you think of this connection between loving God and loving others? Does one or the other feel more difficult for you? Which one? What about it is difficult?

PRAY

Talk to God about the difficulties you experience in this area. Openly share with him your feelings about your struggle. Listen for what he might have to say.

LIVE

C. S. Lewis wrote, "It may be possible for each of us to think too much of his own potential glory hereafter; it is hardly possible for him to think too often or too deeply about that of his neighbor. . . . The dullest and most uninteresting person you talk to may one day be a creature which, if you saw it now, you would be strongly tempted to worship. . . . There are no ordinary people."[28] How does this suggestion alter the way you view others you know? How does it alter the way you view yourself? As you go through your day, ponder these ideas more, but also be ready to ponder-in-practice: As you come across "God's children" during the day, look for small ways to love them.

WALKING IN THE TRUTH

2 JOHN 4-6

⁴I rejoiced greatly to find some of your children walking in the truth, just as we were commanded by the Father. ⁵And now I ask you, dear lady—not as though I were writing you a new commandment, but the one we have had from the beginning—that we love one another. ⁶And this is love, that we walk according to his commandments; this is the commandment, just as you have heard from the beginning, so that you should walk in it.

READ

Focus on these verses, but read all of 2 John, if possible.

THINK

If you grew up in the church, you know that love is a critical ingredient in the life of a follower of Jesus. This ingredient may seem elementary, and believers often talk about love. But that's for good reason: Love is the very nature of God! John reminds us: "And this is love, that we walk according to his commandments; this is the commandment, just as you have heard from the beginning, so that you should walk in it."

On a scale of one to ten (with one being the lowest and ten being the highest), how would you rank your "love quotient"? How might your friends rank your love quotient? What is needed for you to grow in your understanding and expression of love to others?

What would your life look like if you were "walking in the truth"?

PRAY

Ask God to help you see the direct correlation between love and following his commands.

LIVE

Love God. Study his commands. Follow them.

FELLOW WORKERS FOR THE TRUTH

3 JOHN 5-11

⁵Beloved, it is a faithful thing you do in all your efforts for these brothers, strangers as they are, ⁶who testified to your love before the church. You will do well to send them on their journey in a manner worthy of God. ⁷For they have gone out for the sake of the name, accepting nothing from the Gentiles. ⁸Therefore we ought to support people like these, that we may be fellow workers for the truth.

⁹I have written something to the church, but Diotrephes, who likes to put himself first, does not acknowledge our authority. ¹⁰So if I come, I will bring up what he is doing, talking wicked nonsense against us. And not content with that, he refuses to welcome the brothers, and also stops those who want to and puts them out of the church.

¹¹Beloved, do not imitate evil but imitate good. Whoever does good is from God; whoever does evil has not seen God.

READ

Read the passage carefully, imagining that John is writing specifically to you.

THINK

What opportunity have you had recently to show someone hospitality or in some way help someone who is trying to do good? How did you respond to that opportunity? What do you notice about the motives and priorities behind your action (or nonaction)?

PRAY

Lay before God what you have remembered about that opportunity and what you have discovered in your heart. Maybe you will rejoice with him about the victory you experienced in overcoming a temptation to be greedy or mean-spirited, or perhaps you will feel sadness at a missed opportunity.

LIVE

Brainstorm with God what it might look like for you to take steps toward being more hospitable to others. Think about some gifts you have to offer to others (such as your good cooking, your listening ear, your encouragement). Perhaps some of your gifts you are glad to share, while others you're hesitant to offer to others. Regardless of how you feel about each gift, write down what you have that could be helpful to someone.

Now think of a specific person who would be helped by your hospitality. Offer your list to God, and ask him what he would have you offer to this person. Don't force yourself to give something you can give only grudgingly; remember, "God loves a cheerful giver" (2 Corinthians 9:7). Be open to take this small step toward hospitality, and be open to how God may change your heart as you do it.

356
357

DAY 357

GOD ENCOUNTERS

On this seventh day, review and reflect on all you have read this week. Take the time to revel in the ways you've encountered God in the past six days.

DAY 358

EXPANDED PASSAGE: JUDE

GRACE VERSUS LAWLESSNESS

JUDE 3-8

³Beloved, although I was very eager to write to you about our common salvation, I found it necessary to write appealing to you to contend for the faith that was once for all delivered to the saints. ⁴For certain people have crept in unnoticed who long ago were designated for this condemnation, ungodly people, who pervert the grace of our God into sensuality and deny our only Master and Lord, Jesus Christ.

⁵Now I want to remind you, although you once fully knew it, that Jesus, who saved a people out of the land of Egypt, afterward destroyed those who did not believe. ⁶And the angels who did not stay within their own position of authority, but left their proper dwelling, he has kept in eternal chains under gloomy darkness until the judgment of the great day—⁷just as Sodom and Gomorrah and the surrounding cities, which likewise indulged in sexual immorality and pursued unnatural desire, serve as an example by undergoing a punishment of eternal fire.

⁸Yet in like manner these people also, relying on their dreams, defile the flesh, reject authority, and blaspheme the glorious ones.

READ

Read these verses aloud, including all the passion you sense from Jude.

THINK

Think about the meaning of *sensuality,* or *lawlessness.* Now compare that to what you know *grace* to be. What differences do you see between them?

PRAY

Sit in silence and think back on experiences you've had with lawlessness — times you've done whatever you felt like, turning your back on what was right. Now consider experiences you've had with grace. Ask God to show you one of these experiences to focus on. Recall the details: What was it like for you? What was going on around you? What were you feeling about what you'd done wrong?

If you focus on an experience of grace, recall how God made that grace known to you — maybe through another person or through something you read. What did it feel like to be presented with that option? What was it like to take God up on his grace?

If you focus on an experience of lawlessness (when you did not open up to God's grace), were you aware of any other options at the time? What motivated you to choose the route you took? What did you feel later, after the dust had settled?

LIVE

Ask God what he wants you to take away from this time with him and his Word. Be assured that "for those who love God all things work together for good" (Romans 8:28). This doesn't mean that we'll feel happy right away or all the time but that God does want to see us restored. Walk through today pondering the grace of this reality.

THE ALMIGHTY

REVELATION 1:4-8

⁴John to the seven churches that are in Asia:

Grace to you and peace from him who is and who was and who is to come, and from the seven spirits who are before his throne, ⁵and from Jesus Christ the faithful witness, the firstborn of the dead, and the ruler of kings on earth.

To him who loves us and has freed us from our sins by his blood ⁶and made us a kingdom, priests to his God and Father, to him be glory and dominion forever and ever. Amen. ⁷Behold, he is coming with the clouds, and every eye will see him, even those who pierced him, and all tribes of the earth will wail on account of him. Even so. Amen.

⁸"I am the Alpha and the Omega," says the Lord God, "who is and who was and who is to come, the Almighty."

THINK

Revelation is a surreal book, full of visions and events that usually stir up more questions than answers. But from one perspective, the book is not as complex as it seems. Revelation displays the final piece of God's magnificent and victorious story for people. In short, the book could be summarized with two words: God wins. And because of this, it propels us into overwhelming gratitude. Revelation is about worship.

READ

Read the passage aloud, noting the characteristics and actions of God.

PRAY

Lie on your back in stillness (outside, if possible, where you can see the sky). Focus on the magnificence of God's character and how he brings victory to humanity. As you think about who God is, whisper these words to him:

> God, you are the Alpha and the Omega.
> God, you are The God Who Is.
> God, you are The God Who Was.
> God, you are The God Who Is to Come.
> God, you are The Almighty.

Express your gratitude to God in whatever heartfelt way you wish.

LIVE

Live your life today in complete and total thankfulness for who God is and for the plan he's had in mind all along. Use your life as a palette to display your grateful response to him as the victorious Almighty.

LISTEN

REVELATION 2:7,10-11,17

[7]He who has an ear, let him hear what the Spirit says to the churches. To the one who conquers I will grant to eat of the tree of life, which is in the paradise of God. . . .

[10]Do not fear what you are about to suffer. Behold, the devil is about to throw some of you into prison, that you may be tested, and for ten days you will have tribulation. Be faithful unto death, and I will give you the crown of life. [11]He who has an ear, let him hear what the Spirit says to the churches. The one who conquers will not be hurt by the second death. . . .

[17]He who has an ear, let him hear what the Spirit says to the churches. To the one who conquers I will give some of the hidden manna, and I will give him a white stone, with a new name written on the stone that no one knows except the one who receives it.

READ

Read the passage aloud slowly.

THINK

Sit down (if you aren't already sitting). Read the passage aloud again, standing up each time you read, "He who has an ear, let him hear what the Spirit says to the churches."

When you're finished, stand up again and ponder what God might have been trying to say to you recently about your life with him, about your behavior toward others, about your deepest self, about how you could be salt and light in the world. What recurring themes have you noticed in Scripture? Among friends? From wise Christians you've read about? At church gatherings?

Now lie down on the floor with your arms outstretched above you, if you can. Ask God what he wants to say to you today. Wait expectantly. Don't be bothered if nothing specific comes to you. Consider this practice as one of the most important things you'll ever do: listening to God and inviting him to speak to you.

PRAY

Talk to God about learning to listen to him. Ask God to show you how he speaks to you most frequently.

LIVE

Sit in the quiet, and lavish yourself with the thought that God seeks you out to speak to you. You get to live an interactive relationship with God.

BEFORE THE THRONE

REVELATION 4:2-8

²At once I was in the Spirit, and behold, a throne stood in heaven, with one seated on the throne. ³And he who sat there had the appearance of jasper and carnelian, and around the throne was a rainbow that had the appearance of an emerald. ⁴Around the throne were twenty-four thrones, and seated on the thrones were twenty-four elders, clothed in white garments, with golden crowns on their heads. ⁵From the throne came flashes of lightning, and rumblings and peals of thunder, and before the throne were burning seven torches of fire, which are the seven spirits of God, ⁶and before the throne there was as it were a sea of glass, like crystal.

And around the throne, on each side of the throne, are four living creatures, full of eyes in front and behind: ⁷the first living creature like a lion, the second living creature like an ox, the third living creature with the face of a man, and the fourth living creature like an eagle in flight. ⁸And the four living creatures, each of them with six wings, are full of eyes all around and within, and day and night they never cease to say,

"Holy, holy, holy, is the Lord God Almighty,
who was and is and is to come!"

READ

Read the passage once aloud, and get a feel for what is happening. As you read it a second time, do you notice a common theme? Write it down.

THINK/PRAY

Close your eyes and imagine what's described here: the amber and the emerald, the thunder and the lightning, the torches and the sea. See if you can sense the awe of the place. What does it feel like to be there?

Listen as the four living creatures begin to chant, "Holy, holy, holy." Speak these words to God a few times. Share with him what they express for you. Think about what holiness means to you, but not for long. Return your attention to the God who was and is and is to come. Join the four living creatures in their worship again: "Holy, holy, holy."

LIVE

What is one way you could worship God today? Perhaps you know a poem or song that puts words and emotion to your love for him today; read it, play it, sing it. Perhaps you have a special skill like dancing, surfing, or art; perform that for him today. Maybe there is a specific action you could take that would honor him. Do it. Maybe you'll want simply to tell him what you like about him.

BEFORE THE THRONE

REVELATION 7:9-12

⁹After this I looked, and behold, a great multitude that no one could number, from every nation, from all tribes and peoples and languages, standing before the throne and before the Lamb, clothed in white robes, with palm branches in their hands, ¹⁰and crying out with a loud voice, "Salvation belongs to our God who sits on the throne, and to the Lamb!" ¹¹And all the angels were standing around the throne and around the elders and the four living creatures, and they fell on their faces before the throne and worshiped God, ¹²saying, "Amen! Blessing and glory and wisdom and thanksgiving and honor and power and might be to our God forever and ever! Amen."

READ

Stand up and read this passage aloud in a loud and excited tone of voice, imagining yourself before the throne of God.

THINK

Have you heard it said that our sole purpose in life is to worship God? Read again the words that the worshipers sing in this scene. How does this relate to your worship of God?

"Salvation belongs to our God." What has God saved you from, specifically?

"Blessing and glory and wisdom and thanksgiving and honor and power and might." What comes to mind when you think about these words? What are you feeling about the God described by them? Why?

What might this passage have to do with shared worship in church each week?

PRAY

Why is God worthy of your worship? Consider lying down on your face before him as you tell him (with specifics), just as the angels, elders, and creatures do in this passage.

Go on to worship God as you communicate with him. Respond to him with thankfulness, authenticity, honesty, and passion.

LIVE

Take out a piece of paper or your journal. Write down a few sentences or paragraphs telling God how grateful you are for him and for what he has done, is doing, and will do. Include gratitude directed to the Lamb of God. Start and end with the phrase "Amen."

Then read your writing aloud to God as an act of worship.

NO MORE DEATH

REVELATION 21:1-11

¹Then I saw a new heaven and a new earth, for the first heaven and the first earth had passed away, and the sea was no more. ²And I saw the holy city, new Jerusalem, coming down out of heaven from God, prepared as a bride adorned for her husband. ³And I heard a loud voice from the throne saying, "Behold, the dwelling place of God is with man. He will dwell with them, and they will be his people, and God himself will be with them as their God. ⁴He will wipe away every tear from their eyes, and death shall be no more, neither shall there be mourning, nor crying, nor pain anymore, for the former things have passed away."

⁵And he who was seated on the throne said, "Behold, I am making all things new." Also he said, "Write this down, for these words are trustworthy and true." ⁶And he said to me, "It is done! I am the Alpha and the Omega, the beginning and the end. To the thirsty I will give from the spring of the water of life without payment. ⁷The one who conquers will have this heritage, and I will be his God and he will be my son. ⁸But as for the cowardly, the faithless, the detestable, as for murderers, the sexually immoral, sorcerers, idolaters, and all liars, their portion will be in the lake that burns with fire and sulfur, which is the second death."

⁹Then came one of the seven angels who had the seven bowls full of the seven last plagues and spoke to me, saying, "Come, I will show you the Bride, the wife of the Lamb." ¹⁰And he carried me away in the Spirit to a great, high mountain, and showed me the holy city Jerusalem coming down out of heaven from God, ¹¹having the glory of God, its radiance like a most rare jewel, like a jasper, clear as crystal.

READ

If you can, skim the expanded passage once quickly to get a broader perspective on the context of these verses. Then read this excerpt three times slowly.

THINK

Among all the images and names given in this passage — for the believers, for God, for the way life will be then and what will happen — which stands out to you? Consider "the dwelling place of God is with man" or God "wip[ing] away every tear from [our] eyes." Can you believe that this will someday be reality?

PRAY

Offer God your belief or disbelief in the promise of his coming kingdom. Thank him for the promise of it, even if you struggle to believe. Ask him to help you hope in it. Sit in silence for a bit, and be aware of him hearing you and looking at it all with you.

LIVE

What might be different in you (even if it's just the tiniest shift in perspective), knowing that a place is radiant like a most rare jewel waits for you?

DAY 364

GOD ENCOUNTERS

On this seventh day, review and reflect on all you have read this week. Take the time to revel in the ways you've encountered God in the past six days.

LIVING DAILY FOR GOD

One year. Perhaps the beginning of a life lived for him. What was it like? What did you discover that made you stop and really think about this almighty, all-knowing, paradoxical God? What fired your curiosity? What frightened you?

And as he revealed himself to you, how did God work in your life? Where has he led you in this past year? Through the valleys or to the peaks of the mountains? A little of both? On the way, what did you discover about him? About yourself? How has he changed who you are to make you more the person he wants you to be?

Take the things you have learned and put into practice this year and let them become part of the life God has planned for you. Don't let the discipline of reading and studying his Word languish. You're on a roll! Keep up the good work, because God is with you. As he promises in his Word, "God is faithful, by whom you were called into the fellowship of his Son, Jesus Christ our Lord" (1 Corinthians 1:9).

NOTES

1. *The Book of Common Prayer* (San Francisco: HarperSanFrancisco, 1983), 55.
2. Henri Nouwen, *The Inner Voice of Love* (New York: Image, 1999), 98.
3. C. S. Lewis, *Mere Christianity* (New York: Touchstone, 1996), 87.
4. *The Book of Common Prayer*, 81.
5. Nouwen, 101.
6. Peter Kreeft, *Three Philosophies of Life* (San Francisco: Ignatius, 1989), 89.
7. Summarized from Richard J. Foster, *Prayer: Finding the Heart's True Home* (San Francisco: Harper Collins, 1992), 87–90.
8. William Johnston, ed., *The Cloud of Unknowing* (New York: Doubleday, 1973), 47.
9. W. E. Vine, *An Expository Dictionary of Biblical Words*, eds. Merrill F. Unger and William White (Nashville: Thomas Nelson, 1985), 18.
10. C. S. Lewis, *The Problem of Pain* (San Francisco: HarperSanFrancisco, 2001), 91.
11. David Jacobsen, *Clarity in Prayer* (Mills Valley, CA: Omega, 1979), 93.
12. Jan Karon, *These High, Green Hills* (New York: Penguin, 1996), 301.
13. C. S. Lewis, *The Lion, the Witch and the Wardrobe* (London: HarperCollins, 1998), 75.
14. Bruce L. Shelley, *Church History in Plain Language* (Nashville: Thomas Nelson, 1995), 3.
15. Oswald Chambers, *My Utmost for His Highest* (Uhrichsville, OH: Barbour, 2006), 52.
16. Teresa of Avila, *Interior Castle: The Collected Works of St. Teresa of Avila,* trans. Kieran Kavanaugh, OCD and Otilio Rodriguez, OCD (Washington, DC: ICS Publications, 1980), 2:309.
17. These questions adapted closely from Emilie Griffin, *Wilderness Time* (San Francisco: HarperSanFrancisco, 1997), 47.

18. Julian of Norwich, *Revelation of Love*, ed. and trans. John Skinner (New York: Doubleday, 1996), 13.
19. *The Book of Common Prayer*, 337.
20. Margaret Silf, *Going on Retreat* (Chicago: Loyola, 2002), 40–41.
21. Chambers, 193.
22. Bernard of Clairvaux, in Foster, 168.
23. Ruth Haley Barton, *Sacred Rhythms* (Downers Grove, IL: InterVarsity, 2006), 117.
24. John Dalrymple, *Simple Prayer* (Wilmington, DE: Michael Glazier, 1984), 109–110.
25. Foster, 61.
26. That the World May Know Ministries, "Rabbi and Talmidim," *Follow the Rabbi*, March 7, 2007, http://community.gospelcom.net/ Brix?pageID=2753.
27. Douglas V. Steere, *Prayer and Worship* (New York: Edward W. Hazen Foundation, 1938), 34.
28. C. S. Lewis, *The Weight of Glory* (Grand Rapids, MI: Eerdmans, 1965), 14–15.

INDEX

SOLO is intended to immerse you in the beauty and depth of the Bible through *lectio divina*. It is not a topical Bible or a concordance. However, if you are looking for a reading on a specific subject, the following index of topics and day numbers may be of assistance. It is not meant to be an exhaustive list of the topics covered by the Scripture passages discussed in this book.

ABOUT THE AUTHORS

Jan Johnson is a retreat leader and spiritual director and has written more than fifteen books, including *Invitation to the Jesus Life*, *Enjoying the Presence of God*, *Savoring God's Word*, and *When the Soul Listens* (all NavPress).

J. R. Briggs is the cultural cultivator of The Renew Community and is the founder of Kairos Partnerships. As part of his time with Kairos Partnerships, he serves on staff with the Ecclesia Network and Fresh Expressions U.S. J. R. and his wife, Megan, have two sons, Carter and Bennett, and live in Lansdale, Pennsylvania.

Katie Peckham has an MA in spiritual formation and soul care from Talbot Seminary and works as a spiritual director in Orange County, California. She enjoys training for triathlons and traveling with her husband and daughter.